THE COLLABORATION OF NATIONS

THE COLLABORATION OF NATIONS

A Study of European Economic Policy

Edited by
Douglas Dosser, David Gowland and Keith Hartley

Martin Robertson · Oxford

First published in 1982 by Martin Robertson & Company Ltd.,
108 Cowley Road, Oxford OX4 1JF.

British Library Cataloguing in Publication Data

The collaborations of nations.
1. European Economic Community Countries
– Economic policy
I. Dosser, Douglas
II. Gowland, David III. Hartley, Keith
338.94 HC241.4

ISBN 0-85520-389-7
ISBN 0-85520-395-1 Pbk

Typeset by Unicus Graphics Limited, Horsham, West Sussex
Printed and bound in Great Britain at The Pitman Press, Bath

Contents

PART III: MICROECONOMIC CASE STUDIES IN EUROPEAN COLLABORATION

Notes on Authors

Stephen A. Baker previously Research Fellow at the Institute of Social and Economic Research, University of York, now teacher at Clark University, USA. He is currently completing research on the costs and benefits of monetary union. He has contributed 'Theory and Practice of Commercial Policy' in *Surveys in International Economics* (1981).
(Chapters 4 and 9)

Douglas Dosser is Professor of Economics at the University of York and previously taught at Edinburgh and several US universities. He has been consultant to the Commission of the European Community on tax harmonization and economic and monetary union, and part-author of numerous books on these subjects, including *Economic Integration and Monetary Unification* (1973), *Economic and Monetary Union in Europe* (1974) and *Economic Union in the EEC* (1974).
(Chapters 3 and 8)

David Gowland is Lecturer in Economics at the University of York and Director of In-Service Training. He has previously worked in the Bank of England and as a consultant to the 10 Downing Street Policy Unit. His books include *Monetary Policy and Credit Control* (1978) and *Modern Economic Analysis* (1979).
(Chapters 1 and 7 and the section on Banking in Chapter 2)

Keith Hartley is Reader in Economics at the University of York. He has previously taught at the Universities of Hull and Illinois, US. In 1977 he was made NATO Research Fellow. His teaching and research interests lie in defence, industry, labour and public choice. His recent books include *Microeconomic Policy* (1981) and contributions to *The Structure of European Industry* (1981).
(Chapters 2 and 10)

Brian Hillier is Lecturer in Economics at the University of York. He has held posts at the University of Durham and in the Government Economic Service. His recent articles in *Public Finance* include 'Does Fiscal Policy Matter?' (1977), and 'A Note on Bond Finance and Stability' (1980).
(Chapter 6)

Theodore Hitiris is Senior Lecturer in Economics at the University of York. He was previously employed in the Ministry of Economic Co-ordination and the Center of Planning, Greece. His teaching and research interests lie in international economics. He is author of *Trade Effects of Economic Association with the Common Market* (1972).
(Chapter 5)

Alan K. Maynard is Reader in Economics at the University of York and Director of the Health Economics Graduate Course. He has worked for the EEC Commission, OECD, and the Royal Commission on the Distribution of Income and Wealth, and the National Health Service. He is a contributor to *The Organisation, Financing and Cost of Health Care in the European Community* (1979).
(Chapters 11 and 12)

Preface

Collaboration between nations involves a study of social choice. Different societies have to determine whether collaboration is likely to be worthwhile and how it can be 'best' achieved. An obvious starting point is the analogy with individuals who voluntarily sacrifice some of their independence to create households and to join groups (such as trade unions); or, adjacent regions might agree to combine to form a single nation state (like the USA). A similar approach can be used to analyse collaboration between nations: what is it; why does it emerge; which policies are available, and what are the problems? This book considers such questions in a European context, with the EEC providing a classic case study in international public choice.

Nations have to choose whether to apply to join the EEC club, whilst its members have to determine the criteria for admission to the group (such as entrance fees). Negotiations arise over the policy objectives of the club or international grouping, and the choice of macroeconomic and microeconomic policy instruments. In addition, performance indicators are required to assess whether the club is achieving its declared objectives. This book analyses these issues and problems in three sections.

Part I provides a general framework outlining the theory of international collaboration. It considers why nations collaborate and the alternative forms of collaboration. Inevitably, questions arise as to whether economic analysis offers any guidelines for a European economic policy. A public choice approach cannot ignore the effects of the political market on policy formulation. Policy objectives and performance indicators necessitate an analysis of integration and its measurement: what is integration and has it been achieved?

Objectives are achieved through macroeconomic and microeconomic policy instruments. Part II concentrates on the macroeconomic issues, policies and problems which are involved in European collaboration. Both monetary and fiscal policies are assessed and particular attention is given to the costs of collaboration in terms of the sacrifices of national sovereignty over domestic policy instruments. Part III considers European microeconomic policies.

Case studies range from the Common Agricultural Policy to industry, competition and advanced technology policies. Inevitably, policy changes involve some groups and regions in losses, hence the final chapter outlines the arrangements for compensation in the form of social policy.

The book has a number of unique and novel features. The emphasis is on an economic analysis of public policy, general principles and problems of collaboration rather than a detailed description of EEC institutions. The book provides a comprehensive coverage and critical evaluation of *both* macroeconomic and microeconomic policies, reflecting the results of major research projects in this field. Within macroeconomics, distinctive contributions embrace interdependence and integration, debt management and real income transfers. A further distinctive, and less conventional, contribution is the inclusion of a range of microeconomic case studies, such as advanced technology, defence, industry and competition policies. Each chapter in the book outlines the policy problem, presents an analytical framework, identifies the costs of collaboration, provides a critique and considers alternative solutions. In some cases, the authors have been encouraged to suggest alternative policies, some of which involve major departures from current EEC policy. The result is a text which is suitable for second and third year university economics students, as well as an introduction for graduate students; considerable parts should also be of interest to general readers. Of course, our efforts at an analytical and comprehensive coverage of the problems and policies involved in international collaboration have been subject to the usual constraints of space.

The book is a result of *collaboration* between a group of York economists with similar research and teaching interests, and a common intellectual approach to policy issues. Some of the research was supported by the SSRC studies of the Common Market and defence policy as part of the Public Sector Studies Group at York. Douglas Dosser developed a workshop for the discussion of European economic problems: this book is the outcome of the research workshop.

The authors are grateful for advice, assistance and comments from colleagues in the Economics Department and the Institute of Social and Economic Research at York. Thanks are due to Professor Wiseman for research facilities and to those who struggled with the typing, especially Mary Grace and Barbara Dodds.

Douglas Dosser
David Gowland
Keith Hartley
July 1981

PART I

The Theory of Collaboration

CHAPTER 1

The Theory of International Associations

The Framework

Nations collaborate. They have collaborated with – and against – each other since time immemorial. This poses few formal problems for the analyst, however much he might deplore the consequences of such actions on his private life. It is relatively straightforward to treat nations as if they were persons, at least if one implicitly accepts some organic theory of the state. It is then assumed that states, like persons, act to maximize perceived utility. There is a long tradition of such analysis in both political and strategic theory, from Machiavelli and Clausewitz onwards.

Collaboration has often involved the creation of an international association. This may be defined as an institution to which member states adhere and which has an existence independent of its members. Hence it has many of the characteristics of a firm or club. This definition excludes international agreements which only provide for collaborative action. For example an agreement by *A* and *B* to simultaneously invade *C* would not necessarily involve the creation of an international association. If, however, they set up a joint military command then an international association would have been set up. There are many such international associations in existence, amongst them NATO, the UN, UNESCO, IMF, BIS, and the EEC, which is of especial interest to the authors of this book.

However, the existence of such international associations has to be explained. There is no obvious reason why utility-maximizing nations should agree to set up institutions designed to formalize their collaboration. This is exactly analogous to the problem of why individuals set up clubs. In fact, the theory of international associations is a special case of the theory of clubs. This theory was developed in seminal articles by Buchanan (1965) and Ng (1973). Important extensions to theory were made by Berglas (1976) and Helpman and Hillman (1977). The area was recently surveyed by Brennan and Flowers (1980) who clarified and extended the analysis in a number of important areas. This literature has concentrated upon the problem of optimal club size, Buchanan arguing that it should be such as to maximize the average benefit per member whereas Ng argued that total benefit should be maximized. Almost necessarily this means that 'Ng clubs' would be bigger than 'Buchanan clubs'.

Unfortunately there are three serious limitations to the use of this theory for the purpose of international associations. The first is that the analysis assumes that all individuals are identical. This assumption cannot be made when analysing international associations. It is clearly invalid, in that nations do differ far more significantly than individuals. Perhaps more seriously, many international associations exist in part because of the differences between their members. For example, Greece's major contribution to NATO is its (by definition) unique location which is useful both for radar stations and naval bases. The US, on the other hand, contributes military and economic power to the alliance. This complementarity of Greece and the US makes a mutually beneficial alliance possible whereas two identical nations might not form an alliance of this type – if Greece had America's power, or the US Greece's location, neither would need the other.

Secondly, the existing literature by implication considers only a very special type of club. Almost invariably it provides only a single product (although Berglas considers the possibility of a multi-product club based upon joint costs). This restriction in turn involves the further restriction that the good is a price-excludable public good subject to congestion. Other types of good cannot be considered within the framework of a single product club whereas in a multi-product club a much richer range of goods can be comprehended. This is clearly essential in the case of international associations as some provide pure public goods (e.g. NATO whose security is also provided to Ireland, Switzerland and other non-members). Others provide almost pure private goods – e.g. IDA loans.

The standard analysis also assumes that the club is to be closed-entry, see the next section of this chapter. Finally, the theory as presently developed is static. This means that no attention is devoted to the problem of club formation – it is assumed to exist if it is beneficial for it to exist. This is clearly invalid. One should consider when a club will be formed and at what costs. Moreover the static nature of the analysis means that it is impossible to discuss the time dimension of a club in existence. Should a club be permanent or temporary? The analysis of Buchanan *et al.* offers no answer to this question. The next two sections attempt to sketch a framework in which these questions might be tackled.

An alternative approach to the existence of international associations is much more simplistic but in some cases more productive. This is to apply the Paretian social welfare model to the problem of international relations. If one important addition to the basic model is made this seems a very useful approach to many EEC problems. The basic model says that a change would be desirable if it were possible to compensate all losses such that no-one is worse off and at least some persons (i.e. nations in the present case) better off. Usually this is refined to include Scitovsky's criterion that it must not also be an improvement to reverse the change. In the international model, it is crucial that the compensation must not be hypothetical. Every member must be actually better off. To achieve this it may be necessary to require either the payment of actual compensation or a package deal involving several areas. Examples of both are legion, especially in the tortuous history of the EEC. Furthermore the principle of the *juste retour* so decried by many analysts of the EEC is clearly grounded in Paretian welfare economics. No nation should be made worse off by its membership of an international association. If a nation is worse off, or perceives itself to be, the international association should either be reformulated or dissolved. Britain's membership of the EEC is a classic case of this. It can be argued that the 1973 terms of entry violated Pareto criteria. The result has been unfortunate for both Britain and the EEC as an institution as revealed in the continual wranglings over the UK's contribution to the EEC budget.

Indeed the implications of welfare economics for the budgetary and social policies of any Federal body especially for the EEC are considerable (see Chapters 8 and 12). A frequent criticism of welfare economics, or rather of misplaced applications of it, is that too little attention is placed upon what a utility function might contain and too little upon the nature of the alternative instruments available to achieve a given end. In the case of international associations, the last section of this chapter attempts to defeat this criticism in advance.

The Formation of an Association

A club will come into existence only if group action is beneficial in the sense that all the founder members must expect it to produce net benefits for each of them individually. However, this condition while it is necessary is by no means sufficient. It says nothing about the process whereby a club is formed. Moreover, it says nothing about which club will be formed. In Europe in the 1950s there were at least ten possible economic associations with different memberships and different functions (such as a free trade area, customs union, common market etc.). All satisfied the net benefit criteria. None was dominant in that it was preferred by all possible members. Thus it became a matter of bargaining which association evolved and what its rules were. (The Buchanan–Ng analysis is not applicable here because it assumes identical members.) Perhaps of even greater importance, it is necessary to say when a club will be formed and how it will evolve over time. This problem is tackled in various subsequent chapters. However, there is also a need for a general theory of the formation of associations and their development which would suggest a framework for answering the questions:

(1) Which association?
(2) When will it be formed, if at all?
(3) How many members?
(4) What form (see next section)?
(5) How will it develop?

There seem to be two possible approaches to this problem. The first is to adapt the burgeoning and fascinating literature produced by political scientists about coalition formation. A survey of the early work in this area has been provided by Brams (1975, 1976). Important subsequent work includes the collection edited by Hinckley (1976). This is not the place to summarize this important work but one of its crucial results can be applied to the problem of international associations. This is the 'minimal size' rule first developed by Riker. This proposition argues that conditions will normally have the minimum number of members necessary to achieve their goal. Extra members are actually a liability as their presence will lead to disruption as the coalition evolves towards the optimal size. This result can be modified in the present context if a new member yields benefits not foreseen at the time of the formation of the original association. However, in general it would seem that a stable association should not seek to attract new members. Indeed, one could go further and say that Riker's work implies that an open-ended association must be unstable. This result is examined in various contexts below. In particular it is of obvious relevance to the EEC.

An alternative approach would also use game theory but would start from a different premise. It would argue that the coalition results are very specific and that many of their assumptions are invalid. Riker, for example, used a fixed positive-sum game model. Other work in international relations, especially war gaming, has used negative sum or variable sum games. Critically, the coalition literature assumes an independent game. The consequences of either playing a series of interdependent games or concurrently playing several inter-related games needs further exploration. The results in Chapters 5 and 6 below can be interpreted in this context. Finally, one might develop the idea of a super game or meta-game model of international associations (see Brams, 1975). In this context, the minimal size rule might no longer be valid. More importantly, it might become clear under what conditions the rule is valid. It is already clear that another result of game-theoretic political science is vital to an understanding of the EEC and other international associations. This is that effective power is neither directly related to formal power (like nominal voting strength) nor to military and economic power, see Brams (1976) for an application of this model to the EEC Council of Ministers.

This section is necessarily very superficial and tentative. It has, however, sought to raise in a theoretical context a number of vital issues that are discussed in Parts II and III below. These relate to the formulation of an association, its development, the role of alternative associations, the optimal membership and the question of who controls the association.

Types of International Association

The existing literature on the theory of clubs has considered only a closed entry club providing (usually) a single product which is a price-excludable public good subject to congestion. As a contribution to the theory of club, this chapter presents a taxonomy of international associations based upon three dichotomies. The rationale of each type of club is considered and applied to the international association. Later in the book, in Parts II and III all the chapters consider the appropriate form of international association in their respective fields. This is a study of which form of club is the most appropriate in their area.

General or Specific?

The first choice that the founder-members of an association have is that it can be either specific to a single purpose or have multiple objectives and functions. The UN, the EEC and the OECD are all general associations which have multiple functions. On the other hand, NATO, the Bank for International Settlements and Interpol are all specific associations. The existence of specific associations is easy to explain. It is less clear why general associations exist. It would seem optimal to belong to a (large) number of different specific associations rather than one general one. It is unlikely that the optimal membership of each association would be the same. For example, in the early 1950s it became clear that the optimal membership of the European steel community, the European agricultural community and the European defence community were not identical. Nevertheless, whilst the last was detached, the first two were linked as the EEC. This meant that both an apparently sub-optimal agricultural international association and a sub-optimal steel one were formed. What rationale can there be for multi-purpose clubs of any sort? A similar problem was considered by Becker (1975) who hypothesized that the existence of marriage carried a similar theoretical problem. He suggested that the prevalence of the multi-purpose implicit-contract relationship of marriage needed explanation. Without necessarily accepting the validity of Becker's specific application, one may borrow some of his insights into the rationale of multi-purpose associations, as is done below.

Berglas considered the problem in his seminal work and suggested that joint supply was a possible reason for multi-purpose clubs. This is clearly one very good reason for linking activities. His idea may be generalized by considering factors, especially capital goods, that may yield output for both activities even if there is no joint supply in the strict sense. The possibility of achieving cost minimization by such a multi-purpose club is considerable.

The other possibility of cost minimization was stressed by Becker who argued that transactions costs were likely to be reduced by general, multi-purpose associations. He considered this idea in great detail and it is unnecessary to expand on his analysis. However, neither of the cost minimization arguments for multi-purpose club appears to be relevant to international associations, especially irrelevant to the EEC. It cannot be argued that the European Commission is a cost minimizing device of any sort. Indeed one has only to compare the smooth effective workings of the BIS or the relatively smooth workings of NATO with the Byzantine, tortuous paths of the EEC's attempts to devise, say, a common policy on insurance companies to realize how much the existence of the EEC has done to slow down the progress of economic integration, and to realize at how much less cost these goals could have been achieved by separate associations. It is difficult to think of any joint outputs in this sense in the EEC context and, a priori, the small number of participants should ensure low transactions costs if the nations of the world, or of Europe, sought to create many specific organizations.

It, therefore, seems necessary to consider an alternative explanation for the existence of multi-purpose associations. The most obvious seems to me to be the possibility of facilitating bargaining. To return to the formation of the EEC, German participation in the agricultural community was essential to France, as Pfillimin made clear when he launched the green pool plan in 1951. This was because of both social catholic and economic reasons. On the other hand, it was almost certainly against Germany's interests to join whereas the reverse was true in steel. Thus West German participation in the agricultural plan, ultimately the CAP, at enormous direct and indirect cost to Germany was the price of French involvement in the steel plan. This is an over-simplified account of the negotiations that led to Messina as other ideas and other bargains were involved. Nevertheless this was one crucial element of the EEC package. If this analysis is correct, then bad tempered bargaining is not to be deplored, as the Euro-fanatics so often do, nor is it proof that the EEC is failing, rather the attempt to facilitate national goals by bargaining across different issues is the essence and *raison d'être* of the EEC. Similar analysis can be used in the private sector. If *A* has th power to veto a golf club, and *B* the power to veto fox hunting because both own land vital to the activity in question and *B* is a fanatical lover of the chase and *A* of the links then a multi-purpose club dedicated to both golf and fox hunting could emerge. Less fanciful but less clear cut examples abound. Finally general clubs might evolve from single purpose ones as the members discover other mutual interests; the road from the Zollverein to the North German Confederation is a classic example.

Closed or Open?

An association may be closed in its membership, like the OECD, or be open to all and sundry, like the UN. The degree of openness may vary, for example all existing members may have *liberum veto* (as in CENTO) or entry fees may be levied. Entry may require the consent of a single member or a majority or a qualified majority. Entry may be conditional, for example an old boys' association, and depend on meeting certain criteria of background (the Oxford Society) or intellect (MENSA).

Obviously some entry conditions amount to a closed club, for example *liberum veto*. It is interesting to note that many closed entry clubs permit transferability of membership so a marketable property right is created. Seats on the US stock markets and membership in US golf clubs are often traded in vigorous active markets.

The major determinant of the degree of openness is probably the nature of the output of the association. Where it is a public good not subject to congestion then openness is likely to be the rule – ILO, WHO. Where the output is subject to excludability and rivalry, then very stringent conditions will apply – EEC. The only complicating factor is that some nations may wish to veto newcomers for extraneous reasons, e.g. objections to Spain's membership of NATO for reasons other than defence ones (in this case a desire not to give a seal of respectability to Franco). In general, closed or restricted entry is likely to be the norm in any multi-purpose organization where the facilitation of bargaining is the major *raison d'être*.

Permanent or Temporary?

An association may be permanent, or at least for an indefinite period, or for a specific limited period, defined either in terms of time or of some state variable. The EEC is an example of the first category, the European Payments Association the second. On the whole if an association is dedicated to a specific purpose(s) a limited duration is more likely to emerge than if it is a forum for bargaining over time. All game theorists agree (see for example Brams) that optimal solutions are far more likely to emerge in repeated games than one off ones, and still more likely if the game is played indefinitely. Thus the rarity of open, limited, general associations is not surprising.

In summary, the three dichotomies produce eight types of association as in Table 1.1.

TABLE 1.1

	Entry	*Time*	*Example*
Specific	Open	Permanent	WHO
Specific	Open	Limited	any war time alliance
Specific	Closed	Permanent	CENTO
Specific	Closed	Limited	EPA
General	Open	Permanent	UN
General	Open	Limited	EDC (abortive)
General	Closed	Permanent	EEC
General	Closed	Limited	OEEC

The Goals and Instruments of an International Association

The goals of an international association may be the national interest of the members. In this case, possible objectives may in some cases include economic integration (see Chapter 4). Alternatively, the benefits as an association may accrue to those responsible for making the decision to form or to join it. In this case one must look to the economics of politics or the theory of bureaucracy for an explanation. A country may join so that its leaders acquire extra patronage to practise 'clientalist' politics (Italy and the EEC) or to permit its leaders to strut a large stage (Benelux membership of EEC). A mixed association is possible – a different member may have different objectives, this seems to be very much the case with the EEC. One of the major themes of this book is to explore carefully the goals of international economic policy.

Once established, the functioning of an international association is best examined within the *targets and instruments* framework. One of the themes of this book is the examination of a number of instruments that have been considered to achieve the goals of an economic association, especially the EEC. The general result seems to be that there is no 'royal road' to success. This is not surprising as similar results were obtained in the narrow context of tax harmonization. This result seems to be especially true in a macroeconomic context (see Part II). It is impossible to rely on one instrument or on a limited set of goals as the result is likely to be instability. Indeed the limitations to the targets and instruments framework are more striking than the opportunities to maximize broadly specified national utility functions. The environment in which policy makers operate is constantly changing and so, therefore, are the constraints facing them. As trade patterns change and both technical progress and market forces tend to increase the level of international trade, insulationist options are foreclosed. Hence the need to measure and define the degree of integration of economies (Chapters 3 and 4). It is a truism to say that policy making cannot be studied apart from its institutional framework but the implications of structures for policy are too often ignored. Structural differences are vital to policy making, a theme of Chapter 7 and Part III. Moreover, changing technology may provide an opportunity to try to manipulate structures as well as further constraints on the actions of policy makers (Chapter 10).

If the changing environment means that greater co-ordination is necessary, a number of consequences follow. Paretian welfare economics may offer a framework of analysis for international collaboration but as stressed above, there is a crucial addition. Compensation must be actual not hypothetical. The attempt to compensate losses is not simple in either theory or practice (Chapters 8 and 12). Some forms of co-ordination seem to imply a progressive trend towards ever closer integration and an ever-greater loss of national sovereignty (Chapters 5 and 6). Such developments are not welcomed by most statesmen nor by most of the citizens of the countries of the world. Attempts to combine co-ordination and freedom for individuals have led to the development of rules of the game embodied in a notional 'social contract'. Attempts to find equivalent social rules for countries have so far proved to be in vain (Chapter 7). Co-ordination is on the one hand necessary and on the other is not without its disappointments and frustrations. These largely theoretical and macroeconomic conclusions derived in Part II can be contrasted with the empirical evidence of microeconomic collaboration in practice presented in Part III. Agriculture is a notorious example of the dreadful consequences that sprang from the highest ideals of Pflimmin's green pool and its social catholic origins (Chapter 9). Patchier results seem to be obtained in other areas (Chapter 11). Whether multi-purpose general organizations are better equipped than single-purpose specific ones is crucial to any normative analysis of international associations. Defence and high technology provide interesting contrasts in the different ways of pursuing collaboration (Chapter 10). However, before considering the theory and practice of policy making there is one crucial question to be answered – is there a need for a policy at all, or can co-ordination be left to the market?

CHAPTER 2

The Need for a European Economic Policy: Market or State Solutions?

Controversy and the Policy Instruments

Controversy surrounds many of the EEC's available range of macroeconomic and microeconomic policy instruments. At the macroeconomic level, fiscal policies involve debates about tax harmonization and the Community Budget, especially burden-sharing and the relationship between a nation's contributions and its receipts. Monetary policy has been dominated by the search for monetary integration through the creation of such institutional arrangements as the European Monetary System. At the microeconomic level, policies embrace product and factor markets. There are policies for the creation of a common market with free trade in goods and services and factor mobility between member states, together with a common external tariff. The Community is also involved in competition, consumer protection and transport policies. Elsewhere, there are various industrial measures, involving re-structuring and the support of 'key' sectors such as energy and high technology. Conflicts are inevitable, especially between measures aimed at re-allocating resources between declining and expanding sectors, on the one hand, and job preservation, on the other. In this context, there are Community policies for the protection of specific economic sectors, such as agriculture, coal and steel (for example, Common Agricultural Policy; European Coal and Steel Community). Distributional considerations are reflected in the Regional Development and Social Funds: the former provides Community aid to 'problem' areas and the latter aims to improve employment opportunities for workers in the common market through, for example, re-training and re-settlement. Further measures aim to protect workers from unhealthy and dangerous employment conditions, and to promote industrial democracy.

Not surprisingly, the member states have different attitudes towards the various Community policy instruments. Such disagreements can reflect differences in policy objectives, disputes about the underlying economic models, as well as controversies over the 'appropriate' policy solutions. Often, disagreements are reflected in summit conferences, lengthy meetings between Ministers, demonstrations and lobbying by interest groups, before the inevitable compromise and 'agreement'. Agriculture, fisheries, energy, regional imbalances, monetary integration and the Community Budget are the classic examples of the EEC's political process. Predictably, each member state will aim to protect its 'national interest' and try to maximize the gains for its interest groups of producers, taxpayers and consumers. In such a bargaining environment, compromises and agreement on a specific policy issue, such as agriculture, might reflect each member state's views about the benefits and costs of other aspects of the Community's policies. For example, one nation's agreement on agricultural policy might be dependent on concessions and favourable treatment towards its Budgetary contributions and receipts. Such a political environment is unlikely to be conducive to the formulation of policy measures based on orthodox economic criteria.

The general question arises as to whether economic analysis can explain the extent and form of current EEC policies. Why does the EEC need macroeconomic and microeconomic policies; why does it intervene in specific markets and what explains the form of intervention? This chapter will outline general principles, with specific policy applications analysed in Parts II and III. Two issues will be considered:

(1) Does economic analysis offer any guidelines for a *European* economic policy? If so, what might be the features of such a policy and how do they compare with current arrangements?
(2) How has policy been affected by the economics of the political market? In particular, can EEC policy be 'best' explained by a model containing voters, vote-conscious politicians, governments seeking re-election, budget-sensitive bureaucracies and income-maximizing interest groups?

International Associations and Social Welfare: What are the Benefits of a Multi-nation Club?

A Paretian-type social welfare function is an obvious starting point. Countries aiming at optimum resource allocation will obtain economic benefits from the *worthwhile* removal of *international* market failures. Within the world economy, there are two general sources of failure in private markets. *First*, externalities, including public goods. Examples of economic benefits which can be appropriated by groups of nations include defence and military alliances as well as the case of common property resources such as fisheries, together with coastal and atmospheric pollution. Other examples are the enforcement of contracts and law and order (such as Interpol); and the creation of monetary stability and a common currency which will reduce both uncertainty and the costs of searching for mutually beneficial trade and exchange. *Second*, there are market imperfections as reflected in tariff and other barriers to international trade, together with indivisibilities where an activity is too costly to be undertaken by one nation only (such as the European Space Agency; collaborative on aerospace projects: see Chapter 10). The pursuit of self interest and individual utilities will lead countries to exploit any worthwhile opportunities for collective action through international groupings. On this basis, optimality will be reflected in a diversity of international agreements, associations and clubs. Not all the sets are mutually exclusive and there are examples of interlocking membership. Thus, European nations together with the USA and Canada form the NATO military alliance; a European sub-set of this group are members of the EEC; similarly, the UK was involved in collaborative aerospace projects with EEC members *prior* to joining the Community. In other words, the EEC is not the only international organization allowing European nations to exploit the benefits of collective action.

New international associations will be formed and existing ones will change their membership so long as there are *expected* to be net benefits to the participants (see Chapter 1). Both the benefits from, and the costs of forming, an international group have to be considered. Such arrangements are not costless and involve substantial transactions costs in search, negotiating, bargaining and enforcing international agreements and contracts. Changes in technology and in relative factor prices will affect the opportunities and transactions costs of forming or expanding an international association. Changing tastes and preferences within societies (a role for education and information?) will also affect national attitudes towards multi-nation groupings. In this context, can the EEC be viewed as a social welfare maximizing club, aiming to 'correct' major market failures and achieve an optimum allocation of resources (Hartley (1977b), Chapter 2)?

The EEC and Optimum Resource Allocation

There are obvious examples of EEC market-improving policies, namely, the creation of a common market in goods and services and the removal of some of the restraints on factor mobility. In these cases, benefits have been obtained from trade creation, increased competition and reduced *X*-inefficiency. Elsewhere, though, EEC policy seems to have been more intent on preventing, replacing or eliminating private markets. The CAP is a classic example of an EEC policy which favours producers rather than consumers (see Chapter 9). Other instances of Community distortions include member government procurement policies which act as barriers to free trade within the EEC, as well as subsidies to domestic industries for jobs, balance of payments and technology objectives (see Chapter 10). Similarly, the EEC has interfered with changing comparative advantage by introducing selective policies to protect declining industries, thereby favouring producers rather than consumers. Examples include the attempts to restrain certain imports, as with the Multi-Fibre Agreements of 1974 and 1978, and the cartel-type arrangements for shipbuilding and steel (Donges, 1981). Nor should it be concluded that EEC regulatory policy necessarily favours consumers. Economic models of regulation suggest that producers are likely to be the beneficiaries. Also, within the labour market, the EEC has made no effort to create human capital banks to provide funds to *individuals* who are unable to obtain finance for *worthwhile* human investments (for example, education, training, search, mobility: Hartley and Tisdell (1981)). Finally, there are cases where market forces have resisted official EEC efforts at 'integration', as with consumer and producer opposition to some product standardization (e.g. Euro-beer). Such attempts at standardization are worrying for two reasons. First, they reflect a static view of competition which completely neglects the dynamic nature of rivalry with its entrepreneurial search for profitable opportunities and the diversity of consumer preferences. Second, EEC bureaucrats tend to confuse intermediate and final outputs, using the number of Community directives as performance indicators. Obviously, they believe that common policies, standardization, harmonization and directives are 'good' and that more are desirable, regardless of costs. Further insights into the behaviour of the EEC can be derived by examining specific policy areas. Two examples will be outlined, namely defence and banking. The former is a policy area where there are obvious opportunities for a state agency to 'correct' market failure; the latter is a useful illustration of state intervention hampering integration, as well as showing the microeconomic foundation of monetary policy.

The EEC and Public Goods: the Case of Defence

Defence is often regarded as a classic example of a public good and one where there are potential gains from collective action through a military alliance (Olson and Zeckhauser (1968); Kennedy (1979); Hartley and McLean (1981)). But defence policy is not within the EEC's remit. This *appears* to be a further deficiency if the club is to be regarded as a market-improving agency. However, most Community states are also members of a specialist military alliance, namely NATO. In this way, European nations can participate in a much wider collective defence arrangement than would be available within the EEC. None the less, aspects of the NATO alliance have potential implications for the EEC, particularly debates about burden-sharing and weapons standardization policy.

Debates about burden-sharing within the EEC sometimes involve proposals for the inclusion of national defence expenditures as part of any total assessment of Community burdens. Table 2.1 provides an indicator of relative burdens within NATO based on the percent-

TABLE 2.1
Defence Burdens: EEC and NATO

Country	*Defence expenditure as a percentage of GNP* 1950	1960	1970	1979
Belgium	2.8	3.9	3.3	3.3
Denmark	1.8	3.1	2.8	2.4
France	6.3	7.4	4.6	4.0
W. Germany	n.a.	4.6	3.7	3.3
Greece	6.6	5.4	5.6	5.8
Italy	4.2	3.7	3.0	2.3
Luxembourg	1.5	1.2	0.9	1.0
Netherlands	5.4	4.5	3.8	3.3
United Kingdom	7.3	7.3	5.6	4.9
USA	5.5	9.9	8.7	5.2
EEC median	4.8	4.5	3.7	3.3
Total NATO	5.4	8.2	6.7	4.3

Notes:

(i) Data for 1950–70 based on GNP at factor cost: current prices.
(ii) 1979 data based on GDP at market prices.
(iii) Total NATO figures are averages for all NATO members.

Sources: NATO Facts and Figures, Brussels, NATO Information Service, 1976; Cmnd. 7826-I, *Defence in the 1980s*, London, HMSO, 1980, p. 86.

age of gross national product (GNP) devoted to military spending between 1950 and 1979. Differential burdens exist between Europe and the USA as well as between the European members of the alliance. Britain is amongst the pact leaders, whilst Luxembourg is an example of a 'free riding' small nation. On the basis of relative burdens, the UK has often claimed that its military contribution should be brought more into line with that of its major European allies. Admittedly, such comparison have their limitations. There are international differences in the definitions of defence and GNP, and many nations use 'cheap' conscripts whilst the UK relies on an all-volunteer force. Nor does aggregate military spending provide an indicator of defence *output* and the extent to which armed forces contribute to national, as distinct from collective, defence. For example, with the UK a more accurate indicator of its NATO contribution might be its annual expenditure on BAOR and the RAF in Germany, which exceeded £1,600 million in 1981. Clearly, these are substantial sums which might be difficult to ignore in future debates about burden-sharing within the EEC.

A concern with the rising cost of weapons and 'wasteful duplication' has led to greater emphasis on weapons standardization policy and proposals for creating a more competitive European defence industry within a NATO common defence market. This would require eliminating much of the 'waste' associated with twelve national rather than one European procurement effort. It would also involve a re-structuring of inefficient European defence industries to eliminate duplicate development work and to exploit the scale economies from long production runs (Callaghan, 1975). Thus, proposals for weapons standardization policies are inevitably associated with industrial policy, and the latter is of obvious concern to the European Commission. However, the advocates of weapons standardization often envisage industrial solutions involving 'healthy and controlled competition', with 'fairness and equity' in procurement. Such arrangements are unlikely to create a competitive weapons market with all NATO contracts allocated on the basis of comparative advantage and reflecting free entry, competitive bidding and fixed prices. Instead, the desire for 'controlled competition' and 'fairness' is likely to result in regulated, imperfect markets with non-competitive cost-plus type contracts. The result is likely to be an inefficient industrial structure with work allocated on the basis of equity rather than comparative advantage, so providing all NATO members with opportunities for participation. Producer groups are likely to be the beneficiaries (see Chapter 10; and Hartley (1981b).

The EEC and Private Goods: the Case of Banking

Monetary policy is of crucial importance to the EEC (Chapters 5–7). Moreover, financial services are vital to most firms and it has often been argued that the integration of the separate American capital markets in the late nineteenth century was a crucial step in the integration of the American economy from a series of regional markets to a national whole. Hence it is not surprising that the EEC has devoted considerable attention to financial markets both as part of the embryonic attempts at European Monetary Union and directly to facilitate the development of a common capital market. In the process, it has produced a series of draft directives. These policies were of especial interest to the UK in that a rather complacent belief that the City would become the financial centre of the EEC seems to have been a major factor in Britain's decision to join the EEC (Readman, 1974). Moreover, the Bank of England and Treasury claimed that a major reason for their volte-face on banking supervision involved in the 1976 White Paper and 1979 Banking Act was motivated by the need to satisfy the EEC's Fourth Draft Directive on banking regulation and supervision (discussed in Gowland (1978)). Ironically, whilst the EEC has produced a series of embryonic mice in the form of draft directives on banking, insurance and so on, as a result of its mountain of deliberations, European, indeed world, capital markets have moved rapidly towards unification independently of, and often in spite of, the EEC. An example of this is the growth of the Amsterdam stock market as a European stock exchange offering a range of services not available elsewhere in Europe such as Chicago-style traded options and treasury bill futures. This expansion has not been welcomed by the EEC Commission who have been worried about the consequences of a European security market not being restrained by the strait-jacket of the Commission's regulatory ambit.

The conflict between market forces working to integrate markets and the EEC seeking to thwart the growth of such unified markets in the name of integration is best seen in the case of banking. Over the last twenty years the growth of the Eurocurrency market has created an integrated world-wide banking market (Crockett (1977), Gowland (1979, Chapter 3)). There are disagreements about some of the impacts of these developments but none about its effect in integrating the economies of the Western world. This development has rather paradoxically proved extremely unwelcome to the EEC.

There are a number of reasons why the EEC has not responded

favourably to the integration of banking markets. One reason is that the integration has taken place across a wider area than that covered by the EEC. This has been associated with an expansion of American banks in European centres. Both developments are inimical to the 'little Europe' or 'Charlemagne mentality' and to the latent anti-Americanism often implicit in EEC policies (the term 'Charlemagne mentality' was originally coined by Schumacher in the early 1950s and used later by De Gaulle to describe what they regarded as the inward looking nature of the EEC and its excessive concentration on a rather narrow area). More significantly, the growth of Eurocurrency markets has made it much harder to maintain fixed exchange rates (Crockett (1977), Gowland (1979, Chapter 3)). This is very unwelcome to the EEC as all the plans for monetary union have taken the attainment of fixed exchange rates as their starting point.

It has often been argued that the desire to achieve fixed exchange rates involves a confusion of ends, consequences and means (Wood, 1974). One view is that if integration were achieved a consequence would be that exchange rates would not vary; but fixed exchange rates would not bring the attainment of union or integration nearer, even if it were possible. Others have argued that a market solution is more appropriate and in particular that freedom to hold the currency of one's choice is the key to integration – not fixed parities (Hayek, 1978). The validity of such arguments is irrelevant. The crucial point is that the 'state solution' to monetary integration – fixed exchange rates – has been in conflict with the market solution – Eurocurrency markets. The EEC has either produced or encouraged a whole string of policies which hamper the operations and growth of the Eurocurrency market. Some are designed to do this, especially the exchange control intended to facilitate the workings of the EMS. In other cases the effect may be unintended (e.g. two-tier exchange rates). EEC banking regulations are not conducive to the operations of the Eurocurrency market, or rather would not be if implemented. They are designed for national banks rather than multi-national ones (as was argued in an editorial in *The Banker* in September 1978). Thus, banking is a classic example of state intervention which hampers market forces working to integrate economies.

The Choice of Policies

Various explanations can be offered to rationalize the EEC's policy 'mix' which ranges from private market solutions to market-improving as well as market-displacing measures. Technocrats would view the diversity as reflecting conflicts between objectives and the search for as many instruments as there are targets. Another possibility is that the EEC is not aiming at a Pareto optimum, with its emphasis on consumer preferences and individual utilities; nor might it be seeking Kaldor–Hicks gains. Instead, policy might reflect the view that individuals are not the best judges of their welfare and that private markets result in an undesirable distribution of income (see Chapters 11 and 12). If so, what are the components of the EEC's social welfare function, always assuming that optimization of some target(s) is an empirically valid approach to explaining behaviour? Alternatively, geographical constraints reflected in its current membership could explain why the EEC might be failing to exploit all the worthwhile gains from collective action. For example, would a larger European Community create net benefits and what is the optimal size for this *form* of association? Clearly, in terms of comparative advantage, any European trading bloc will be 'too small' to capture all the potential gains from international specialization and division of labour available within the world economy. And yet, there are substantial transactions costs in reaching agreement on the wide range of economic and political issues associated with the EEC form of international association. Countries will have different social welfare functions with different targets and weights and any increase in membership might accentuate diversity. This is especially likely in policy areas which are evolving, where the existing members have yet to formulate and operationalize objectives, so making it much more difficult (too costly) to completely 'screen' new applicants and assess their 'suitability'. Problems are accentuated where there is a lack of theory and empirical evidence on the policy implications of 'integrating' nations with different social welfare functions, different economic structures (like agriculture, manufacturing), public sectors of varying sizes and efficiencies as well as money, capital and labour markets with varying degrees of specialization (see Chapters 3 and 4, and Part II). Furthermore, each nation's policy-makers (e.g. central bankers, civil servants) will be experts on the most efficient policy instruments within their economy: hence, they are likely to oppose Community measures which they believe to be 'inappropriate' for their domestic economies or where they have no previous experience.

At a more general level, the existing mix of EEC policies might be rationalized as second (or *n*th) best solutions. Technical and policy created constraints might prevent the achievement of a Pareto optimum, so limiting the appropriateness of piece-meal policy recommendations based on Paretian principles. Even so, the identification of *policy*-created constraints can be informative in suggesting that governments might be pursuing other objectives, such as their re-election. Indeed, references to EEC summit conferences, bargaining and agreements suggest that an economics of the political market might provide an alternative explanation of Community behaviour. If so, the possibility arises that government and state solutions can fail (see also market failure).

The EEC, State Solutions and the Economics of Politics

Policy choices will be determined by the political market place of voters, politicians, governments, bureaucrats and interest groups. Within the EEC, member states will have different structures for their political markets. A nation's constitution will determine its voting and collective choice rules and, within such constraints, transactions costs will further affect market structure. And, just as private markets can 'fail', so too can political markets 'fail' to fully and accurately satisfy voter preferences. In democracies, the supply side can be imperfect whilst competition is infrequent and discontinuous, so that voters are unable to re-contract continuously. Also, competition might be of the 'all-or-nothing' type with the majority party obtaining the entire market. Nevertheless, various devices allow individuals to register their preferences and so overcome any apparent deficiencies in a nation's constitution and its voting rules. The possibilities include log-rolling, political participation (such as new parties), interest groups, private provision and international mobility. Within the EEC, there are obvious opportunities for log-rolling with individual Ministers reaching private vote-trading arrangements exchanging their less valued for their more valuable preferences. Such exchanges also provide opportunities for interest groups to influence policy. After all, vote-conscious Ministers can always present an EEC agreement as a national 'victory' for his farmers or fishermen, spreading the resulting costs over large numbers of widely diffused and unorganized consumers and taxpayers. An extra 1 per cent on, say, food prices can always be presented as one of the prices which has to be paid to reap the benefits from membership of the European club. Further understanding of EEC political markets can be obtained by considering the behaviour of parties, governments and bureaucracies.

The Economics of Politics and Bureaucracies: Predictions and Examples

In democracies, policy formulation will be influenced by the desire of governments for re-election and by the vote-maximizing behaviour of rival political parties. Significantly, models of the economics of politics predict that vote-sensitive governments will favour producers more than consumers (Downs (1957); Mueller (1979)). Producer groups embracing firms and trade unions can afford the substantial investments in information to influence government policy in their favour, and the potential returns make such activities worthwhile. These groups can use their specialist knowledge to provide expert and persuasive information showing political parties that their activities are in the 'national interest' and make a 'socially desirable' contribution to jobs, technology and the balance of payments (and hence votes). They might try to 'buy' monopoly rights by purchasing protection from competition. They lobby for tariffs and import controls, or the regulation of prices and restrictions on the entry of 'unreliable' firms offering 'inferior and unsafe' products. Examples within the EEC include agricultural prices, air fares, drugs, subsidies to firms and state support of high technology projects. The result is that governments will tend to over-supply special interest legislation favouring producer groups (Hartley and Tisdell (1981), Chapters 3 and 15; Olson (1965)). In addition, policy choices will be influenced by bureaucrats.

Bureaucracies are usually monopoly suppliers of information, goods and services to the governing political party: competing bureaucracies are condemned for 'wasteful duplication'. As monopolists, bureaucrats can pursue self-interest with budget-maximizing behaviour enabling them to satisfy their preferences for salary, power and prestige. They are experts on their agency's production function with implications for the quantity and efficiency of public sector output. Opportunities for discretionary behaviour are reinforced by the bureaucrat's employment contract which is often incompletely specified and lacking in efficiency incentives. In this market environment, budget-maximizing bureaucracies have every incentive to over-estimate the demand for, and under-estimate the costs of, their preferred policies and projects (Niskanen, 1971). Bureaux can stress the total gross social benefits of a project (such as jobs, technology); they can formulate programmes which will be supported by producer groups likely to benefit from contracts and they can suggest policies which are potential vote-winners for a government (for example, subsidies to firms in marginal constituencies). They will obviously favour bureaucratic solutions in the belief that all these are good and more are desirable, regardless of cost. Examples include administrative procedures to control inflation, Keynesian aggregate demand management, economic planning, re-distribution in kind rather than cash, support for the public regulation of private industry, and a preference for selective rather than open competition in awarding government contracts (Hartley, 1980). In total, economic models predict that bureaucracies will be associated with allocative and technical inefficiency. On this basis, it is likely that industries and services supported by monopoly ministries and state agencies will be 'too large'.

It might be thought that bureaucratic behaviour can be controlled by voters and vote-conscious politicians. But usually at the ballot box, voters are only able to express their EEC preferences in a general form. Frequently, votes are for a package of policies rather than a specific issue such as the CAP, monetary integration or the Community Budget. Does a vote for, say, the UK Conservative Government of 1981 mean that the voter supports *all* aspects of current EEC policy or does it reflect a preference for higher defence spending, an independent nuclear deterrent and the pursuit of price stability? In addition to the problems of identifying voter preferences, a government can find that it is costly to achieve compliance with its objectives. How can a President, a Prime Minister, a Cabinet or a Secretary of State ensure that their wishes are actually implemented by the bureaucracy? Problems arise because bureaucrats are experts on the possibilities of varying output as well as on the oppotunities for factor substitution. Although some of these substitutions can result in perverse outcomes for a government (consider potential vote losses from public expenditure cuts: see Hood and Wright, 1981), they might be too costly for any individual Minister to monitor, police and eliminate completely. In these circumstances, bureaucrats have opportunities for satisfying their own preferences rather than the voters. Such discretionary opportunities are likely to be even greater at the EEC level, given the relative independence of the Commission and the limitations of the European Parliament as a controlling authority representing European voters.

Conclusion: Do We Need a European Economic Policy?

The need for a European economic policy will depend upon the views of potential gainers and losers and the arrangements for compensatory payments both within and between members states (for example, regional policy). Questions have to be asked as to *who* is maximizing *what* for the benefit of *whom*? For some products (e.g. defence), specialist international associations embracing European and North American member states might be ideal; elsewhere a European-based multi-product club of the EEC type might be socially optimal. Much will depend on the expected benefits and costs of international associations of different sizes, forms and degrees of product specialization. Presumably, a country will continue to be a member of an international organization so long as membership is expected to be worthwhile.

This chapter has also outlined some of the explanations for the extent and form of current EEC policies. One model explains policy in terms of the pursuit of a Paretian-type social welfare function. In which case, EEC policy would be characterized by market-improving measures designed to favour *consumers*. The frequency with which Community policy favours *producers* suggests an alternative model based on the economics of politics and bureaucracies. Here, there are specific roles for governments seeking re-election, interest groups and budget conscious bureaucrats, all of which appear to influence EEC policy. Even so, there are opportunities for developing the model at the Community level. For example, the Council of Ministers might be analysed in terms of small group bargaining behaviour, with individuals acting like trade unions and employers making initially high claims and low offers, respectively. And bargaining is likely over, say, farm prices where industrial nations will prefer low food prices and agricultural countries will demand favourable terms. Subsequent behaviour might be modelled using the Hicksian analysis of resistance and concession curves related to the expected duration of disagreements, including threats to withhold payments to the Community Budget or to hinder negotiations elsewhere (Sapsford, 1981). Obviously, a more detailed analysis is required. Subsequent chapters will outline some of the possibilities and problems within their specialist areas. A logical starting point is policy objectives and the EEC's concern with integration. What is integration; why is it desirable and has it been achieved?

CHAPTER 3

Economic Integration and its Realization in the Public Sector

The Concept of Integration

Integration, convergence, and co-ordination are concepts much employed recently to describe either trends or desires in the creation of a European Community economy, as distinct from nine national economies with trading links. However, there appears not only to be little agreement on whether the Community economy is integrating or converging, but confusion as to how this is to be interpreted or measured.

The main corpus of technical literature has concentrated on trade patterns.[1] Certainly, data availability is at its best here particularly in *ex post* studies, where many variations are practised in measuring changes in trade brought about by 'integration', whilst *ex ante* studies predict what might happen depending on import price elasticities from this or that removal of tariffs between groups of nations.

The concept of 'integration', and its measurement, is at its most unambiguous in these trade studies. But by now this approach must be considered *simpliste*. By these measures, the EEC has shown unremitting 'integration' over many years, and indeed the UK would be indicated as a constantly integrating member. But many would hardly accept these propositions, especially for the UK and the EEC for the last few years.

Clearly the concept of 'integration' has to be multi-dimensional. Various economic series have to be convergent, in some sense of the term. Several recent papers (for example in Hodge and Wallace (1981)) have analysed trends in GDP growth per head, gross value-added per employee, inflation rates, money supply growth, etc., in an effort to extend the areas of economic activity which ought to be included in studies of 'integration'.

However, the position is left in a highly unsatisfactory state. Different observers stress different series, the measurement of many is difficult if not impossible, the idea of weighted combinations meaningless. Is the Community economy integrating, converging, unifying?

The idea of this chapter is to attempt some elucidation of the situation in the following way. First, a sharp distinction is drawn between the positive and normative approaches; meaning can only be given to the question normatively. And then, it all depends on the normative 'model' one uses to view the EEC.

Positive and Normative Approaches to Integration

Progress in European Community economic development means different things to different observers, and no unique indices are possible. Since *integration* is often used as a synonym for progress, its meaning is also likely to be complex. The interpretation of these concepts is embedded in the most fundamental perception by an individual or political group as to what the Community is, and should become.[2]

For example, to take an extreme case, those with an individualistic outlook on the state may see the 'integration' of society as offering wider choice – of jobs, products, leisure pursuits, freedom to travel – whilst those preferring a collectivist viewpoint emphasize equality, participation, etc. It is not difficult to find socio-economic trends which *diverge* as an integral part of the integration process for the first observer, but which should *converge* for the collectivist.

The distinction between a positive and normative approach should be sharply drawn; the above interpretations fall in the normative category, but let us clarify the positive side first. At any given time in the Community economy, we can observe ten national trends in a variety of economic and socio-economic statistical time-series. The commonest economic ones are: per capita GDP and regional incomes, employment levels, product and factor prices, trade, investment, movements of labour and capital, and sectoral disaggregations of these between agriculture, manufacturing and services, and between particular industries; also money supply and rates of interest, social security payments, tax rates.

The time-trends of any set of these are determined by endogenous economic decisions within the Community, and exogenous factors, principally technological change and other unforeseen and uncontrolled world events, such as the oil crisis. A further distinction is useful within the endogenous category – decisions in the private sector unrelated to Common Market policy, and decisions in the public domain that may be similarly unconnected but that may be pursuant to the development of the EEC. The observations of nine time-series at any one time is a result of all of this, playing on an inter-connected system.

In a highly simplified and stylized two-nation world with the countries trading with each other:[3]

from
$$Y_t = E_t + X_t - M_t + A_t,$$
$$Y_t^* = E_t^* + M_t^* - X_t^*,$$

where E_t = exogenous expenditures, A_t = autonomous, and imports M_t = exports $X_t^*, M_t^* = X_t$, and

$$E_t = aY_{t-1}, \qquad X_t = b^*y_{t-1}^*, \qquad (a < 1, b^* < 1)$$
$$E_t^* = a^*y_{t-1}^*, \qquad M_t = bY_{t-1}, \qquad (a^* < 1, b < 1)$$

we have

$$Y_t = (a - b)\, Y_{t-1} + b^*Y_{t-1}^* + A_t,$$
$$Y_t^* = (a^* - b^*)\, Y_{t-1}^* + bY_{t-1}.$$

The generation of time paths of national incomes Y and Y^*, given a shift in autonomous expenditure A can diverge or converge according to the size of parameters, a, a^*, b and b^*. Thus one set of parameters is consistent with 'integration' whilst another set is not. But no set could be contrasted with another *a priori* as representing an 'integrating' economy.

If we extend our stylized model of the Community economy to include, say, GDP per head and a sectoral division of Y into agricultural and industrial output, divergence or convergence of trends can again be produced by parameter values which could not be designated as 'integration' parameter values or the opposite on *a priori* grounds.

Upon what basis can any ordering of states (parameter values and generated time paths of economic variables) on an integration scale be based? In truth, the concept of integration has no meaning in positive economics. The attempt to try to base such on 'trade' relies on picking out that one sector and ignoring developments in other areas, e.g. GDP per head, industrial output, etc.

Normative Models of Integration

Any meaning to be attached to 'increasing integration' must be derived in normative economics. Consequently any ordering of states of integration depends on one's choice of normative model of the Common Market.

Whilst recognizing the existence of gradations and combinations, between them we could characterize four normative models; they are characterized by the vision they offer of how the Community should work, and what the prospectus of the economic development of the Community should be. In some cases this is explicit; in others, it is implied in shorter-run or institutional recommendations.

The four normative models are:[4]

(1) The Treaty of Rome Economy – keeping as close as possible to the letter and spirit of the Treaty's provisions.
(2) The EMU Model – incorporating EMS and some of the features envisaged for Economic Union.
(3) The Federal Finance System – following MacDougall (EEC, 1977) and Forte (1979) with considerable income transfers.
(4) The Inter-Governmental Model – a smoother working of present arrangements taken as a final outcome.

Each of these models has different implications for per capita GDP and regional incomes, employment, product prices, factor prices, trade, investment, movements of labour and capital, output of agriculture, manufacturing and services, and particular industries: also for social security payments, money supply and rates of interest, main tax rates. They have different implications because they set out to achieve different results by different policy decisions.

There could be some confusion as to whether the above 'models' are, in fact, positive or normative. A proposed clarification is this. There is a positive description of the current Community economy which we could take to be that part of the LINK model comprising the nine member-states. This positive model generates time-paths of the principal economic variables listed. The 'normative' models would then form a basis to decide whether the Community economy was 'integrating' or 'progressing', possibly coming to different answers, of course. As an example, whether GDP per head in different member-states or regions was equalizing or diverging would gain a differing value in different models.

But further, the normative models could be used to guide institutional change which would indeed affect the parameters of the positive (LINK) model and help toward the generation of time-series which accorded with that model's normative ideas.

Thus, whilst LINK remains *the* positive model, the various normative models have two roles, (i) to permit *evaluation* of the trends implicit in the actual LINK model, (ii) to guide *policy action* in changing LINK equations to produce the desired effects sought by particular normative schools of thought.

We now look summarily at the four normative models to understand what they seek as regards some principal economic areas: trade policy, factor movement, sectoral policy, regional and social policy, monetary and fiscal policy, income distribution, and conjunctural policy. We shall then concentrate on the public finance series as a special illustration of our general theme.

General Characteristics of the Four Models

The Treaty of Rome Economy represents, of course, the most 'market-oriented' approach to the Community, with stress on the idea of a single market for the Twelve, that is, the abolition of customs, fiscal and other economic barriers. It is therefore strong on trade; factor movement, tax harmonization and monetary and capital market unification. Little interest is consequently shown in social policy, income redistribution or demand management.

The one major counter-tendency is the agricultural policy, which is founded in the Treaty, and which tarnishes the pure form of this market approach – unless it be argued that the most marketized Western economy would still protect the agricultural sector for reasons of security. It is perhaps best to exclude this aberration in evaluating the model. Or, it could be regarded as a temporary phenomenon in the minds of the framers of the Treaty, to disappear when Community agriculture was restructured and modernized (see Chapter 9).

Monetary unification also presents some classification problem. It is usually lumped in with 'Economic and Monetary Union' whereas more strictly it belongs to the market approach just outlined. It eliminates barriers created by different currencies and exchange rates and unifies business conditions.[5] On the other hand, unlike agriculture, it does not have much specific basis for its implementation in the Treaty of Rome. It should, however, be included; it is an aspect of 'negative' integration (see Machlup (1977)), removal of obstacles, which characterizes the market or (mostly) Treaty of Rome approach.

When we come to Economic Union, we turn to what has been called 'positive' integration. Generally in this, the manifold 'interventionist' policies of the modern member state, both in production and welfare, are to a degree to be performed by Community institutions. Industrial, regional and social policy become important Community areas, and hence require major Community budgetary and financial developments to service them. Fiscal instruments may have to play an active role, not just a neutral one, and thus the implications for these as other economic policy variables may need to take a quite different course compared with the Treaty of Rome economy.

These 'positive' integration measures of Economic Union involve substantial Community expenditures of a *programme* type – direct or indirect subventions to industrial sectors, and regions, and social expenditures ranging from Community unemployment benefit to Community health and education systems. The interest is not redistributive *per se*, although there may be some such effect; and when there is, it is mainly inter-personal (see Chapters 8 and 12).

This approach is to be distinguished from the Federal in that, whilst the latter also involves a substantial financial operation on the part of the Community, this is one of income transfers from richer to poorer states or regions, along the lines of the federations of USA, Canada and Australia. The MacDougall Report (EEC, 1977a), which is the acme of this approach, envisages an interim Community budget of 2 per cent of Community GDP and a final target of 20 per cent, aimed principally at this redistributive goal.

This Federal approach aims more explicitly at equalizing incomes per head around the Community than even Economic Union. Whilst doing so however, it is much more devolutionist than union. The member states are left far more to decide on their degree and type of intervention in productive enterprise and welfare services.

Actually, it is still a special brand of federalism that MacDougall exhibits.[6] A federal structure is not necessarily accompanied by a large income transfer system, and even when it is, one has to be careful not to fall into the trap of individual equalization of living standards (personal incomes and public services) whereby member states become only administrative agencies. In most fiscal federal approaches, some evening-up of fiscal capacity is envisaged with member-state autonomy over a wide margin of the degree of (local) taxation and types of public expenditures. In some expressions, mobility is emphasized in federalism more than equalization (see Tiebout (1956)) so people have a choice between tax-expenditure patterns as well as employment. Does such a federal model differ from the Treaty of Rome approach? It does in that some budgetary transfers are still encouraged in order to prevent polarization, the rich moving to the low tax regions steadily worsening the fiscal capacity of poorer states.

The Federal model of the MacDougall type, with substantial transfers, or the more restrained Tiebout type, differs essentially from the Inter-Governmental model, where more and more, the principle of *juste retour* is asserted by nation-states. This is the most current, most realistic, and perhaps the most probable outcome of the attempt at European economic integration. Its success criteria are almost perverse: little further encouragement to factor mobility, a limited Community budget, little redistribution across member-state borders, strongly autonomous powers for member states in economic and social policy.

Public Finance in the Four Models

The expected and desired development of tax revenues and public expenditures for a Community budget will be quite different according to which of the four background models we have in mind. There are really four major elements of the public finances to discuss in each case, two on the revenue side, two on the expenditure side.

Revenue can be provided by a Community tax or by borrowing. Of the three Community 'taxes' as at present, the common external tariff and the agricultural levies are minor, and can only provide a diminishing relative, and maybe even absolute, proportion of budgetary revenue. All the weight must therefore fall on the value-added tax or other taxes. Within 'other' taxes, direct personal and business taxes can be excluded for the foreseeable future, so only other indirect taxes need be considered (Denton (1981), Dosser (1974), EEC (1978a)). Different borrowing possibilities – in the different models – are the only major alternative to indirect tax revenues.

The expenditure side of the Community budget can be divided for our purposes between programme expenditure and inter-state or inter-regional transfers. The former have their rationale as Community 'public goods' – the allocative side of resource use, the latter are explicitly for redistributive purposes.

The means of finance, and the use of that finance by the Community, sharply distinguishes our different models in their public finance aspect.

The Development of Indirect Tax Revenues

To start from the present position, the sources of revenue for the very small European budget are the proceeds of the common external tariff, of the agricultural levies (neither of which are expected to grow greatly over the years) and a part of member states' value-added tax receipts, with zero longer-term borrowing (i.e. the budget is balanced).

The VAT amount, being that raised by a near-to-1 per cent rate on private consumption expenditure around the Community (soon the 1 per cent legal limit will be reached), is of course only a fraction of the VAT actually raised by member-state governments. No other indirect tax revenues – excise duties – are received by the Community, although much is raised.

The small pre-existing amount of Community tax revenue, is predicated on achievement of a degree of 'tax harmonization' as raising it on a 'Community base' requires the application of that same base in each member state. This has been achieved by the Sixth Directive – with certain derogations allowed to member states in practice.

The development of further tax revenues for the Community has strong implications for future tax harmonization, whilst other aims in the fiscal area, for example, the abolition of fiscal frontiers, do the same. Hence, the expected and desired course of tax harmonization plays a key – and different – role in the integration process according to one's standpoint.

The starting point is that of eight Directives on VAT and on Excises. The VAT has a common base nominally, covering all consumer expenditures, but less general exemptions, such as small businesses, banking etc., and special derogations, food and medical products, books and newspapers, clothing and footwear for particular member states. Whilst consumer expenditure forms a base of around 50 per cent of GDP in member states, approximately half of this is excluded in a country like the UK with its extensive derogations (although the Community's 1 per cent rate yield has to be paid over on the underogated base).

The pre-existing differences in VAT rates in the member states are very wide, and each has multiple rates. In Table 3.1 we give the standard rate in each member state, and also the 'effective' rate (VAT revenue as a percentage of total consumption expenditure) which allows for the differences in exemptions. This is to look at the VAT just from the revenue-raising point of view. This major tax also has a possible function in national conjunctural or anti-inflation policy, and in social policy modifying market-determined income distribution.

We can see that it is still principally a national tax, only a vestigial Community tax. Now in which direction further developments should go depends on the Community model. Possible directions are:

TABLE 3.1
VAT Rates in Community Member States

	Standard nominal rate (%)	*Effective rate (%)*
UK	15	7.5
Netherlands	18	9.6
Luxembourg	10	6.6
Italy	14	6.9
Ireland	20	7.2
France	17.6	10.8
Denmark	20.25	10.1
Belgium	16	9.3
West Germany	13	6.9
EEC	1	1

(*a*) Convergence to a uniform (nominal or effective) rate, with no further switches of revenue to the Community;
(*b*) No convergence, but steady increases in the Community take starting from the initial 1 per cent;
(*c*) Convergence with steady change of destination of revenues.

Each of these courses would be fully legitimate in different concepts of the Community and would represent 'progress' or 'integration'.

In the pure Treaty of Rome model, the weight would fall on (*a*). The most important aspect of the tax harmonization for this view lies in the abolition of fiscal frontiers, following the disappearance of customs frontiers. Further, the single market concept implies that firms anywhere in the Community – and they can locate anywhere under the right of establishment – face the same sales tax schedules in the interests of free and equal competition. Once rates are the same everywhere in the Community, the principle of taxation can change from being based on the place of consumption of goods to the area of origin or production, and fiscal frontiers disappear (as rates outside the Community border remain different, the destination principle has to remain for extra-Community trade – otherwise Community producers could be undercut by low-taxed foreign suppliers).

Now this is the only development to be looked for. Social and regional policy is at a minimum in the Treaty of Rome model, and conjunctional policy uncalled for (unemployment and inflation to be dealt with by market adjustments). The Community budget need not grow beyond market-regulating functions, and there is spare revenue for this as the agricultural policy declines.

However, not only convergence of rates is essential but concentration on a single rate for all products, very desirable. Not only is simplicity and economy (in public and private sector cost) served, but there is no social reason why some consumer products in the Community should be taxed more than others – with the consequential resource-diverting effects.

Movement toward this full-base common uniform rate has three grand revenue consequences (*a*) the ending of derogations for member states, (*b*) the re-allocation of current revenues as the change from destination to origin principle occurs, (*c*) a change in the balance of member-state tax revenues as their VAT rates rise or fall to the common rate.

The 'average' uniform rate recently mooted is 15–17 per cent, but with one reduced rate, 3–5 per cent for food. On such a basis, major re-alignments of indirect tax revenues would occur for France and Denmark in a downward direction, and Luxembourg and the UK in an upward one. In the case of the UK, for example, consumer goods produced here whether domestically-consumed or exported would carry a somewhat higher tax rate, but more significantly, the untaxed (or zero-rated) half of consumer expenditure would be drawn into the tax net. Member states would be faced either with increases in the total tax burden – Germany, UK and Luxembourg – or decreases – France and Denmark, or have to make compensating changes in other taxes.[7]

In spite of the difficulties, alignment and the abolition of fiscal frontiers remains a prime target of Community policy, as expressed by the Commission. The prize is a move nearer a 'common market', with one more distortion supposedly removed – that due to differences in sales tax imposed on businesses (and consumers) resident in different parts of the Community.

All this is within the context of the Treaty of Rome economy. When we come to Economic Union, a different picture emerges in two great respects: an increasing tranche of VAT revenues needs to be transferred to the Community budget, and a conjunctural aspect of member-state VAT rates has to be acknowledged. We have to think of a two-part VAT, where the Community rate will be uniform, 2 per cent or more, but the second part may be left as a variable, for demand management and social policies in member states. This is in direct contrast with alignment; it involves purportedly, a 'cost' of an inefficient resource allocation in the Community, but a social benefit of managed demand, distributional and labour policies. Of course, both sides of the equation are shot through with qualifications. The supposed gain from alignment, lost in this model, may need to refer to effective rates, not nominal, and in any case, the removal of one source of distortion may not improve a generally distorted resource allocation (see Dosser (1981)).

On the use of the VAT for various economic and social effects, confidence has fallen in the efficacy of manipulating tax rates as inflationary/deflationary devices, especially when subsequent money wage bargaining may neutralize the tax-inclusive price change just wrought. And as a social instrument, the VAT's progressivity is uncertain and uneven.

However, the indices of progress are going to be quite different in this case of Economic Union. The target is to increase the percentage of VAT going to the Community (needing a common assessment base), leaving a variable rate within member states. The question further arises as to the control of those variable rates. In Economic Union this would steadily pass to the Community, for use in an overall Community strategy in the management of economic activity and social policy around the Community.

The Federal model also requires an increasing flow of tax finance to the Community budget. It has this in common with Economic Union. However, the federalist is likely to be *more* interested in undistorted conditions of business through abolishing differences in tax rates, and *less* interested in member-state or regional demand management through tax manipulation, so may favour alignment and the abolition of fiscal frontiers whilst seeking an increasing transfer of VAT revenues to the Community. For regional policy, the Federal model has its grants-in-aid system as instrument.

Finally, the Inter-Government approach, with its interest in national autonomy and *juste retour* would seek little development away from individual and autonomous national tax-rates with national contributions to the Community budget. The percentage on a purely notional common base is simply a formula to calculate the contribution. Complete discretion is retained to fix the national VAT rate, the actual tax base, number of rates, and to vary them, all in the interests of national conjunctional and social policy. If anything, 'progress' would manifest itself in a less rigid assessment basis for national contributions to the Community budget to make *juste retour* more easily attainable – various pay-back mechanisms and other abrogations of the common-base assessed amounts are a move in this direction.

We can see then that the three conceivable courses of direction for the VAT (and later Excises) listed earlier each correspond with a view of the Community: convergence with no further transfer with the Treaty of Rome, non-convergence with transfer for Economic Union, and convergence with transfer to Federation. Non-convergence and non-transfer accords with the Inter-Governmental approach.

Community Public Debt-Finance

At present, the Community budget is crucially different from national budgets, not only in size, but in that only tax finance is possible. In national budgets of Community member states, up to 25 per cent of budget revenue comes from the issue of bonds. Would this not prove to be a means of significantly increasing the size of the Community budget whilst avoiding the political difficulties involved in increasing Community taxes? The answer is intimately bound up with monetary union, and will distinctly vary with the Community model assumed. Unlike some other aspects of economic policy, one has to be more speculative about the philosophy behind each model in this case, because this matter is not often explicitly discussed by the supporters of each approach (for a general discussion, see Woolley (1974)).

The Treaty of Rome makes no explicit reference to debt finance. But it variously recommends capital market integration and the removal of obstacles to competition so, as earlier, it is easy to view monetary integration as a Treaty policy. This is a necessary condition for Community bond issues.

Monetary union (not pseudo-monetary union – just the freezing of exchange rates, see Corden (1972)) is usually keyed to the transfer to the Community of the power to create money, which is, of course, one form of Community debt issue. The question arises: can the power to issue bonds be left in national hands, once money issue has been transferred? The answer is firmly in the negative: 'With monetary union, the Community authorities will be obliged to control not only the money supply in the EEC but also the size and maturity composition of the debt issued by the member countries. Only if this is done can there be a monetary policy at Community level that is not undermined by independent manipulation of their debt by member countries' (Woolley, 1974). Essentially the term structure of interest rates is otherwise out of the control of the central authority, and monetary management by the controller of the money supply thwarted (see also Chapter 7).

But once transfer of the bond issue is also passed to the Community, dramatic consequences follow. The finance of member-state budgets by the issue of debt has to be governed by the Community, who 'ration' the issue of bonds and their type. Given that ration – and on what principles? – the member state can only increase public expenditure by increasing what taxes remain as autonomous national taxes.

Returning to the Treaty of Rome economy, we arrive at a rather puzzling result. We have earlier characterized the public finance attitude of the Treaty as a small-budget one (especially when the CAP disappears), and it is not too fanciful to feel that large Community budget deficits would not be in the spirit of the Treaty of Rome.

On the other hand, the vast structure of European public debt fulfils a need, for example as a repository of institutional funds such as pension funds, which it would be very far-fetched to imagine being replaced by company issues.

Thus, the Community itself would not need to issue bonds on a substantial scale for the finance of its own budget deficit, but it would control and determine issues to finance member-state deficits. The bonds may continue to be nominally ascribed to the member-state government but to all intents and purposes – being placed on a Community-wide market, quoted on all member-state stock exchanges, denominated in the Community currency, and paying common rates of interest – they would be Community bonds.

The single, unified economy of the Treaty of Rome would be fulfilled, with the member-state bond issues like those of local authorities. The remaining paradox is that deficit finance would be eschewed by the central government authority whilst the substantial deficits of the sub-units would supply the substantial European bond market.

When we come to Economic Union, these paradoxes fall away, and we have an altogether more recognizable situation. A large Community budget is acceptable, both for industrial and welfare programmes and for stabilization policy. It is highly desirable that secular expansion, and short-run variation, be facilitated by deficit financing. Probably the bulk of the bond market is ultimately supplied by direct Community issues. Bond finance of member-states continues, but under full and direct control of the Community authorities. The problems of equitable distribution, or burden sharing, curiously enough are eliminated for deficit finance of the Community budget, but accentuated for member-state budgets where a whole dimension of a nation's budget, not just that corner which is the size of its net contribution to the Community, becomes a matter for the central authority.

Obviously, the logical consequences in the field of debt finance in Economic Union take us far down that road which the approach intends us to go. Economic power concentrates at the centre. Community operation of regional and social policy, financial relations with extra-Community powers (Community deposits with the IMF), is facilitated, member-state economic autonomy is atrophied.

When we turn to the federal approach to the Community, the role of debt financing of the central budget changes again. Like Economic

Union, a substantial budget is called for, but since the main intent is redistributional, the pattern of financial burdens and benefits must be clear and determinable. Grants or expenditures, however financed, fulfil this need, but debt revenue sources do not. Community bonds may be subscribed by residents of richer regions, but they receive market-determinant remuneration, unlike taxes more heavily imposed on the wealthier. So the revenue side would not assist the redistributive programme; its realization by deficit finance is inferior to the use of tax finance unless the latter is strictly non-progressive.

The federalist may further be less interested in deficit finance if his interest in short-term conjunctural policy is minimal compared with the longer-term redistributive role of the Community budget.

Finally, all of the arguments against the use of Community debt to finance Community budget deficits, or indeed member-state deficits, combine together in force in the Inter-Governmental model. The pattern of payments and receipts by member-states need to be clear to effect *juste retour*. The Community budget should remain small, a book-keeping exercise, not perform a conjunctural or redistributive role. And member states need to retain control over the size of their public expenditures and how this is to be financed, issuing national bonds for secular finance or short-term demand management, of a type suited to their national financial structures. Of course, this implies no progress down the road to monetary union, beyond pseudo-union (fixed internal exchange rates) which is precisely all that is allowed in current circumstances.

Public Expenditures in the Four Models

We shall deal more summarily with the expenditure side,[8] for it will easily be seen that the desirable development of public expenditures is sharply distinguished in our four approaches.

Since the Treaty of Rome contained few recommendations for Community industrial or regional, social or welfare expenditure (agriculture being an aberration to the theme), the Treaty is consistent with a low Community tax (as we have seen) and expenditure profile, and therefore not much transfer of spending power from member states. It could be argued that the single economy concept implies common social and welfare services, or at least is inconsistent with markedly different welfare regimes in member states, but the Treaty does not appear to recognize this (see Chapter 12).

In the case of Economic Union, we might say that the single economy concept is extended to the single community concept. Not only productive expenditure – aids to and interventions in industry – become more of a Community responsibility (using the increased and transferred tax and bond revenues) but the homogeneity of the European 'nation' demands equal treatment of citizens as regards health, welfare, education, etc. The expenditures of the Community budget are therefore substantial and of a programme type, redistribution between member states or regions only a by-product.

In the federal system, however, whilst the Community budget may be substantial it is a redistributive agent, helping to equalize the fiscal capacity of member states or regions, who continue to hold autonomy over their industrial and welfare programmes. Of course, the last two models represent 'pure' cases, and in practice, we would only expect particular 'federal' budgets to veer in one direction or the other, as those of the USA, Canada and Australia do. Finally to the current situation of the Inter-Governmental model: minimal Community expenditure, returned to member states, mainly by programme expenditure, in proportion to their contributions. But there is no proper Community 'public goods' expenditure, not even defence, and any significant redistribution between members is ruled out (see Chapters 2 and 10).

Conclusions

The implications for the development of Community tax revenues, bond issues, and public expenditures are sharply different according to the model of the EEC in which the discussion is set. Therefore the observed time-series of these variables will represent 'integration' to some and the lack of it to others, and the aims of policy in each will be quite different for the various 'philosophies' of the Common Market. Hence, with strong forces pulling in different directions, it is not surprising that we observe the actual progress of policy as one of fits and starts, declarations never realized, plans thwarted.

Perhaps the best illustration lies in the field of tax harmonization and tax revenues for the Community. The early aim as regards the VAT was the uniformization not only of the base, but conformity to a single common rate throughout the Community, and the establishment of the origin principle in intra-Community trade. At the same time, further tranches of the common rate would be transferred to the Community budget. In the event, rates have, if anything, increased in divergence and multiplicity. At the same time, the Commission still hanker after the abolition of tax frontiers, which entails fairly close alignment of VAT, and the abolition of the derogations from the VAT base (see EEC (1980b)). Also, of course, increases above the yield of a 1 per cent rate should go to the Community budget (see EEC, 1978a). Whilst these propositions flow from the Commission, individual nation-states alter VAT rates to suit their own convenience, and absolutely resist increases in the percentage going to the central budget. The Commission has gone from a Treaty of Rome model toward Economic Union, the member states (whilst remaining supporters of the EEC) work within the Inter-Governmental model. Federalists would seek a different scenario in tax and budget affairs yet again. All seek 'integration' in the EEC but their normative attitudes determine the actual progress of economic variables desired or achieved. Their interpretation of the time trend of economic time-series in the Community will differ. These trends are examined in the next chapter, where statistical difficulties also present themselves in addition to these philosphical problems.

Notes

1. Trade studies are reviewed, and added to, in El-Agraa (1980b).
2. Some way along this road has been taken by Machlup (1977).
3. The counterpart in practice is the LINK model.
4. We could have included a fifth – the Parallel State (Pinder, 1978), but the detailed characteristics are not yet much worked out.
5. Monetary union itself has several meanings, ranging from simply the narrowing of exchange rate margins between member states to central Community control of monetary policy.
6. Of a vast literature on fiscal federalism, see Oates (1972) and Musgrave and Musgrave (1980).
7. Some of the quantitative consequences are worked out in EEC (1980b).
8. Where these are redistributive, the subject is examined more fully in Chapter 8.

CHAPTER 4

Convergence and the Relationship between the Members of the European Community: Some Indices

Collaboration and Convergence

The importance of the relationship between the economies of the members of the European Community (EEC), and changes in the relationship (convergence or divergence), depends on the policy background considered (see Chapter 3). In this section we shall illustrate by examples why certain relationships are relevant to the present policies of the EEC, and to proposed policies.

Under the most recent important policy innovation, eight of the nine members of the EEC – the exception being the UK – have joined the European Monetary System (EMS). The practical aim of the EMS is the same as its predecessor the 'snake', to reduce the degree of exchange rate instability. If this objective is to be achieved it is desirable that the differences between the EEC members' economic performances should be reduced. In particular the more alike are the members' inflation and growth rates, the less likely it is that pressures to alter parities will develop from divergent trends in competitiveness. Regardless of the eventual outcome of the EMS, it is probable that the members will continue to intervene in some way to stabilize exchange rates and that these considerations will continue to be important.[1]

The relationship between inflation rates is particularly relevant to the long-run objective of monetary unification. Vaubel (1978) argued that the divergence of inflation rates raised the cost of transition to monetary union (pp. 4–5), while Laidler (1978, p. 54) used the disparity of inflation rates in the autumn of 1977 as a basis for arguing that it was undesirable to move toward monetary union at that time. Monetary union entails a common monetary policy, therefore the relationship between money supply growths is of interest as an indication of the extent to which members have similar monetary objectives. Monetary union also entails capital market unification, and the similarity of interest rates appropriately measured is important as an indication of the extent of capital market integration (see Argy and Hodjera (1973)).

The relationship between the general economic performances of the EEC members is relevant to the discussion of the feasibility desirability and possible role of public finance, and stabilization policy in particular, at a Community level – as envisaged by the MacDougall Report (EEC, 1977a). If a degree of similarity exists between the members of the EEC, the co-ordination of economic policy at a Community level to achieve a common objective or a common policy, may be more efficient than independent action at national levels. The MacDougall Report considers the possible role of redistribution policies at a Community level. The justification put forward for intervention is that integration may confer net gains in the aggregate but 'does not necessarily raise the economic welfare in all areas' (p. 60). The cost of an effective redistributive policy is directly related to the disparity between the member states to be reduced. For example, one might expect Community policy objectives to include: income levels (see Chapter 8), growth of income or productivity, and unemployment levels. One reason for Community policies to redistribute incomes is to ensure that potential Pareto improvements become actual improvements (see Chapter 2).

We have shown that given a set of objectives for the Community, the cost of pursuing those objectives is influenced by the relationship between the members. Alternatively, the policy objectives may be adapted because of relationships, for example Dosser *et al.* (1974) argued that 'As autonomous integration proceeds the Community cycle tends to become consolidated, and should correspondingly be dealt with by Community instruments' (p. 21). (Autonomous integration arises 'from trade and factor inter-penetration which is only in part . . . controlled by the action of the public authorities' (p. 21).) Rather than consider the appropriate policies for a given group of countries, in principle it is possible to consider the appropriate group for a given policy, by examining the relationships between a number of countries (for instance see Baker (1980)). For example, persistent chronic inflation problems in a potential member could imply that the country would not be able to take part in an EEC monetary system.

Finally, an important reason for examining convergence is simply that the members have declared this to be an objective, e.g. 'The council is convinced that both the development of the Community and the greater stability of intra-Community exchange relations require that the economic policies of the member states should converge and their economic situations be brought into closer alignment' (*Bulletin of the European Communities*, 11/76, para. 2202).

Types of Convergence and Measurement Problems

Convergence may be defined simply as a process of coming together. A basic distinction can be drawn between the convergence of values in the long run which we shall call 'trend convergence', and increases in the relationship between short-run fluctuations (this form of convergence can be classified according to the nature of the fluctuation, and is described in detail below). Absolute trend convergence may be defined as a reduction through time in the absolute difference between two series. Relative trend convergence exists when the absolute difference between two series at each point of time, divided by the average of the absolute values at that time, is falling. In general absolute convergence does not imply nor is it implied by relative convergence, although absolute convergence (divergence) accompanied by an upward (downward) trend in the mean does imply relative convergence (divergence).

Short-run fluctuations from long-run trends may be cyclical in nature. It is not clear whether increased interdependence will lead to the coincidence of the peaks of one series with the peaks, or with the troughs, of another series. We may define a tendency towards coincident peaks as pro-cyclical convergence, and a tendency towards the coincidence of peaks and troughs as counter-cyclical convergence. For example, when trade increases between two countries counter-cyclical growth may emerge if the growth of one country is at the expense of the other.[2] Conversely, pro-cyclical convergence could emerge from a multiplier reaction between the two with both gaining or losing simultaneously. Short-run fluctuations need not be of a regular cyclical nature, although it is common to find variations in growth or employment described as cyclical fluctuations. A more general concept is that of residual convergence which describes an increase in the relationship between short-run deviations from trends, without the deviations being restricted to any particular pattern. (As with cyclical convergence a distinction could be drawn between pro-residual convergence and counter-residual convergence.)

While the concept of convergence between two countries is not unambiguous, it can be refined to reduce the ambiguity. When a number of countries are involved it is more difficult to arrive at a general conclusion. A summary result necessitates the averaging of a number of relationships. As an illustration of this problem, in Figure 4.1 we show GNP per capita in EUAs for six countries. The relationship between Belgium, France, Germany and Netherlands was clearly a close one throughout the period, but at certain times there appears to have been convergence, and at others divergence.[3] It is clear that Italy and the United Kingdom have diverged from the other four

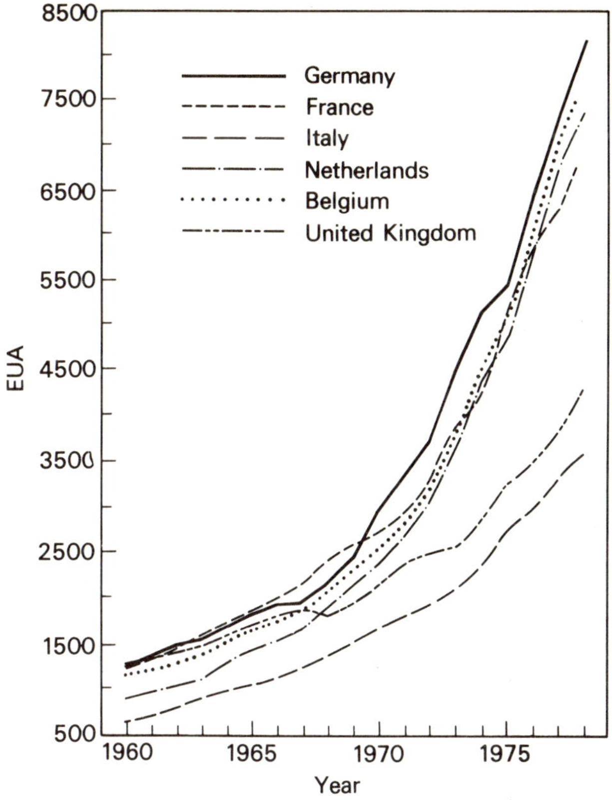

Figure 4.1

members, and converged together. For the group as a whole, the spread across the group has widened from 653EUAs–1286EUAs in 1960, to 3604EUAs–8187EUAs in 1978. (Italy–United Kingdom, and Italy–Germany respectively.) There has clearly been absolute divergence between the top and the bottom countries, but relative divergence has been slight.

The measurement of convergence can be affected by the choice of, and changes in, the units of measurement. Indices of production, prices etc. express the value of a weighted average of goods for one year against the same average for a base year. In Figure 4.2 we show two (imaginary) index number series, *A* and *B*, measured to base 1970 = 100. We might conclude that the series converged (relatively and absolutely) before 1970 and diverged (relatively and absolutely) subsequently. If we adjust the series to base 1960 = 100, *A* and *B* becoming *C* and *D* respectively, then there appears to be relative and absolute convergence throughout. The problem arises because the

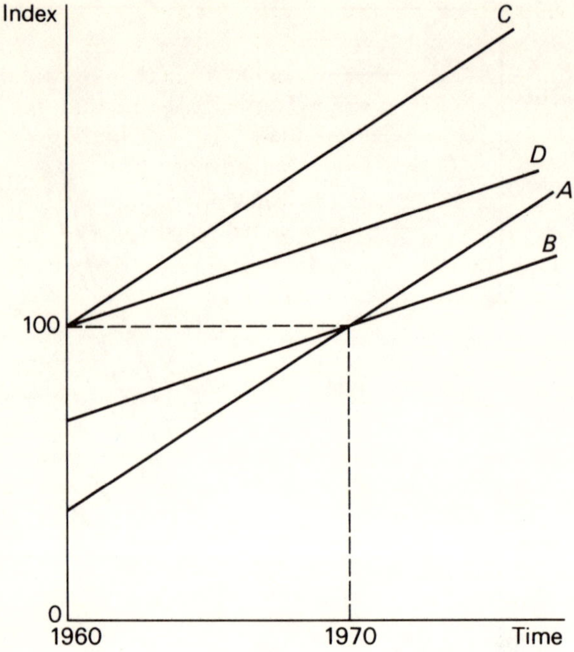

Figure 4.2

series are ordinal not cardinal measures, and comparisons between the values of the two series are meaningless. To avoid this problem we have used growth rates which do not depend on the units of measurement of the series.

Apart from this problem of index numbers, international comparisons are notoriously difficult to make. Indices of production prices etc., not only contain different goods but the weightings given to the same goods differ between countries. Unfortunately this problem is unavoidable and is not removed by using growth rates. Therefore, all comparisons derived from indices should be evaluated within these limitations. Even if we use absolute prices we cannot avoid these problems, because the relationship between prices within each country differs. The ability of any price or index to summarize the characteristics of any economy is limited.

Trade and Interdependence

One would expect the relationship between countries to be stronger the greater the amount of trade between them. An economy with a large external sector will be more susceptible to external influences than a relatively closed economy, and if a high proportion of trade comes from a particular source that source is likely to exert an influence. This transmission mechanism is generally accepted, thus Cairncross (1974) states, 'It is common ground that the increasing inter-penetration, or inter-dependence, of the economies of member countries makes for a synchronization in short-term fluctuations in economic activity and usually intensifies them' (p. 36). One can use this form of inter-dependence to support the argument for a Community policy (or for the co-ordination of national policies) e.g. the Werner Report (EEC, 1970b) argued that inter-penetration had had adverse consequences for the member countries: 'The increasing inter-penetration of the economies has entailed a weakening of autonomy for national economic policies. The control of economic policy has become all the more difficult because the loss of autonomy at the national level has not been compensated by the inauguration of Community policies' (p. 8).

In Table 4.1 we show the ratio of foreign trade (exports plus imports) to GDP measured in current values for the member coun-

TABLE 4.1
Trade as a Proportion of GDP

	BE	*LU*	*DE*	*FR*	*GE*	*IR*	*IT*	*NE*	*UK*
1960	0.67	1.65	0.69	0.28	0.37	0.77	0.28	0.98	0.42
1961	0.69	1.67	0.64	0.27	0.36	0.84	0.28	0.96	0.40
1962	0.68	1.64	0.63	0.26	0.36	0.82	0.28	0.95	0.39
1963	0.70	1.62	0.63	0.26	0.36	0.88	0.29	0.96	0.39
1964	0.73	1.62	0.65	0.26	0.37	0.88	0.28	0.94	0.39
1965	0.73	1.61	0.63	0.27	0.38	0.78	0.29	0.92	0.38
1966	0.73	1.56	0.61	0.28	0.39	0.79	0.30	0.90	0.37
1967	0.72	1.49	0.59	0.27	0.40	0.77	0.31	0.87	0.38
1968	0.77	1.52	0.60	0.27	0.41	0.83	0.32	0.87	0.42
1969	0.83	1.56	0.60	0.30	0.43	0.82	0.34	0.90	0.43
1970	0.85	1.64	0.62	0.30	0.43	0.82	0.35	0.96	0.44
1971	0.85	1.61	0.62	0.31	0.43	0.79	0.35	0.96	0.44
1972	0.84	1.67	0.60	0.32	0.42	0.75	0.37	0.92	0.43
1973	0.93	1.64	0.66	0.34	0.44	0.84	0.40	0.96	0.50
1974	1.06	1.81	0.75	0.43	0.52	1.05	0.51	1.10	0.61
1975	0.92	1.75	0.69	0.37	0.50	0.98	0.49	1.01	0.56
1976	0.98	1.72	0.71	0.40	0.53	1.04	0.52	1.05	0.58
1977	1.05	1.63	0.60	0.41	0.53	1.13	0.48	0.99	0.60
1978	1.03	1.63	0.57	0.39	0.51	1.16	0.48	0.95	0.57
1979	1.12	–	0.62	0.42	0.54	1.25	0.52	1.04	0.58

Notes: BE, DE, FR, GE, IR, IT, LU, NE, UK, denote: Belgium, Denmark, France, Germany, Ireland, Italy, Luxembourg, Netherlands and the United Kingdom, respectively.

Source: IFS, May 1978. All countries 1960–76 (LU 1960–75). Data used national accounts lines (90c + 98c)/99b. Subsequent figures from IFS September 1980 and December 1980.

tries.[4] There has been a steady rise in the value of this ratio for most members (GDP has increased, but foreign trade has increased at a faster rate). As an indicator of the susceptibility of members to the influence of other members this ratio is inadequate as it does not distinguish between trade with EEC and non-EEC countries.

In Tables 4.2 and 4.3 we show the proportion of total imports and exports respectively accounted for by other EEC partners. (The increase in the membership of the Community from six to nine members is reflected in a break in the series at the end of 1971.) With the exception of Ireland and Denmark the share of the EEC in the total exports and imports of each country increased during the sixties. Since 1972 there has been relatively little change except for the UK. The oil crisis may be responsible for the fall of the EEC share of imports – the values for 1974 are lower than those for 1973 in all cases, however this would not explain the fall of export shares in 1974 for all members (except the UK). It is interesting to note that the UK was increasing both its imports and exports with EEC countries even before membership.

We would expect to observe an increasing share of the EEC trade

TABLE 4.2
Share of Imports from EEC* in Total Imports (%)

	BE-LU	*DE*	*FR*	*GE*	*IR*	*IT*	*NE*	*UK*
1960	47.9	38.5	29.4	29.9	–	27.7	45.8	14.6
1961	50.6	39.4	31.5	31.3	–	29.5	49.2	15.4
1962	51.0	37.8	33.6	32.5	–	31.2	50.2	15.8
1963	52.5	35.9	35.8	33.4	15.4	33.0	51.6	16.0
1964	53.3	35.4	37;4	34.9	15.6	32.7	52.0	16.6
1965	54.5	35.6	38.8	38.1	15.3	31.3	53.4	17.3
1966	55.9	34.4	40.9	38.5	13.4	32.5	54.0	18.5
1967	55.6	32.7	43.4	39.6	14.6	34.6	54.5	19.6
1968	54.9	32.7	47.5	41.5	16.4	36.2	55.4	19.8
1969	57.4	33.6	50.5	43.6	15.5	38.7	56.7	19.4
1970	58.8	33.2	48.9	44.4	16.5	41.1	55.9	20.1
1971	63.0	31.8	50.1	46.8	16.5	42.4	54.5	21.4
1972	71.1	45.9	56.0	53.9	69.3	49.2	62.3	31.6
1973	70.6	45.9	55.4	52.2	71.7	48.0	61.0	32.8
1974	66.1	45.5	47.6	48.1	68.3	42.4	57.4	30.0
1975	67.2	45.8	49.8	49.5	69.2	43.0	56.9	32.4
1976	67.5	47.2	50.0	48.2	69.4	43.6	55.2	32.2
1977	67.4	47.7	49.4	49.0	68.1	43.0	54.8	38.5
1978	69.1	49.7	51.4	50.1	70.2	44.7	57.4	38.0
1979	67.3	50.0	50.1	49.3	75.4	44.2	56.4	40.8

* The definition of the EEC changes for the years 1972 onward to include the Nine rather than the Six.

Source: Basic Statistics of the Community, Statistical Office of the EEC.

TABLE 4.3
Share of Exports to EEC* in Total Exports (%)

	BE-LU	*DE*	*FR*	*GE*	*IR*	*IT*	*NE*	*UK*
1960	50.5	29.5	29.8	29.5	–	29.6	45.9	15.3
1961	53.2	29.1	33.5	31.7	–	31.3	47.6	17.4
1962	56.8	28.4	36.8	34.0	–	34.8	49.2	19.3
1963	60.8	28.8	38.2	37.2	7.5	35.5	53.3	21.1
1964	62.6	28.1	38.8	36.4	11.5	37.8	55.6	20.6
1965	61.9	27.4	41.0	35.2	12.9	40.2	55.7	20.0
1966	62.8	25.4	42.3	36.3	11.0	40.6	55.6	19.2
1967	63.0	22.9	41.3	36.8	8.5	38.7	54.9	20.0
1968	64.3	23.3	43.0	37.6	9.0	40.1	57.4	20.2
1969	67.6	23.0	47.8	39.8	11.1	42.5	60.1	21.6
1970	68.5	22.7	48.8	40.2	11.6	43.0	62.0	21.8
1971	68.6	22.4	49.4	40.1	8.5	44.7	63.7	21.0
1972	73.8	43.1	56.3	46.9	78.0	50.3	74.1	30.1
1973	73.1	45.6	56.1	47.1	76.0	50.1	72.6	32.3
1974	69.9	43.1	53.2	44.9	74.1	45.4	70.8	33.4
1975	70.5	45.0	49.2	43.6	79.4	45.1	71.1	32.3
1976	73.7	45.7	50.6	45.7	75.8	47.8	72.1	35.6
1977	71.2	44.3	50.4	44.9	76.5	46.6	70.4	36.6
1978	71.6	47.9	52.5	45.8	77.7	48.0	70.9	37.8
1979	72.8	49.0	52.8	48.3	77.6	49.4	72.6	41.8

* The definition of the EEC changes for the years 1972 onward to include the Nine rather than the Six.
Source: Basic Statistics of the Community, Statistical Office of the EEC.

in total trade but the proportion will not expand indefinitely. Obviously the share cannot exceed 100 per cent, and given that the EEC is not self-sufficient in all commodities, an upper bound is to be expected. The upper bound will not be the same for all members since the type of imports, and the source of imports, will vary across the Community according to the type of industrial activity in which each member specializes. We can conclude from the tables that as the share accounted for by the EEC has increased the potential for disturbances to be transmitted from one Community member to another through trading links has grown. This need not imply that the actual interdependence of the members has increased for other factors may be operating.

McKinnon (1974) examined the relationship between domestic stability and the degree of openness. He found that there was a *positive* relationship between stability and openness – the more open economies being the most stable. This can be taken as grounds for questioning either the assumption that fluctuations are transmitted through the external sector, or, that the fluctuations which are transmitted through this sector are likely to be destabilizing. If disturbances are mainly of domestic origin, an open economy which passes on these disturbances to other countries through trade, may be more stable than a closed economy which must absorb the full impact of a domestic disturbance. Thus, by simply observing the proportion of trade with EEC members has increased we cannot conclude that inter-dependence has increased.

Measures of Convergence

Dispersion Methods

If we measure the dispersion of a variable, say the rate of inflation, across countries at one point in time, and compare it with the dispersion at another point, we have an indication of convergence which will be shown by a falling dispersion rate. We shall employ two measures of convergence: the standard deviation (SD), and the coefficient of variation (CV) which is a measure of relative dispersion (CV equals SD divided by the mean). As the series are likely to exhibit trends relative dispersion should be examined as well as absolute dispersion, because it is independent of the units of measurement: a deviation of 5 units from a mean of 10, may have different significance to a deviation of 5 from a mean of 100. In Tables 4.4 and 4.5 we show the SD and CV (respectively) of a number of variables for the members of the Community over the period 1960 to 1979.

The SD of inflation rates is clearly higher after 1973 than before, although this break does not occur using the CV (because the average inflation rate is higher after 1973). The SD of income levels grows continuously from 278.2 in 1960 to 2967.3 in 1979, but the CV is more stable and mainly varies between 0.25 and 0.35. Neither the SD nor the CV of the growth of GDP or the money supply show any continuous tendency to converge or diverge. The SD of interest rates is higher from 1974 on, but this pattern is not shown in the CV results. The SD of unemployment rates varies little, but the CV is lower after 1974 than before (because of an increase in the average level of unemployment).

From these results it is clear that convergence is not a general phenomenon, certain variables converge at certain times in various ways, and diverge at others. In the terminology developed above, after 1973 there is evidence of absolute trend divergence of inflation, incomes and interest rates, but the relative differences do not change. There is relative trend convergence of unemployment rates but absolute differences do not change.

TABLE 4.4
Standard Deviations

	Growth of consumer prices	*Level of GNP per capita*	*Growth of GDP*	*Growth of money supply*	*Rate of interest*	*Un-employment (%)*
1960	1.245	278.2	–	3.704	1.766	2.174
1961	0.750	301.8	–	4.625	1.354	2.024
1962	1.899	324.1	1.716	5.287	0.858	1.724
1963	1.822	337.4	1.487	3.802	0.845	1.669
1964	1.554	336.1	2.000	1.718	1.177	1.729
1965	0.786	404.0	1.247	3.146	0.537	1.893
1966	1.538	439.6	1.487	4.148	0.654	1.757
1967	1.836	455.9	2.048	3.495	1.378	1.428
1968	1.970	496.8	1.390	2.824	1.446	1.454
1969	1.998	561.6	1.797	4.838	1.599	1.565
1970	1.612	618.0	1.658	6.938	0.991	1.798
1971	1.757	691.4	1.138	5.798	1.157	1.822
1972	1.102	839.8	1.314	2.339	1.766	1.932
1973	1.594	1230.7	1.087	4.896	2.590	1.794
1974	3,726	1417.6	2.187	4,342	1.668	1.442
1975	5.769	1647.9	1.379	3.257	2.353	1.505
1976	4.603	1900.4	1.197	3.644	3.681	1.800
1977	4.376	2188.3	1.260	4.824	2.335	1.876
1978	3.032	2667.6	1.308	6.882	3.022	1.859
1979	4.188	2967.3	0.950	7.534	2.985	1.975

TABLE 4.5
Coefficients of Variation

	Growth of consumer prices	*Level of GNP per capita*	*Growth of GDP*	*Growth of money supply*	*Rate of interest*	*Un-employment (%)*
1960	0.819	0.252	–	0.514	0.284	0.848
1961	0.326	0.252	–	0.539	0.333	0.915
1962	0.461	0.249	0.372	0.538	0.245	0.836
1963	0.445	0.242	0.381	0.355	0.212	0.786
1964	0.340	0.237	0.321	0.208	0.230	0.904
1965	0.190	0.242	0.317	0.364	0.106	0.946
1966	0.387	0.246	0.466	0.531	0.109	0.879
1967	0.488	0.240	0.491	0.463	0.248	0.542
1968	0.497	0.251	0.250	0.347	0.245	0.551
1969	0.417	0.255	0.297	0.607	0.214	0.696
1970	0.304	0.253	0.348	1.053	0.134	0.795
1971	0.272	0.253	0.326	0.477	0.217	0.729
1972	0.166	0.258	0.296	0.158	0.285	0.663
1973	0.182	0.300	0.184	0.417	0.261	0.674
1974	0.271	0.311	1.115	0.584	0.163	0.442
1975	0.411	0.310	−1.298	0.236	0.310	0.296
1976	0.400	0.343	0.235	0.246	0.362	0.321
1977	0.415	0.347	0.497	0.410	0.423	0.315
1978	0.414	0.337	0.415	0.473	0.323	0.307
1979	0.451	0.316	0.284	0.602	0.226	0.344

Dispersion measures have been used elsewhere, e.g. Salant (1977),[5] Argy and Hodjera (1973). They are attractive as they provide a single figure which describes each period. However, this attraction is gained at the expense of an information loss, because one statistic cannot fully describe the data.

Cluster Analysis

The similarity between the EEC members was examined by assessing the similarity of the members with each other and with non-member countries using cluster analysis. Cluster analysis is a technique(s) which groups a number of entities, in this case *N* countries, which are represented by numerical characteristics, which in our analysis were time-series observations, into a smaller number of 'clusters' according to the similarity between the countries. Cluster analysis is not specifically a time-series technique, although our data took the form of *N* series of a variable measured for *p* periods through time it was treated as *N* collections of *p* different variables. The assumption on which the analysis is based is that it is meaningful to compare the value of a variable at a certain time in one country with the value in another. The similarity between each pair of countries is calculated from the *p* observations of each country. In this study each country was considered to be a point in *p* space and the similarity measure the Euclidean distance between points. These similarity measures are used to group the countries into clusters, each set of clusters being dependent on how stringent the criterion for grouping is which we select. As we relax the criterion for clustering more countries will merge together (as the 'permitted' distance between them rises). We can rank the clusters according to a measure of the distance between the countries which have merged. Such a procedure yields the 'dendogram' which shows how the countries cluster together as the distance measure rises. Eventually all the countries merge into one.[6]

The method of analysis we adopted is based on the work of Ward, the program and method used are described in Wishart (1978). One advantage of using cluster analysis in this way is that it does not necessitate the adoption of distributional assumptions since the *p* observations are treated separately as *p* variables which are comparable across countries at any time. We examined three variables, inflation (CPIG), growth of industrial production (IIPG) and the growth in the number unemployed (UNG); IIPG and UNG were seasonally adjusted.[7] Each variable was measured quarterly and the data used covered two periods: 1960–69 and 1970–79. The dendograms are shown as Figures 4.3–4.8.

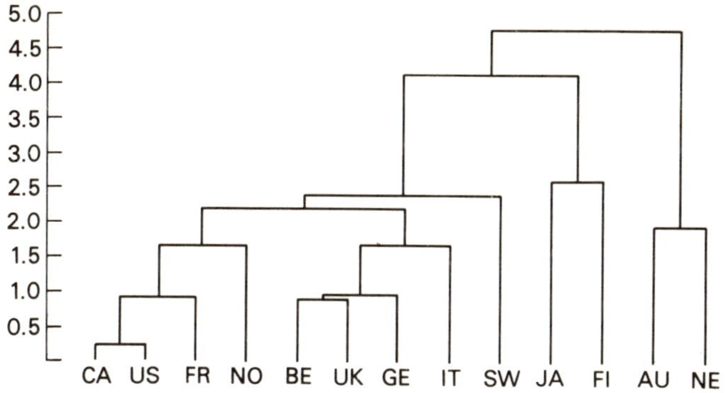

Note: AU, BE, CA, FI, FR, GE, IT, JA, NE, NO, SW, UK, US; denote: Austria, Belgium, Canada, Finland, France, Germany, Italy, Japan, Netherlands, Norway, Sweden, United Kingdom, United States, respectively.

Figure 4.3 CPIG 1960-69

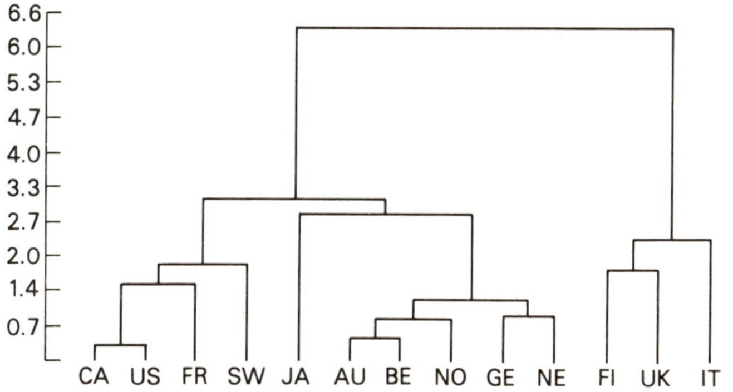

Figure 4.4 CPIG 1970-79

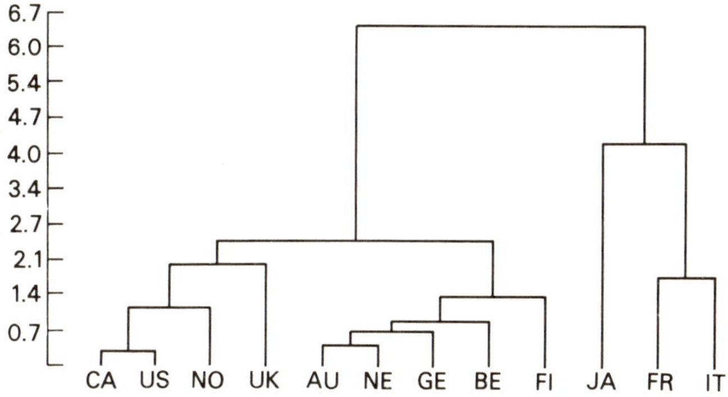

Figure 4.5 IIPG 1960-69

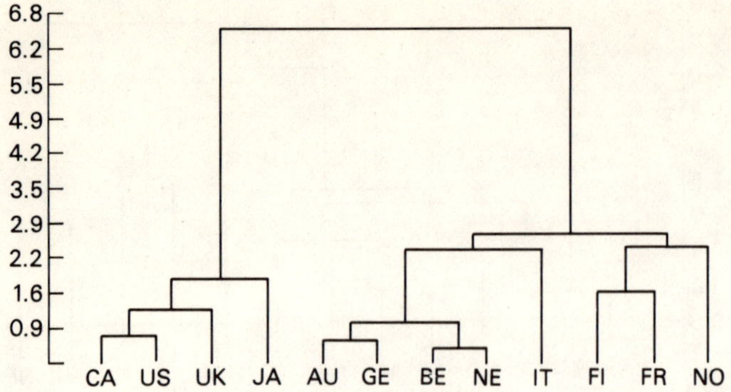

Figure 4.6 IIPG 1970–79

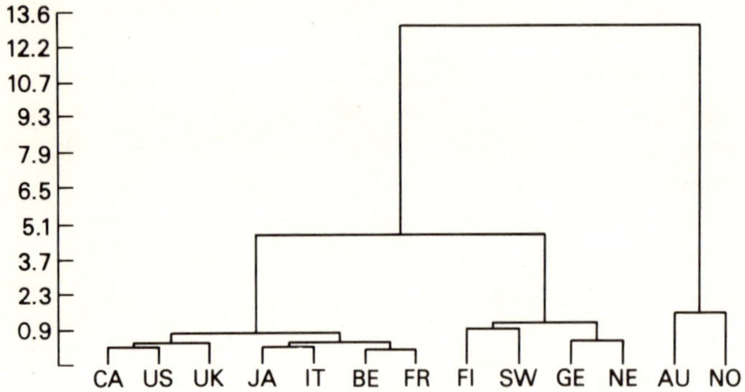

Figure 4.7 UNG 1960–69

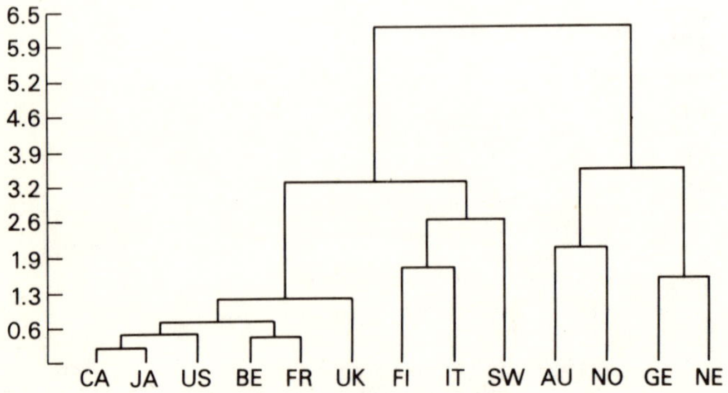

Figure 4.8 UNG 1970–79

Overall the dendograms do not support the hypothesis that over this limited range of characteristics the EEC is a grouping of countries with more similarities with each other than with other countries. There are some reassuring results which support the method, e.g. Canada and the United States cluster with each other first in all but one case, and Austria, Belgium, Germany and the Netherlands cluster together quite quickly in most cases. The method is too crude to allow one to say definitely whether the Community members were more or less alike during the seventies than during the sixties, but there does not appear to be strong evidence of either convergence or divergence. Cherif and Ginsburgh (1976) used cluster analysis[8] and found that 'in some cases more clearly than in others ... the EEC countries have a tendency to form relatively homogeneous groups ... there is however ... no clearcut indication of a trend towards greater homogeneity' (p. 76).

Correlation

In order to assess the relationship between short-run fluctuations we calculated the monthly rate of change of three series: the consumer price index (CPI), the index of industrial production (IIP), and the number of people unemployed (UN); IIP and UN were seasonally adjusted in each separate sample period.[9] The sample period was split into two, 1970–74 and 1975–79, and correlation coefficients were calculated between countries. The results are shown in Tables 4.6–4.8. In the upper right triangle we show the coefficients for the first period, and in the lower left triangle those for the second period.

For the CPI only three of the fifteen correlations are higher in the second period than in the first, most of the correlation coefficients are positive. Values of $|r|$ greater than 0.25 are significant at the 95 per cent level: eleven are significantly different from 0 in the first

TABLE 4.6
The Correlation of Inflation Rates

	BE	*FR*	*GE*	*IT*	*NE*	*UK*
BE	–	*0.66*	*0.25*	*0.72*	*0.25*	*0.42*
FR	−0.11	–	*0.15*	*0.67*	*0.21*	*0.61*
GE	0.33	0.02	–	*0.15*	*0.13*	*0.27*
IT	−0.16	−0.04	−0.08	–	*0.36*	*0.34*
NE	0.17	0.42	0.08	0.15	–	*0.46*
UK	0.40	0.27	0.46	0.04	0.23	–

Note: The numbers in the upper right triangle (italicized) are the results from the first sample period (1960–69).

TABLE 4.7
The Correlation of Changes in Production

	BE	FR	GE	IT	NE	UK
BE	–	*−0.02*	*−0.01*	*−0.01*	*−0.08*	*−0.09*
FR	0.12	–	*−0.03*	*−0.01*	*0.27*	*0.14*
GE	0.05	0.18	–	*−0.11*	*0.05*	*0.05*
IT	−0.16	−0.87	−0.05	–	*0.18*	*−0.01*
NE	0.00	0.13	−0.25	−0.07	–	*0.10*
UK	0.03	0.39	0.03	−0.36	0.16	–

Note: The numbers in the upper right triangle (italicized) are the results from the first sample period (1960–69).

TABLE 4.8
The Correlation of Changes in Unemployment

	BE	FR	GE	IT	NE	UK
BE	–	*0.13*	*0.02*	–	*−0.17*	*−0.97*
FR	0.09	–	*0.10*	–	*−0.24*	*−0.09*
GE	0.10	0.06	–	–	*−0.04*	*0.09*
IT	–	–	–	–	–	–
NE	−0.04	0.01	0.00	–	–	*0.19*
UK	−0.04	−0.08	−0.07	–	−0.07	–

Note: The numbers in the upper right triangle (italicized) are the results from the first sample period (1960–69).

period, and five in the second. These results suggest that members experience similar inflationary disturbances, and the relationship is stronger in the first period. Of the fifteen correlations for IIP, eight are higher in the second period. Only one correlation is significantly different from 0 in the first period, and four in the second. There is an element of convergence, but the relationship between changes in production is weak. Finally, of the ten correlations for UN, four are higher in the second period. However, with one exception the correlations are not significantly different from 0, and this suggests that monthly changes in unemployment levels are not related.

Conclusion

In this chapter we have examined the concepts of convergence and divergence, and the relationship between the members of the EEC using annual, quarterly and monthly data. It was found that there are similarities between the members, but that these similarities are not increasing. Also the relationship between members of the EEC does not appear to be stronger than the relationship between members and non-members. The consequences of interdependence and convergence for macroeconomic policy are considered in Chapter 5.

Appendix: Data Sources

Annual

Consumer prices	Percentage in consumer price index, IMF, *International Financial Statistics* (IFS), various issues.
GNP per capita	*National Accounts of OECD Countries: 1960–1971*, OECD, subsequent data from OECD *Main Economic Indicators* (MEI), various issues.
Growth of real GDP	OECD, *Economic Outlook*, No. 27, July 1980.
Money	Percentage increase in M1, IFS.
Rate of interest	Treasury bill rate for BE, NE and UK; call money rate for FR; IR, official discount rate; IT, medium term bond rate; GE, 'three months money'. MEI for BE, FR, IR, NE, and UK; IFS for IR, and *European Economy*, November 1979 and Supplement, for GE.
Unemployment	Percentage of civil active population. *European Economy*, November 1978 and July 1980.

Quarterly

CPIG	Quarterly change in consumer price index, MEI.
IIPG	Quarterly change in index of industrial production, MEI.
UNSEG	Quarterly change in total unemployed, MEI.

Monthly

CPI	Monthly change in consumer price index, MEI.
IIP	Monthly change in index of industrial production, MEI.
UN	Monthly change in the number unemployed, MEI.

Notes

1. This does not mean that fixed and adjustable parities is the best policy for the Community, see Johnson (1971).

2. For example, Neubauer (1973) emphasizes the importance of cyclical convergence with respect to trade: 'It would seem that the policy of monetary integration can be successful only if trade cycles in the Community are sufficiently synchronised' (p. 135), i.e. he argues that pro-cyclical convergence is desirable. This argument runs counter to that of Baker (1980) who argued that the saving of reserves from monetary union increases as the members' trade balances become more negatively correlated.
3. The data are taken from *European Economy*, November 1979, EEC, D-G for Economic and Financial Affairs, Brussels.
4. Balassa (1975) says: 'Calculating the ratio of exports or imports to GNP is not an appropriate indicator, in part because exports and imports are expressed in value terms while GNP is value added, and in part because GNP includes non-traded goods' (p. 191). This criticism is relevant to Table 4.1 (but not to Tables 4.2 and 4.3).
5. Salant (1977) discusses whether or not a decrease (increase) in dispersion necessarily accompanies an increase (decrease) in the transmission of fluctuations. He concludes that there is not necessarily a relationship between the two (pp. 172–5).
6. The author would like to thank John Illingworth for helpful comments and guidance with cluster analysis, although any errors are the sole responsibility of the author. One problem encountered using cluster analysis is that (in the simple form adopted here) the countries are treated as equals. For the first cluster the 'most similar' form a cluster which results in the minimum increase in the 'within group sum of squared deviations' (see Anderberg (1973), pp. 142–5). For subsequent groupings it may be undesirable to use this cluster (e.g. comprising the average values of Luxembourg and United States) as the basis for analysis. No attempt was made to weight the values as it is not clear what weights (if any) should be used, and any weighting is arbitrary.
7. Seasonal adjustment of unemployment and production was carried out using a moving average.
8. Cherif and Ginsburgh also used principal components analysis. Their results did not suggest the existence of a 'Common Market factor'.
9. The correlations and adjustments were carried out using the TSP computer program.

PART II

Collaboration in Macroeconomic Policy

CHAPTER 5

Progressive Interdependence and Economic Integration: (a) A General Case

Customs Union and the Path of Integration

When countries agree to form a customs union they take a political decision that involves progressively increasing economic interdependence which necessarily leads to more advanced stages of economic integration. Increasing economic interdependence through trade and factor movement renders the instruments of domestic economic policy progressively ineffective and restricts national autonomy in the choice of, and ability to reach, policy targets. Internationalization of the causes of economic problems may require the internationalization of solutions and the exercise of policy at the supranational level. For example, national monetary autonomy does not exist under fixed exchange rates and capital mobility. However, free factor movement and, hence, capital mobility within a fixed exchange rate area is one of the basic requirements and aims of common markets. Therefore, formation of a common market is a move towards unification that implies considerable loss of national economic sovereignty. Consequently, its success as a stage within a dynamic process depends on the degree of commitment of the member countries towards both political and economic integration.

In the following we examine the aims and the effectiveness of national economy policy within the confines of a customs union which is gradually progressing towards greater interdependence. We specifically argue that advanced forms of economic integration give rise to problems of policy co-ordination and harmonization that generate the need for new negotiations and agreements, which impose constraints upon the members and inevitably lead to more integration. Consequently, customs union is not a form of static equilibrium which countries can freely choose to adopt but a stage within the dynamic progress towards advanced integration. Although the following analysis is theoretical, the case of the EEC will be used as an example of integration-in-practice.

The aim of the EEC is to promote economic interdependence between the member states (Treaty establishing the EEC, Article 2). This can only be achieved by co-ordination, that is consultation and co-operation in the choice of targets and the use of instruments, and by harmonization of the economic policies of members states. This kind of progressive interdependence ultimately leads to integration and conditions analogous to those of internal markets. However, the Treaty provides only general outlines of procedures and policies that must be followed for the harmonization of policy objectives (for example Articles 103, 104, 109). On the other hand, the piecemeal approach towards integration adopted by the EEC gives rise to a period of conflict between the national economic objectives of member states and the group objectives of the Community. Solutions to problems of this nature which would mark the progressive or regressive character and the aims of the EEC are not readily available in the Treaty. During the process of integration countries transfer part of their real sovereignty over the design and exercise of economic policy to a supranational authority in exchange for some actual or potential benefit. Since this exchange is voluntary, one must assume that the participating countries have decided that they can achieve their objectives better within than outside the Community.

The next section of this paper presents a general outline of the problems that member countries are faced with in the course of exercising national/domestic economic policy during the process of integration. The third section examines policy conflicts and possible solutions in short-run stabilization analysis. The last section presents briefly the conclusions of the study.

Integration and Macroeconomic Policy

Definitions

The well-known progressive forms of economic integration are (see Balassa, 1962): *Customs Union*, which involves free trade for commodities within the union and the equalization of tariffs in trade with non-member countries; *Common Market*, where not only trade restrictions but also restrictions on factor movements are abolished; *Economic Union*, which involves the suppression of restrictions on commodity and factor movements within the union and some degree of harmonization of national economic policies; and *Total Economic Integration*, which presupposes the unification of monetary, fiscal and other policies and the setting up of a supranational authority whose decisions are binding for member states. These involve progressive loss of national autonomy, and the forging of new elaborate international agreements (see Johnson, 1968). Ultimately, the establishment of supranational institutions is required.

On the other hand, a looser degree of international interdependence is the *Free Trade Area*, where trade restrictions between the participating countries are abolished but each country retains its own trade restrictions against non-members. In the case of a free trade area the need for harmonization additional to what is already required of countries engaged in world trade is nominal and can be handled by existing intergovernmental channels of negotiation and consultation.

Integration and Stability

As the degree of integration rises, intervention in the market in the form of 'harmonization' becomes more intensive. Abolition of restrictions on intra-market trade and unification of national tariff schedules disturbs the *raison d'être* of tariff policy, that is the economic and social reasons on which each member country had based trade intervention prior to the establishment of the customs union. Thus, not only tariffs as an instrument of national policy are lost, but also the targets of that policy are altered by participation in the customs union. Similarly, free movement of factors of production will probably change the stock of productive resources available to a country and, consequently, the pattern, the pace and the limits of domestic economic growth. Therefore, harmonization is actually a package of interventionary policies the need for which arises from the emerging divergence between free market tendencies within a customs union and the conflicting short-run objectives of individual member states. Thus, if the main economic objective of countries participating in a customs union is to increase their individual welfare, it seems more likely that not all of them will succeed without some form of harmonization. A customs union cannot be mutually beneficial for all participants without a policy of transfer payments to the members that will lose from the operation of the market mechanism within the customs union (Riezman, 1979). Thus, free trade in commodities and factors of production within the area of a common market is not a viable practical proposition, unless it is accompanied by such policies that would provide a sort of equality in the benefits and costs of liberalization. But, this kind of intervention simply raises the degree of interdependence and integration. Therefore the intermediate forms of economic integration are from practical necessity unstable situations. Consequently, our contention is that there are only two truly stable categories of integration: (*a*) Free Trade Area and (*b*) Total Economic Integration. All other forms simply constitute intermediate and transitional stages in the process of the voluntary integration of national states by piecemeal methods. Moreover, these transitional forms of integration for economic, political, etc. reasons are inherently unstable. Hence, countries embarking upon a stage of intermediate integration, such as a customs union, impose on themselves economic and political constraints that create difficulties in the exercise of their economic policy and even prevent them from attaining certain of their national economic objectives. In an attempt to overcome these difficulties the countries concerned would move progressively and from necessity to either higher stages of integration and more interdependence or less interdependence and looser integration in the form of a free trade area. Intermediate forms of integration are non-viable. The best historical examples of long-surviving unions are completely integrated states or federations of states.

The Case of the EEC

In practice the course of progressive integration may begin with the members of the union adopting as their basic target the unification of markets, free competition, and market determination of commodity and factor prices. Consequently, the members cease to intervene in the markets for commodities and factors of production and dismantle all the existing measures of intervention and unfair competition by 'policy harmonization'. If intervention is still required for the protection of certain sectors or geographical areas, this is arranged by the union authority at the supra-national level in the form of regional policy, common agricultural policy, etc. Exchange rate unification follows, which aims at the same basic target. However, the harmonization of economic policy and the progress towards the establishment of a common market still leave the national authorities of the member countries with problems that they are not always able to solve with the policy instruments left in their hands and within the constraints imposed in the course of pursuing the adopted common targets. Hence, the need for monetary and fiscal unification, which actually comprises the transfer of both the problems and the means and power to solve them by the national authorities to the authority of the common market. Thus, Community welfare is ranked above the welfare of the individual members.

The EEC's explicit intention is to move towards a greater degree of interdependence and co-operation among its members. The Treaty of Rome[1] states that the aim of establishing the EEC is 'to promote throughout the Community a harmonious development of economic activities, a continuous and balanced expansion, an increased stability, an accelerated raising of the standard of living and closer relations between its Member States' (Article 2). In pursuing this aim the EEC member countries will consider their economic policy 'as a matter of common interest. They shall consult with each other and with the Commission on measures to be taken in response to current circumstances' (Article 103). Furthermore, it is stated that in their domestic policy 'each member state shall pursue the economic policy necessary to ensure the equilibrium of its overall balance of payments and to maintain confidence in its currency, while ensuring a high level of employment and the stability of the level of prices' (Article 104). The instruments of policy which member states may employ to achieve the stated objectives include fiscal, monetary and exchange rate policy, provided that 'each Member State shall treat its policy with regard to exchange rates as a matter of common interest' (Article 107), trade controls *vis-à-vis* non-member countries, mutual assistance 'recommended by the Community', and, in the last resort and subject to Community approval, temporary 'protective measures' against other members: 'Such measures shall cause the least possible disturbance in the functioning of the Common Market' (Article 109). Floating exchange rates are not included among the recommended instruments of policy. Thus, the Treaty assumes implicitly a commitment on the part of the members to maintain fixed exchange rates, that is the *de facto* establishment of an 'exchange rate union'. This implicit requirement is in accordance with the international economic system in operation at the time (1955), but it imposes on the members an extra obligation to maintain domestic economic stability. It can be argued that up to this point the Treaty simply deals with the co-ordination of (Keynesian) macroeconomic policies among the members of the EEC for the purpose of maintaining a satisfactory rate of growth and employment together with reasonable stability of prices within an environment of free commodity trade. However, the Treaty provides an outline for the free movement of factors of production at a later stage of the integration process for the purpose of achieving optimization of resource allocation in the wider area of the Community: 'The free movement of workers shall be ensured within the Community' (Article 43); 'Member States shall ... progressively abolish as between themselves restrictions on the movement of capital' (Article 67). Reference to the Treaty of Rome does not, of course, lead to the conclusion that a fully fledged European Union is the explicitly ultimate objective of the EEC. But, on the other hand, free movement of factors of production may indirectly lead towards economic and political unification. During the early stages of integration the member countries are still functioning as independent economic units, but within an environment of added restrictions arising from policy co-ordination and harmonization. These restrictions or constraints may prevent both the member-countries and the Community as a whole from operating efficiently. For example, the freedom of movement of factors of production may entail the gravitation of productive factors from slow-growth areas to fast-growth areas, which will cause economic imbalances and inequality unacceptable to some member states. Optimization will be possible in the longer run, when aggregate concepts of welfare become politically acceptable to the Community-at-large, and a central authority has control over both growth policy and the distribution of community income. Meanwhile in the short run, that is during the intermediate stages of integration, instead of the optimal allocation of resources the members of the EEC are pursuing 'convergence' in the form of *equalization* of economic performance, an objective that conflicts with the target of optimal allocation of production within the area of the Community-at-large and with the aims of the free mobility of factors of production. Convergence imposes constraints on the growth rate of income of individual member countries and thus of the Community in the aggregate. But, although convergence is neither an optimal nor a stable policy target, it may be viewed as a short-run political compromise for sharing the costs and benefits of participation in the Common Market and, probably, for avoiding the emergence of centrifugal tendencies that might reverse the course of integration.[2] 'Convergence' can be very well justified as a policy which is necessary during the dynamic process that will take the EEC countries along the road of economic and political integration. If the formation of a customs union and the policies followed therein are the means for the realization of higher economic and political aspirations, such as the establishment of the United States of Europe, static economic considerations are assigned to a secondary role.

Short-Run Stabilization Policies

Our hypothesis is that countries participate voluntarily in a customs union for the purpose of achieving certain political and economic objectives that otherwise they may not be able to accomplish outside the union. It is therefore interesting to review situations where conflicts in the field of economic policy may arise and study the means by which solutions can be found. Conflicts are expected (a situation also dealt with in Chapter 6) to occur particularly in the intermediate period between the establishment of a customs union and the ultimate stage of complete political and economic union. Our purpose, however, is to examine conflicts arising from operating short-run stabilization policies during the process of integration and to discuss alternative solutions that are considered compatible with the expressed purposes of voluntary political and economic interdependence.

In a multinational Free Trade Area interdependence is loose and more degrees of freedom in the choice of instruments and targets and the exercise of economic policy are available than in a customs union. Hence, in this case the instruments of economic policy are usually ranked according to their 'effectiveness' on national economic targets. The literature on this subject is dealing mostly with a small country which can exercise independent economic policy, so that use of its vector of instruments for the attainment of a set of given objectives does not significantly affect other countries and, therefore, it does not induce counter-offensive policies by the country's trade partners. Interdependence is examined, if at all, with the capital account of the balance of payments as the main link (Turnovsky and Kaspura, 1974). The possibility that the economic policy of other countries may affect at least some of the economic variables of the small country is usually ignored. This one-sided 'independence' has resulted in unrealistic policy recommendations since the small country may frequently have to apply some of its instruments to offset or to supplement the spillover effects of policies originating in other countries. In order to show maximum interactions both in this chapter and in the next, we use a model of two countries only (Cooper (1969); Roper (1971)), which can be visualized as the only two members of a customs union with insignificant extra-union economic relationships. In this case each member's economic policy on domestic targets has a maximum impact on the other country's economy, while balance of payments disequilibria are symmetrical and become the objective of co-ordinated customs union policy. Problems arising from this kind of economic interdependence are demonstrated in the following sections with the use of simple models of external and internal balance in the two-country world of a customs union which is progressing towards more integration. The models are stationary, in that no growth is considered. This assumption renders the conclusions of the analysis more relevant for the short and medium term, when the intermediate stages of integration occur, than for the long run. We should note at the outset that these models assume that the economy operates under the conditions of the short-run Keynesian underemployment equilibrium with constant prices and, hence, identical nominal and real magnitudes. Consequently, the analysis does not deal with problems of price instability and inflation. In fact, while the process of integration is not in itself a cause of inflation, the fixed exchange rates system, which countries committed to integration are expected to adopt, and the progressive loss of autonomy of national monetary policy make inflation a problem of international, i.e. intra-union, dimensions. For similar reasons, the following analysis does not deal with the external economic relations of the economic union.

Two-country models have, of course, obvious limitations. Thus, in the context of integration, the omission of the *outside world* and the relative economic importance of the customs union in world trade present an unrealistic framework that exaggerates both the causes and the outcomes of economic actions and counteractions within the union while it ignores extra-union repercussions. Consequently, the following analysis is presented only as a sketch of basic situations that might describe possible theoretical directions of the process of economic integration, but are not claimed to be realistic projections of the complex problems that accompany the course of economic integration in practice. We assume that the countries concerned trade in both goods and capital, while labour does not migrate internationally. The purpose of the analysis is to show that, even under these simple constraints on national economic policy, problems arise that will generate tendencies for change which lead towards increasing interdependence.

Customs Union

We examine first a small country's policy options outside a customs union.

The country's expenditure sector is given by the identity[3]

$$Y = E(Y, r) + G + T(Y, \gamma),$$
$$E_Y > 0,\ E_r < 0,\ T_Y < 0,\ T_\gamma > 0,\ (1 - E_Y - T_Y) > 0. \qquad (1)$$

The country's income, Y, equals the sum of private expenditure, E, government expenditure, G, and the balance of trade, T. Private expenditure on consumption and investment depends on the level of income and the rate of interest, r. The balance of trade depends on the level of income and the exchange rate, γ, which is defined as the price of foreign currency in terms of domestic currency. The balance of payments, B, of the country equals the sum of the trade balance and the net capital inflow, K. That is

$$B = T(Y, \gamma) + K(r) \tag{2}$$

where $K_r > 0$, on the assumption that the foreign rate of interest remains constant.[4] The country's monetary sector is

$$\begin{aligned} &M = L(Y, r), \\ &L_Y > 0,\ L_r < 0. \end{aligned} \tag{3}$$

The money supply, M, is exogenous, while the demand for money, L, depends on the country's income and the rate of interest. For two policy-determined variables, G and M, and two targets, Y and B (or γ), the policy multipliers are

$$\frac{\partial Y}{\partial G} > 0, \quad \frac{\partial Y}{\partial M} > 0, \tag{4}$$

$$\frac{\partial B}{\partial G} \gtreqless 0, \quad \frac{\partial B}{\partial M} < 0, \tag{5}$$

and for the case of flexible exchange rates,[5]

$$\frac{\partial \gamma}{\partial G} \gtreqless 0, \quad \frac{\partial \gamma}{\partial M} > 0. \tag{6}$$

We assume now that this small country agrees with another country, the partner, to form a customs union and to trade exclusively with each other. Hence, the expenditure sectors for the country under consideration and its partner respectively are:

$$\begin{aligned} &Y = E(Y, r) + G + T(Y, Y'), \\ &T_{Y'} > 0, \end{aligned} \tag{7}$$

$$\begin{aligned} &Y' = E'(Y', r') + G' - T(Y, Y'), \\ &E'_{Y'} > 0,\ E'_{r'} < 0,\ T_Y < 0,\ T_{Y'} > 0,\ (1 - E'_{Y'} + T_{Y'}) > 0 \end{aligned} \tag{8}$$

where the partner's variables are indicated by a prime. Notice also that the partner's balance of payments is equal, but of the opposite sign, to equation (2), so that $B + B' = 0$. At this stage of integration the only agreed link between the two countries is the balance of trade. However, this degree of interdependence cannot last, if changes in the country's rate of interest affect the flow of capital within the customs union. Thus, the system of equations (2), (3), (7) and (8) provides the multipliers

$$\frac{\partial Y}{\partial G} > 0, \quad \frac{\partial Y'}{\partial G} < 0, \quad \frac{\partial B}{\partial G} \lesseqgtr 0, \tag{9}$$

$$\frac{\partial Y}{\partial M} > 0, \quad \frac{\partial Y'}{\partial M} < 0, \quad \frac{\partial B}{\partial M} < 0. \tag{10}$$

Consequently, assuming that the country pursues expansionary public expenditure policy, disturbances in the partner's equilibrium variables will occur, even if the country that initiated the policy changes does not diverge from the implicitly agreed objective of equilibrium in the balance of payments at $B = 0$, which can be pursued by monetary policy. The next step, therefore, is to recognize the interdependences of the two countries through both the current and the capital account of the balance of payments and the expected reaction of each country to the disturbances caused by the spillover effects of the partner's economic policy. For this, we introduce the monetary sector of the partner-country

$$M' = L'(Y', r'), \tag{11}$$

$$L'_{Y'} > 0, \; L'_{r'} < 0,$$

and the modified balance of payments equation

$$B = T(Y, Y') + K(r, r'), \tag{12}$$

where $K_{r'} < 0$. The system of equations (3), (7), (8), (11) and (12) provides the multipliers:[6]

$$\frac{\partial Y}{\partial G} > 0, \quad \frac{\partial Y'}{\partial G} > 0, \quad \frac{\partial B}{\partial G} \gtrless 0, \tag{13}$$

$$\frac{\partial Y}{\partial M} > 0, \quad \frac{\partial Y'}{\partial M} > 0, \quad \frac{\partial B}{\partial M} \gtrless 0. \tag{14}$$

A similar set of multipliers is obtained, if we assume that the balance of payments surplus or deficit affects the equilibrium of the monetary sector (sterilization policy). If each country uses two policy instruments, monetary policy that changes the stock of money supply and public expenditure policy that changes the flow variable G, to pursue two policy targets, that is a certain level of income and a certain position of the balance of payments (or the price of foreign exchange), equilibrium will not necessarily be reached. Thus, assuming that under a fixed exchange rates system one of the countries has full employment and deficit and the other country has full employment and surplus in the balance of payments, policies by either of the two countries directed towards attainment of internal and external equilibrium affect the internal equilibrium of the other country. Interdependence can therefore lead to instability and cyclical disturbances by a process of actions and counteractions in the field of economic policy.[7] It is therefore reasonable to assume that each country recognizes this danger and tries to avoid the disturbances of its own policies on the partner's economy.[8] Accordingly, each country should aim at three objectives, its own income, the balance of payments, and the neutralization of the impact of its policies on the partner's economy which could start the cyclical reactions. These three objectives cannot be achieved by each country acting on its own with the available two instruments of economic policy. Two solutions are possible, the ranking of which depends on the degree of preference for economic interdependence and advanced integration: (*a*) the introduction of freely flexible exchange rates, which will release the monetary policy instrument from the balance of payments objective (or constraint); and (*b*) policy co-ordination between the two countries so that with their four instruments of policy they can attain the targets. Adoption of the first solution would mean that national monies cease to be perfect substitutes and this is a movement towards less interdependence and contrary to the aims of integration. Fixed exchange rates with unrestricted interconvertibility is the only system compatible with the 'internationalism' (Machlup, 1980) implied by commitment to integration. Provided no new money is created by either country, changes in output are thus shared between the partners and the customs union's money stock is redistributed.[9] The second solution is well recognized in the theory and practice of economic policy in interdependent economies which tend to co-ordinate and to harmonize policies and goals. Harmonization is, however, a movement towards more interdependence and a higher stage of integration than that provided by a customs union. It is in fact a step towards the formation of an Economic Union.

Common Market

The relationship between capital flows and the rates of interest in the two countries, equation (12), was of crucial importance for the derivation of the policy multipliers, (13) and (14). Independent interest rate policies in a world of two or more countries within a customs union is, however, a very unrealistic assumption. The use of monetary policy on domestic or balance of payments targets could conflict with the objectives of efficient resource allocation, by deliberately invoking perverse movements of capital. Greater mobility of capital will increasingly mean that the member countries keep their interest rate levels in alignment. Under permanently fixed exchange rates, in the case of policy oriented interest rate differentials, free movement of capital and interest arbitrage will certainly ensure the equalization of interest rates in the two countries (Holmes (1972); Dernburg (1970)). Consequently, the rate of interest will not determine capital flows between the two countries, but rather capital flows and a common rate of interest will be determined simultaneously. This interrelationship raises problems with the degree of effectiveness and independence of domestic monetary policy. Furthermore, to serve their common objective of integration the countries have to establish an exchange-rate union, at least by fixing the exchange rate and co-ordinating monetary policies. We assume therefore that the two countries adopt a system of fixed convertibility between their national currencies, which is subject to periodic adjustments. There is still no explicit integration of economic policy, no common pool of foreign-exchange reserves, and no single supranational monetary authority. Each country has its own reserves and conducts its own monetary and fiscal policies, aware of the international repercussions of national economic policy. The model for two countries is therefore modified as follows:

(*a*) Capital is perfectly mobile so that the same rate of interest, r^*, will be determined in both countries, that is, the capital market is integrated.

(*b*) The balance of payments position will be reflected in the changes of foreign exchange reserves, which will affect the supply of money (no sterilization). Thus, the supply of money consists of foreign exchange, R, and domestic assets, M; the latter is the monetary policy variable of the country. Assuming that in the two-country world, the level of reserves, W, is fixed, we have the identity

$$\bar{W} = R + R'.$$

This formulation transforms the character of the problem of equilibrium in the external sector from that of flow equilibrium (balance of payments, B), to that of stock equilibrium (reserves R).

The two-country model will consist of the following system of equations (Mundell, 1964):

$$Y - E(Y, r^*) - T(Y, Y', \gamma) - G = 0, \quad (15)$$

$$Y' - E'(Y', r^*) + T(Y, Y', \gamma) - G' = 0, \quad (16)$$

$$M + R - L(Y, r^*) = 0, \quad (17)$$

$$M' + \bar{W} - R - L'(Y', r^*) = 0. \quad (18)$$

For target variables Y, Y', R, R', and r^* none of the countries acting on its own can be successful. Co-ordination of policies and instruments will eliminate the overlapping targets and the results become determinate. The effects of changes in the policies of each country have international repercussions. Thus domestic policies under the unlikely regime of flexible exchange rates and perfect capital mobility within the common market[10] provide the following policy multipliers:

$$\frac{\partial Y}{\partial G} > 0, \ \frac{\partial Y}{\partial M} > 0, \ \frac{\partial Y'}{\partial G} > 0, \ \frac{\partial Y'}{\partial M} < 0, \ \frac{\partial r^*}{\partial G} > 0, \ \frac{\partial r^*}{\partial M} < 0. \quad (19)$$

Therefore, the international transmission mechanism remains at work even under a regime of flexible exchange rates, provided that capital is perfectly mobile (Mundell (1964), p. 428). In other words, flexible exchange rates do not insulate the country from foreign disturbances, which can still be transmitted by capital flows. If instead of flexible exchange rates the partner countries adopt the most likely regime of fixed exchange rates, the corresponding policy multipliers are:

$$\frac{\partial Y}{\partial G} > 0, \ \frac{\partial Y}{\partial M} > 0, \ \frac{\partial Y'}{\partial G} \lesseqgtr 0, \ \frac{\partial Y'}{\partial M} > 0, \ \frac{\partial r^*}{\partial G} > 0, \ \frac{\partial r^*}{\partial M} < 0. \quad (20)$$

These multipliers show that an increase in domestic money supply increases domestic and foreign income. The increase in domestic expenditure has ambiguous results on foreign income, since it increases domestic income and induces imports but it also initiates increases in the common rate of interest inducing an inflow of capital which will ultimately equalize the rate of interest in the two countries at a relatively high level. The system will not provide equilibrium solutions if each country desires different rates of growth and attempts to achieve a target rate of interest different (lower) from the one provided by the interdependence of financial-capital markets. Perfect capital mobility results therefore in 'integration' of the monetary sectors of the two economies under either flexible or fixed exchange rates, and it will be a matter of indifference to the individuals in both countries whether they hold home or foreign currency (Kemp, 1977). There is therefore a connection between a *common market*, which involves free mobility of capital, and a *monetary union*, so that countries that have formed a common market move naturally towards a monetary union. This is necessary when the sovereignty over policy actions diverges from the ability to control the members' national economic targets and as the means for achieving the targets of integration. It is not dependent upon arguments for the formation of optimum currency areas.

Monetary Union

Monetary union of countries establishing a common monetary policy under fixed exchange rates is not free of problems. Unanticipated changes in the fixed exchange rate, caused by either intra-union spillover effects of domestic policies in the partner countries or extra-union disturbance, would be highly disruptive (McKinnon, 1979). On the other hand, each member country undertaking a parity commitment – or a 'modest band' pledge – is expected to direct its short-run monetary policy towards the target of fixed parities. This implies that the members have to act jointly, not only in the area of intra-market economic policy, but also in the area of their extra-market trade and monetary deals. Consequently, against the advantages to be gained from monetary union must be set the questions of effectiveness of national economic policy and the cost considerations of the loss of national sovereignty over monetary policy. The internationalization of capital markets – for example through transnational mergers and take-overs, multinational enterprises and so forth – and, at a later stage, the integration of the markets for labour and the internationalization of trade unions render the instruments of national economic policy increasingly ineffective. Thus, free capital mobility under a regime of fixed exchange rates leads to integration of money markets and to progressive loss of national control over domestic monetary conditions. At the same time regional and inter-country differences are aggravated by factor mobility and may call for further increases in interventionary policies which cannot be implemented for lack of alternative policy instruments or control over the choice of targets. Monetary problems in the integrated area should therefore become the responsibility of an integrated monetary authority which will be the sole manager of internal and external monetary affairs at the level of the economic community. Monetary integration will not necessarily require the simultaneous integration of fiscal policies, which, nevertheless, need to be harmonized. However, in the absence of a national monetary sector, for the financing of budget deficits governments will have to rely on their capacity to borrow on the community's capital markets.

Monetary union as envisaged by the EEC involves the formation of 'an individual monetary unit within the international system, characterized by the total and irreversible convertibility of currencies, the elimination of fluctuating margins of rates of exchange and the irrevocable fixing of parity rates'.[11] This has been reiterated in the schemes put forward for the establishment of the European Monetary System (EMS).[12] Consequently, we assume that the two countries form a monetary union by establishing a supranational monetary authority, while they still maintain their national fiscal policy. There is only one currency in circulation issued by the single central bank of the community. The two-country model consists of equations (15) and (16) and the equation of the integrated monetary sector:

$$\bar{W} + M^* = L(Y, r^*) + L'(Y', r^*), \tag{21}$$

where M^* is the exogenous supply of money of the monetary authority. The solutions of the model provide the following multipliers:

$$\frac{\partial Y}{\partial G} > 0, \quad \frac{\partial Y}{\partial M^*} > 0, \quad \frac{\partial Y}{\partial G'} \gtrless 0, \tag{22}$$

$$\frac{\partial Y'}{\partial G} \gtrless 0, \quad \frac{\partial Y'}{\partial M^*} > 0, \quad \frac{\partial Y'}{\partial G'} > 0, \tag{23}$$

$$\frac{\partial r^*}{\partial G} > 0, \quad \frac{\partial r^*}{\partial M^*} < 0, \quad \frac{\partial r^*}{\partial G'} > 0. \tag{24}$$

The effects of fiscal policy on the common rate of interest and on domestic income are positive. Once again, the direction of change of foreign income is ambiguous, because increase in domestic income has positive repercussions on the partner's income through trade effects while the increase in the rate of interest effects the partner's internal balance by an outflow of capital and the subsequent higher cost of investment. Monetary union which involves exchange-rate unification, integration of the capital market and establishment of a single monetary authority, transforms the countries into *regions* of the integrated area and separate balances of payments cease to exist. Monetary policy can now be directed towards the target of growth of the integrated area (or towards the balance of payments of the integrated area and the outside world). Domestic fiscal policies aim at regional problems of employment stabilization and welfare. But while regional problems of inequalities and imbalances can be corrected in the long run through sufficient capital investment, there are limits on the amounts of capital that regions can borrow in the community's markets. Furthermore, there are still short-run problems arising from the harmonization of fiscal policies and the lack of regional monetary policy. These problems remain the responsibility of the community's budgetary authority which may have to establish a mechanism for interregional transfers, such as the Regional Fund of the EEC and, to a certain extent, the CAP. A policy of interregional transfers is indispensable, if the targets within the integrated area are balanced growth, interregional distribution of income, and compensatory adjustments for the inequities which may arise from the enhanced mobility of factors of production within the integrated area. As will be shown in Chapter 6, it is likely that under monetary union national governments will need to co-ordinate all their policies to achieve their targets; this situation has been almost envisaged in the Marjolin Report. In a monetary union 'national governments put at the disposal of the common institutions the use of all the instruments of monetary policy and of economic policy whose action should be exercised for the Community as a whole. These institutions moreover must have a discretionary power similar to that which national governments possess now, in order to be able to meet unexpected events' (EEC, 1975b). In other words, economic integration cannot be achieved without political integration.

The Inexorable Path of Economic Integration

When countries agree to form a customs union they take a political decision that involves progressively increasing economic interdependence which leads necessarily to more advanced stages of economic integration and subsequent loss of autonomy in the design and exercise of their national economic policy. Economic interdependence through trade and factor movement renders the instruments of domestic economic policy progressively ineffective and restricts the choice of policy targets and the ability to reach them. Internationalization of the causes of economic problems may require the internationalization of solutions and the exercise of policy at the supranational level. Thus, national monetary autonomy does not exist under fixed exchange rates and capital mobility and the traditional separation between domestic and external policy becomes invalid. Since free factor movement and, hence, capital mobility is one of the basic requirements and aims of common markets, a move towards monetary unification may be both desirable and necessary. However, monetary unification implies considerable loss of national economic sovereignty and, consequently, it depends on the degree of commitment of countries towards political, institutional and economic integration. The EEC Treaty and subsequent Council Resolutions have laid down a number of objectives which demonstrate a high degree of commitment towards integration, such as: (i) the establishment of a common market by the free movement of persons, goods, services and capital; (ii) free competition and progressive alignment of member states' economic policy; (iii) common economic policies on external trade, agriculture, transport (and, to some extent, energy, regional policy and environment). Therefore, a move towards European Monetary Union follows naturally from the process of integration.

The argument is taken further, in a detailed investigation of the Monetary Union case, in the succeeding chapter.

Notes

1. *Treaty Establishing the European Community*, signed in Rome on 25 March 1957.
2. Short-run inequality in the distribution of benefits and costs is perhaps the main cause of the collapse of the East-African Community (Hazlewood, 1979).
3. We adopt the usual convention of denoting derivatives by subscripted letters.
4. This specification is standard in the simple exposition of Keynesian models and its limitations are well known. Recent portfolio allocation theory has shown that capital flows respond to changes in the interest differential between domestic and foreign money markets, rather than the size of the differences (Tsiang, 1975).
5. The multiplier $\partial B/\partial G$ is positive if $K_r L_y > T_y L_r$, that is if the slope of the *LM*-curve (monetary sector) is greater than the slope of the *BB*-curve (balance of payments) both taken in the *r*-*Y* plane.
6. If $B = 0$ and monetary policy is directed towards the stability of the foreign exchange market, that is γ, the results are similar.
7. For the importance of time lags in the structure of actions and reactions of policy see Cooper (1969) and Roper (1971).
8. Treaty of Rome, Article 109. An alternative plausible assumption usually adopted in this field is that the country will predict the effects of the other country's policies on its own economy and it will act to offset or supplement them to achieve its own objectives; see Cooper (1969), and compare with the Stackelberg equilibrium of duopoly.

9. The EEC Treaty does not explicitly specify a preference for either type of exchange rates system, although there are implicit references to a fixed rates regime. At the time of signing the Treaty nobody could have foreseen that the Bretton Woods system was coming to an end.
10. In this case, $r = r' + \partial\gamma$.
11. EEC Resolution, 9 February 1971.
12. EEC Resolution, 5th December 1978. However, the establishment of the EMS is not necessarily a step towards the ultimate target of a European monetary union.

CHAPTER 6

Progressive Interdependence and Economic Integration: (b) The Case of Monetary Union

Implications of Monetary Union

The previous chapter has commented on the potential policy conflicts that may arise in the presence of international economic interdependence. Such conflicts do not necessarily cause countries to attempt to isolate themselves from the rest of the world, and may, instead, cause them to progress to greater co-ordination of policies or even more advanced stages of integration.

This chapter will build upon the previous one by focusing in detail upon the co-ordination problems facing macroeconomic policy makers using a two-country model similar to the one in the previous chapter. The conclusions which will be reached are that recognition of interdependence and co-ordination of economic policies can improve macroeconomic performance, but that a move to full monetary union, as often discussed in the EEC, may involve some cost in terms of economic sovereignty far beyond the restrictions placed on the monetary policies of the members.

There are four sections of this chapter. The next section presents a geometric model to indicate how interdependence and policy interaction can weaken the autonomy of national economic policy, and shows the potential for gains from co-operation. The third section uses an algebraic model to show more clearly how co-ordination of policies can satisfy the objectives of co-operating governments, as well as to indicate the costs imposed on the governments under various circumstances. Differences in the assumptions underlying the models in these two sections are pointed out; both models are highly simplified but both illustrate the effects of macroeconomic interdependence. Finally, the last section offers some conclusions.

Macroeconomic Interdependence: A Geometric Approach

There are a number of elements involved in the general usage of the term macroeconomic interdependence. First, trade in goods links economies with one country's imports obviously being another's exports. Second, trade in assets means that not only goods but also assets in one country become closer substitutes for those in another. Third, and most important for present purposes, is the small number of influential countries. It is this third element which makes it no longer possible to make the small economy assumption, that is, it is no longer possible to examine an open economy under the assumption that whatever the economy does, the rest of the world remains unaffected. This third aspect of interdependence may be highlighted by analysing a macroeconomic model consisting of two countries. The remainder of this section examines such a model using a geometric approach to illustrate the difficulties facing macroeconomic policy in an interdependent world where policy interactions and repercussions are important. This is not to say, however, that co-ordination is not likely to be important for a large number of small countries all affected by a common external shock such as a bad harvest or oil price rise.

For simplicity it is assumed that the exchange rate between the national currencies of the two countries in the model is fixed, and that the currencies are freely convertible for current account transactions (trade) but that there is no convertibility for capital account transactions so perfect capital immobility holds. These assumptions make it possible to leave aside considerations of fluctuations in the exchange rate and the role of interest rate arbitrage, but still allow interdependence through trade flows. Figure 6.1 illustrates the relevant arguments for the home economy, whilst Figure 6.2 relates to the foreign economy. Taken together the diagrams represent a special case chosen to highlight the effects of interdependence.

The Home Economy

Figure 6.1 consists of four sections. Section (*a*) of Figure 6.1 shows the standard short-run *IS*/*LM* curves representing equilibrium real interest rate, r, and real income, Y, loci in the goods and money markets respectively. Initially both markets are in equilibrium at the combination r_0 and Y_0. However, for r_0 and Y_0 to remain as equilibrium values it is necessary to check other parts of the model to see that nothing is taking place to shift either the *IS* or *LM* curves.

Section (*b*) of Figure 6.1 shows real exports, X, and real imports, M, both rising with the level of home income. The usual small economy analysis shows imports rising with income, but holds exports constant. Here it is necessary to allow for rising imports, which are the exports of the foreign country, causing the foreign

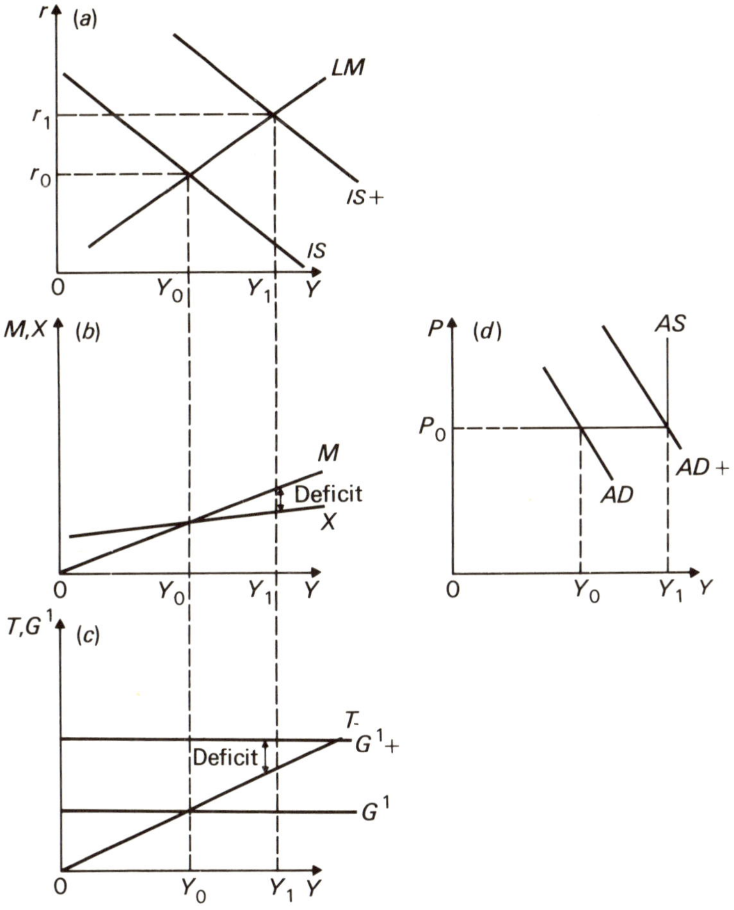

Figure 6.1 The Home Economy

income level to rise. Rising foreign income causes increased demand for imports by the foreign economy, and these imports are the exports of the home economy. The relative slopes of the export and import lines represent the plausible assumption that the direct effect of home income on imports exceeds the indirect effect on exports. Again equilibrium is shown at income level Y_0 where exports equal imports and trade is balanced, which with the assumption of zero capital flows implies that the balance of payments is causing no net flows of money into or out of the economy, and is placing no pressure on the *IS/LM* equilibrium in section (*a*).

The monetary approach to the balance of payments places great stress on the self-equilibrating tendencies in the balance of payments,

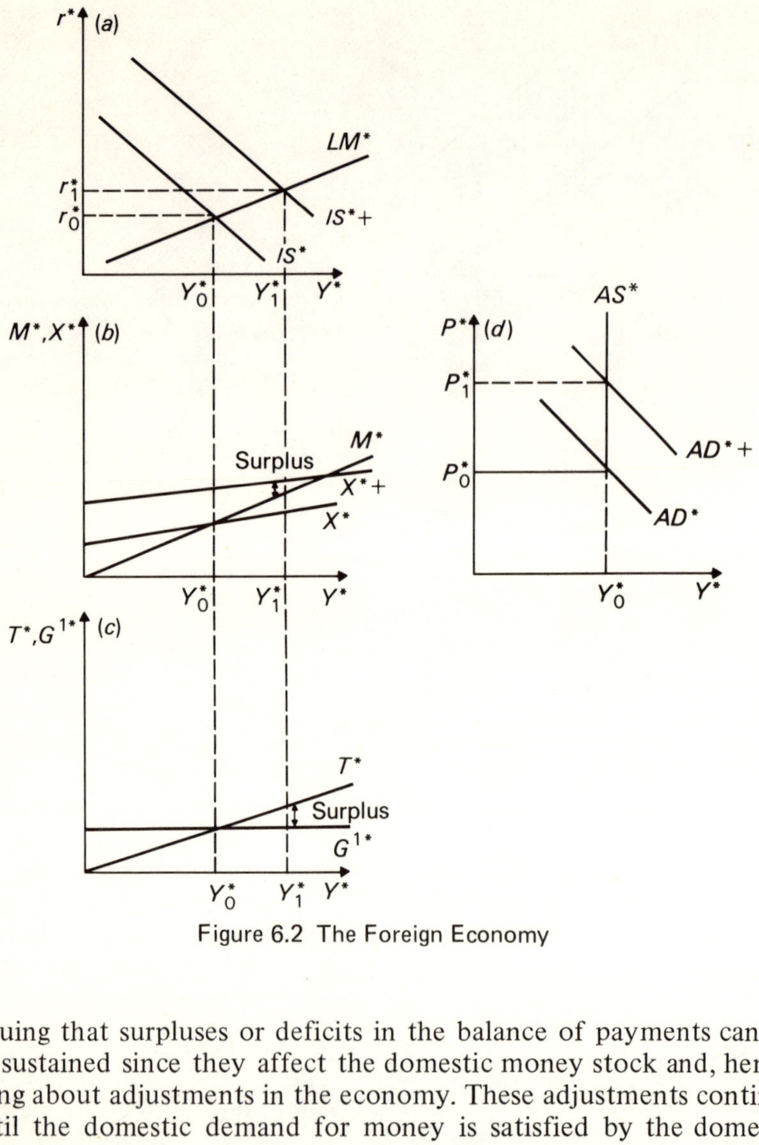

Figure 6.2 The Foreign Economy

arguing that surpluses or deficits in the balance of payments cannot be sustained since they affect the domestic money stock and, hence, bring about adjustments in the economy. These adjustments continue until the domestic demand for money is satisfied by the domestic money stock and the balance of payments is in equilibrium (see, for example, Johnson, 1972). Such stock-flow effects are important, but despite apparent claims to the contrary,[1] they can be recognized in Keynesian models even, in some cases, at text-book level (see, for example, Levacic, 1976). Thus, in the absence of offsetting sterilization policies by the government, surpluses or deficits would affect domestic money stocks and would cause shifts in the *IS*/*LM* sector. The real points at issue are not whether Keynesian open economy analysis is more or less logically consistent than the monetary approach to the balance of payments, but concern instead the stability of the economy, the time-scale to adjustment, and the time-scale over which sterilization policies are feasible.

The balance of payments is not the only means by which domestic money stocks are affected, and it is also necessary to take account of flows into or out of the money stock as a result of government financing. 'Indeed, the government budget constraint and the balance of payments constraint are precisely analogous for an open economy and must be analysed together' (Currie, 1976). Whilst such criticism was directed towards the monetary approach to the balance of payments it would also seem to apply to earlier Keynesian analysis which also, to some extent, neglected the role of government financing.

The government budget constraint does not place limits on government expenditure, but is simply a financing requirement. The government must always finance its spending in one way or another, either by taxation, borrowing or printing money. Section (*c*) of Figure 6.1 shows real taxes, T, rising as a function of income, whilst real government spending inclusive of transfers and interest payments, G^1, is, for simplicity, assumed to be unresponsive to income. The government budget is balanced at Y_0 where G^1 equals T, and so the government budget is not causing any flows into or out of the domestic money or bond stocks and is not disturbing the *IS*/*LM* sector equilibrium.

Whilst standard short-run closed economy models require a balanced budget at equilibrium to prevent disturbance to the money or bond stocks (see, for example, Blinder and Solow (1973)) and standard open economy models require balance of payments equilibrium for the same reason, it is clear that neither condition is necessary when the government budget and balance of payments are both taken into account. It is possible, even if unlikely, that the government could finance a deficit (surplus) by printing (destroying) money whilst domestic money stocks remain constant since the money pumped in (taken out) by the government flows out (in) through a balance of payments deficit (surplus) of equal magnitude to the budget deficit (surplus). However, at income Y_0 both a balanced budget and balance of payments equilibrium coincide.

Finally, section (*d*) of Figure 6.1 shows a reverse-L aggregate supply function, *AS*, with an extreme Keynesian horizontal tail over which price is fixed and quantity varies, and an extreme classical vertical section over which it is price which varies and quantity which is fixed. The aggregate demand line, *AD*, consistent with the discussion so far cuts *AS* at Y_0 and price level P_0.

The Foreign Economy

Figure 6.2 shows the corresponding situation in the foreign economy with equilibrium at r_0^*, Y_0^*, G^{1*} and P_0^*. It is now quite easy to show why policy interactions are important in such interdependent economies, and why governments need to take each other's actions into account. Consider that the home country's government is not satisfied with income level Y_0, but wishes to raise income to the level Y_1 consistent with full employment. If the government assumes that no response will be made by the foreign government to its actions, it may decide to increase real government spending to move the G^1 line upwards to G^{1+} in section (*c*) of Figure 6.1, this causes the demand for goods at any interest rate to rise and shifts the *IS* curve in section (*a*) upwards to *IS*+ causing *r* and *Y* to rise to r_1, Y_1 respectively. Corresponding to the shift in the *IS* curve to *IS*+, is a shift in the *AD* curve to *AD*+ in section (*d*) showing that the price level remains at P_0. Assume that the budget deficit at Y_1 is financed by printing money, which flows out of the economy through a balance of payments deficit of equal magnitude as shown in sections (*b*) and (*c*). Since the domestic money stock is unchanging and the price level constant the new *IS*/*LM* equilibrium appears to be stable.

Even under the small economy assumption it is clear that a continuous balance of payments deficit and depletion of reserves is incompatible with maintaining a fixed exchange rate. The point is that adjustment does not come about by endogenous shifts in the *IS*/*LM* sector, but by exhaustion of the deficit country's stock of reserves, or by pressure being brought to bear upon the government by the other government which would be reluctant to go on building up reserves of the deficit country's currency. Also if capital were mobile then endogenous pressure would be placed upon the exchange rate and interest rate by the capital markets' reluctance to hold assets in the deficit currency.

Examining Figure 6.2 in the present interdependent model it is clear just why pressure will be placed upon the deficit government to reduce its spending, and also why the foreign government may take retaliatory action. The increase in government spending in the home economy will mean that imports by the home economy will be higher than before for any level of income in the foreign economy. In other words, foreign exports will be higher for any level of foreign income and the X^* line moves up to X^*+ in Figure 6.1(*b*). This causes the IS^* line in Figure 6.1(*a*) to move up to IS^*+ apparently yielding equilibrium at r_1^* and Y_1^* in the IS^*/LM^* sector and surpluses in both the balance of payments and government budget as shown in Figures 6.1(*b*) and 6.1(*c*). However, this position is only apparent since looking at Figure 6.1(*d*) it is possible to see that income cannot rise to Y_1^* as aggregate demand increases, but instead prices will begin to rise towards P_1^* and income will remain at Y_0^*. Even if the budget surplus just offsets the balance of payments surplus effects on the money stocks, the rising price level will reduce real money stocks and cause disturbances in the IS^*/LM^* sector and throughout the rest of the model.

The foreign government may well begin to place pressure on the deficit government to reduce its spending and accept some unemployment to ease the inflationary pressure its deficit is causing, and may even retaliate by reducing its own spending and import demand for the exports of the home economy. It is possible that a situation similar to the game situation called prisoner's dilemma will occur. 'If both parties co-operate, high payoffs to both result; if neither co-operate, low payoffs occur. But if one co-operates and the other does not, the payoff to the co-operating is very low and that to the non-co-operating very high' (Hamada, 1974).

The Case for Co-ordination

In the real world there are more than two influential nations and groupings of nations and this complicates matters but without changing the basic idea that interdependence brings with it the potential for gains from co-ordination and the incentive for nations or groupings to place pressure upon one another. For example, it could be argued that a situation similar to the one outlined above has been behind the moves towards monetary union in the EEC as one way of uniting the European economies to place pressure on the USA to attempt to put its monetary policy in order and reduce the outflow of dollars. On the other hand, the USA has urged the surplus countries of West Germany and Japan to take the lead in demand expansion, and some co-ordination of policies has taken place such as the agreement on concerted expansionary policies reached in 1978 following discussions in the European Council and at the Western Economic Summit held in Bonn. However, moves towards greater co-operation even within Europe have proceeded at a sluggish pace, and international relationships have been strained by conflict over major macroeconomic issues. No doubt some of the disagreements have reflected differences in national interests, but some may have been due to misconceptions about the interactions of national policies and objectives.

Returning to the theoretical case discussed above it is possible that both governments could achieve their objectives for income and price level if they co-ordinated their actions. Co-ordination would mean setting some national policies in accordance with international interests, and though this could be interpreted as a loss of economic sovereignty it may be assumed that governments retain ultimate control of their policies and only agree to concerted action when the gains to them exceed the costs. Recognition of interdependence involves acknowledging that countries do not possess autonomous control over their own economies and are involved in a game with other countries. What is important is to establish fair rules of the game and a fair distribution of the benefits of co-ordination.

In order to show more clearly how countries can calculate their co-ordinated policies, the next section uses an algebraic model of two interdependent economies. The following analysis will also show that some types of international co-ordination and integration are more costly in terms of economic sovereignty than others.

Macroeconomic Interdependence: An Algebraic Approach

Assumptions

The model to be developed in this section differs from the one used in the previous section. First, the assumption of perfect capital immobility is replaced by the opposite assumption of perfect capital mobility. Second, prices are now assumed to be constant and all changes in nominal income represent changes in real income. The assumptions of free trade and fixed exchange rates are maintained. In the absence of divergence between spot and forward exchange rates perfect capital mobility implies that the interest rate will be common to both economies, and this will be assumed to be the case in what follows.

Monetary integration has been defined as an exchange rate union combined with capital-market integration (Corden, 1972). This means that exchange rates within the union are permanently fixed and that currencies are freely convertible within the union for either current or capital transactions. It is clear that the assumptions of the model define a system of monetary integration.

On the other hand, the minimum conditions for monetary union are said to be more stringent and to consist of two key elements concerning agreement on a mutually consistent price-level target to which national monetary policies can be adjusted and on the appropriate division of the supply of money from domestic sources among the members of the monetary union (McKinnon, 1979). Clearly the first of these two elements is not applicable to the present model, although the second element will be shown to involve an extra restriction on the policy choices open to members of the union.

It has been argued that 'the only thing that a government gives up when it gives up the right to print its own money is the ability to cause inflation and use inflation as one source of revenue. There are no other restrictions on political freedom of action' (Parkin, 1976). The present analysis clearly differs from Parkin's since recognition of the government budget constraint as well as the balance of payments constraint leads to the conclusion that fiscal policies and fiscal arrangements are the long-run determinants of financial stock variables. Put the other way around, controlling monetary policy and the right to print money will affect fiscal arrangements and fiscal policies, and hence may place restrictions on governments far beyond the direct restrictions on monetary policy.

The model to be used in this section is a model of aggregate demand determination and gives a role to all the elements of government policy, not just monetary policy. The extreme assumption of constant price and varying real income is unfortunate but unimportant in this context, since if the opposite extreme assumption of varying price and constant real income were made the model would simply determine price rather than real income. A more complicated model would allow for variations in both prices and real income. The alternative price – real income assumptions are interchangeable and would not affect the argument that restricting monetary policy also restricts government options on other policies too.

However, this is not to argue with attaching prime importance to the role of money in the inflation problem, but simply to add that monetary and fiscal policy are closely linked. Indeed although it can be established that a bond-financed deficit produces a larger total change in price-level than a corresponding money-financed deficit, it can be argued that bond-financing creates only modest inflation. The high rates of inflation observed in recent years can be explained 'as an essentially monetary phenomenon. But it also appears that this monetary phenomenon is partly determined by the fiscal policies pursued and the fiscal arrangements established. These policies and arrangements condition the money supply process and contribute to determine the longer run monetary growth' (Brunner, 1976). Thus, fiscal and monetary policies are linked by the government budget constraint. Inflationary monetary policies do not occur independently from fiscal policies, but by the same token restricting monetary policies will affect other policy choices.

The Equations of the Model

It is now useful to discuss the equations of the model, although some readers may prefer to skip over these to p. 91. The non-starred equations and subscript 1 represent the home country in terms of the home currency, whilst the starred equations and subscript 2 represent the foreign economy in terms of the foreign currency. In the case of bonds the subscript represents the source or issuing government, and the superscript represents the purchaser's country. The non-starred equations are given in the text, whilst starred ones are listed in the appendix. Unless otherwise specified the variables in the text refer to the home country in terms of the home currency in period t and the subscript $1t$ is implied; similarly those in section 2 of the appendix refer to the foreign country in terms of the foreign currency in period t and the subscript $2t$ is implied. Full notation is given in section 3 of the Appendix to this chapter.

Firstly, consider the government budget constraint

$$G + \sum_{n=0}^{t-1} r_n \Delta B_{1n} \equiv T + \Delta B + \Delta H. \qquad (1)$$

Equation (1) states that total real government expenditure in period t, G, plus interest payments on outstanding bonds, $\Sigma_{n=0}^{t-1} r_n \Delta B_{1n}$, must be financed out of tax receipts, T, or by the sale of bonds, ΔB, or by the printing of money, ΔH. All bonds are perpetuities with fixed interest payments so that the sale of bonds of value ΔB in period t will commit the domestic government to interest payments of $r\Delta B$ in all future periods.[2] The government can buy back bonds, but such actions will show up as negative ΔB in the period in which such purchases occur. As noted earlier, domestic and foreign bonds will be considered to be perfect substitutes so the same interest rate, r, will apply to both bonds. Thus, equation (1) and (1*) allow for the interdependence of fiscal and monetary policies, and for the impact of the government budget upon domestic money and bond stocks.

The private sector in each country is also subject to a budget constraint.

$$L_{1(t-1)} + \frac{\sum_{n=0}^{t-1} r_n \Delta B_{1n}^{1}}{r_{t-1}} + \frac{e \sum_{n=0}^{t-1} r_n \Delta B_{2n}^{1}}{r_{t-1}} + Y_D \equiv L$$

$$+\frac{\sum_{n=0}^{t} r_n \Delta B_{1n}^1}{r_t}+\frac{e\sum_{n=0}^{t} r_n \Delta B_{2n}^1}{r_t}+C+M. \qquad (2)$$

Equation (2) states that the private sector consumption, which consists of domestically produced goods, C, and imports, M, and its end-of-period wealth holding in period t are constrained by its wealth holding at the beginning of the period and disposable income for the period, Y_D. Wealth holdings consist of money, L, plus domestic and foreign bond holdings,

$$\frac{\sum_{n=0}^{t} r_n \Delta B_{1n}^1}{r_t} \quad \text{and} \quad \frac{e\sum_{n=0}^{t} r_n \Delta B_{2n}^1}{r_t} \quad \text{respectively.}$$

The exchange rate, e, represents the domestic currency price of foreign currency.

The private sector is assumed to behave according to the following equations:[3]

$$C = c_1(Y_D, W_{1(t-1)}, r_t, t, e), \qquad (3)$$

$$c_{11} > 0,\ c_{12} > 0,\ c_{13} \gtrless 0,\ c_{14} \gtrless 0, c_{15} \gtrless 0,$$

$$M = m_1(Y_D, W_{1(t-1)}, r_t, t, e), \qquad (4)$$

$$L_t^1 = l_1(Y_D, W_{1(t-1)}, r_t, t, e), \qquad (5)$$

$$B_t^1 = b_1(Y_D, W_{1(t-1)}, r_t, t, e). \qquad (6)$$

The signs of the partial derivatives in equations (4), (5) and (6) are similar to those given for equation (3). L_t^1, B_t^1 represent private sector desired demands for holdings of money and domestic and foreign bonds at the end of period t. Several restrictions are placed upon the partial derivatives in equations (3) to (6) by the budget constraint (2). For example, any increase in disposable income must be either spent on consumption of domestic or foreign goods, or else added to money or bond stocks so that:

$$c_{11} + m_{11} + l_{11} + b_{11} = 1.$$

The joint influence of the budget deficit and the balance of payments or change in reserves, ΔR, on the domestic money stock is shown in equation (7). For simplicity, this assumes a money multiplier of unity so that domestic money supply changes are simply the sum of the changes resulting from the government budget and the balance of payments:

$$\Delta L = \Delta H + \Delta R. \tag{7}$$

The change in reserves arising out of the balance of payments is defined in equation (8) as the difference between exports, X, and imports, M, and the net flow of capital, F, as a result of net bond purchases and net interest payments as defined in equation (9),

$$\Delta R = X - M + F, \tag{8}$$

$$F = \Delta B_{1t}^2 - e\Delta B_{2t}^1 + e\sum_{n=0}^{t-1} r_n \Delta B_{2n}^1 - \sum_{n=0}^{t-1} r_n \Delta B_{1n}^2. \tag{9}$$

The following equations complete the model:

$$Y_D = Y + \sum_{n=0}^{t-1} r_n \Delta B_{1n}^1 + e\sum_{n=0}^{t-1} r_n \Delta B_{2n}^1 - T + \\ + \left(\frac{\sum_{n=0}^{t-1} r_n \Delta B_{1n}^1}{r_t} - \frac{\sum_{n=0}^{t-1} r_n \Delta B_{1n}^1}{r_{t-1}} + \frac{e\sum_{n=0}^{t-1} r_n \Delta B_{2n}^1}{r_t} - \frac{e\sum_{n=0}^{t-1} r_n \Delta B_{2n}^1}{r_{t-1}} \right), \tag{10}$$

$$T = \bar{T} + t_1 \left(Y, \sum_{n=0}^{t-1} r_n \Delta B_{1n}^1, e\sum_{n=0}^{t-1} r_n \Delta B_{2n}^1 \right), \tag{11}$$

$$W_{1t} = L_{1t} + \frac{\sum_{n=0}^{t} r_n \Delta B_{1n}^1}{r_t} + \frac{e\sum_{n=0}^{t} r_n \Delta B_{2n}^1}{r_t}, \tag{12}$$

$$\Delta L_{1t} = L_{1t} - L_{1(t-1)}, \tag{13}$$

$$\Delta W_{1t} = W_{1t} - W_{1(t-1)}, \tag{14}$$

$$\Delta B = \Delta B^1 + \Delta B^2, \tag{15}$$

$$Y = C + G + X, \tag{16}$$

$$\left.\begin{aligned} X_{1t} &= eM_{2t}, \\ M_{1t} &= eX_{2t}, \\ F_{1t} &= -eF_{2t}, \\ \Delta R_{1t} &= -e\Delta R_{2t}. \end{aligned}\right\} \qquad (17)$$

Equation (10) defines disposable income in terms of real income, Y, interest receipts, taxes, and capital gains which are shown in the brackets. Taxes, T, are defined in (11) as consisting of a lump sum and proportionate tax levied equally on earned income and interest receipts, but, for simplicity, not on capital gains. Equation (12) defines wealth, equations (13) and (14) define changes in money and wealth, whilst equation (15) is the equilibrium condition that the sum of the demands for new domestic bonds equal the supply, ΔB, coming from the government budget constraint (1).[4] Equation (16) defines real income in terms of consumption of domestic goods, government expenditure which is assumed to be solely on domestic goods, and exports. Finally, equation (17) shows the interdependence arising out of trade and capital flows, one country's exports being the other country's imports and so on.

The model concentrates on the demand side, and abstracts from explicit consideration of supply side variables and the labour market. Also, net investment is assumed to be zero, not only to limit the number of equations and variables, but to avoid any consideration of growth of the capital stock and potential output, which would be necessary in a more complete model. Nevertheless, the above equations represent a logically consistent model of a two country world which exhibits interdependence and policy spillover effects. Since the model, in spite of the significant simplifying assumptions, is still quite complex it will be used only for the simple purpose of relating targets and instruments in order to see if, given knowledge of the system, the governments could achieve their targets each period.

Targets and Instruments Under Monetary Integration

There are several variables in the model for which the governments may wish to set target values. Taking the Treaty of Rome objectives, for example, would indicate target variables such as income levels (as proxies for unemployment), balance of payments equilibrium, and the exchange rate. The interest rate will be added as a target, since in a fixed exchange rate world with perfect capital mobility the interest rate is common and neither government is likely to wish to leave it to be determined by market forces and the actions of the other country's government. Without further loss of generality it is assumed that the target interest rate is constant since this conveniently sets capital gains equal to zero.

The interdependence of the two economies is obvious with the set of targets to be examined here. The exchange rate and interest rate are common to both countries, and one country's loss of reserves is the other country's gain. Both countries have targets for common variables and these targets must be consistent or it will be impossible for both countries to achieve their targets. Alternatively some compromise might be reached or some game played by the two countries, but it is impossible for the countries to ignore one another and treat the rest of the world as independent.

The policy variables or instruments available to the governments are the levels of government spending, the new supplies of money and bonds, and the tax parameters. This means that between them the two countries have ten policy variables (G_1, G_2, $\bar{T}_1$, $\bar{T}_2$, t_1, t_2, ΔB_1, ΔB_2, ΔH_1, ΔH_2) and six targets (Y_1, Y_2, ΔR_1, ΔR_2, e, r), but there is considerable interdependence since ΔR_1 and ΔR_2 are not independent but related according to equation (17) and the instruments are interrelated too according to the government budget constraints. As is shown in section 1 of the appendix the model indicates that between them the two countries need to use eight of their policy variables to achieve their six targets. The usual result is that as many independent policies are needed as there are independent targets, but in this case there are significant interdependencies amongst both policies and targets and no such simple rule is applicable. All this means that between them the governments have two policies over which they can exercise their discretion, the remaining eight policies must then be co-ordinated in order to achieve the six targets.

Thus, it is possible under monetary integration for each government to achieve its targets for income, interest rate, exchange rate and reserve change, whilst also exercising discretion over one of its policy variables such as government expenditure, possibly to achieve some goal of distribution policy (Peacock, 1979). The proviso must be made that both countries must agree on certain targets, and co-ordinate their remaining policies.

Monetary Union

Now consider that the two countries form a monetary union. This means that they agree upon the new supplies of money to be created by each member government. In other words, they agree to use the one degree of policy discretion available to each of them under monetary integration to set their monetary policies, and lose discretion over their expenditure policies. Forming a monetary union means that governments face an extra restriction upon their freedom of action. However, this is not to say that monetary integration is preferable to monetary union. In practice the degree of interdependence under monetary integration may be so great that members tend to seek monetary union to give them more control over each other's monetary and fiscal policies to control the transmission of inflation from members with strong inflationary tendencies to those with weaker inflationary tendencies. Of course, the inflationary members may be reluctant to submit to such control, and the resulting disagreement between members may cause the break-up of the fixed exchange regime.

The above arguments relate closely to the question of European monetary union. Aside from the possibility expressed earlier that such union would give greater weight to the European economies in negotiations with the rest of the world, and especially the USA, most arguments put forward in favour of European monetary union involve the desire to reduce the instability of the floating exchange rate system with its supposedly harmful effects on trade. Some proponents therefore really just want to see fixed exchange rates and monetary integration, but the above arguments indicate that, in the presence of interdependence, co-ordination of policies will also be necessary to prevent the system from being torn apart by individualist policies on the part of the members, and, furthermore, monetary integration may contain itself a natural tendency to either monetary union or else disintegration. Thus, the model supports those who argue that co-ordination is necessary if fixed exchange rates are to hold within any European monetary system.[5]

On the other hand, it would be possible to have policy co-ordination even under a floating exchange rate regime, and there are still those who argue that such a regime is preferable to a fixed exchange rate regime in the world as it is today. For example, it might not be possible to base a fixed exchange rate regime upon the dollar since the experience with US monetary policy after the Vietnam War has undermined international trust in the stability of the dollar. Similarly, it could be hazardous to place such trust in a European monetary system since success would depend upon the performance of the national governments in the system, as well as 'upon the evolution of the as yet non-existent institutions that would not only co-ordinate policies between the relevant countries, but would also ensure that the policies in question were such as to make the basket of currencies a stable store of value' (Laidler, 1980).

To those who argue that monetary integration or union will place a benevolent discipline upon governments with inflationary tendencies Laidler argues that such discipline will be effective only 'if it arises from domestic political pressure exerted by a general public which does not like inflation but understands its causes'. In the absence of such pressure a government will not accept international discipline, and in the presence of such pressure the international discipline will not be needed. Unable to find trustworthy international institutions Laidler favours a system of floating exchange rates and the extra independence which such a system entails.

This is a contentious area, and others argue that a European monetary system would be worthy of trust, and, moreover, fixed exchange rates would provide governments with an excuse for following the ultimately desirable, but possibly domestically unpopular, tight money policies favoured by Laidler. In any case even floating exchange rates do not completely isolate economies and some interdependence will remain, and, therefore, co-ordination will still offer gains.

Dilemmas in Policy Making in Interdependent Countries

It has been shown that international interdependence involves a weakening of macroeconomic autonomy for individual nations. In such circumstances there are gains to be made from co-ordination of policies across nations, but some types of integration are more costly in terms of economic sovereignty than others and rely upon trust in the international institutions and partners in the system. The scope for co-ordination may, therefore, be great in theory, but limited in practice so long as countries have differing objectives and lack trust in one another.

The economic analysis has been based on quite simple, although logically consistent models, and further work is necessary with more complicated models, and with more than two countries. For example, the simple fixed target approach was adopted, which tends to highlight the difficulties in achieving objectives, and more work is needed using the optimizing approach (see, for example, Niehans (1968), and Turnovsky (1979)) which attaches costs not only to failure to achieve targets, but also to using policies. The optimizing approach indicates trade-offs between targets and instruments absent from the present analysis and tends to stabilize policy use compared with the simpler target-instrument approach used above, which may result in policy instability where it becomes necessary to increase the use of some policy period after period in an explosive fashion. The analyses presented in Chapter 5 and in the present chapter seem to present some unpleasant dilemmas to policy makers. They may try to escape them by trying to find suitable rules of thumb or mitigate their effects by real income transfers, the subjects of the next two chapters.

Mathematical Appendix

1. *Targets and Instruments*

Let the set of targets under monetary integration be Y_1, Y_2, ΔR_1, e and r, and the instruments available be G_1, G_2, ΔH_1, ΔH_2, ΔB_1, ΔB_2, T_1, T_2, t_1, t_2. The set of starred and non-starred equations may be simplified in order to ease the task of relating targets and instruments as follows. For single period analysis equations (14) and (14*) may be omitted as they are needed only as a dynamic link between time periods. Equation (2) may be removed from the system as it is linearly dependent upon equations (1), (7) to (10), (13), (15) and (16); similarly equation (2*) may be removed. The reason for being able to remove (2) and (2*) is that if the government budget constraints and the flow of funds within the model are specified correctly then the private sector budget constraints are implied by the rest of the model, alternatively the government budget constraints could be removed and the private ones retained. Noting (18) and (18*)

$$\Delta B_t^1 = \Delta B_{1t}^1 + e\Delta B_{2t}^1 = B_t^1 - B_{t-1}^1, \tag{18}$$

$$\Delta B_t^2 = \Delta B_{2t}^2 + \frac{1}{e}\Delta B_{1t}^2 = B_t^2 - B_{t-1}^2, \tag{18*}$$

and the assumption of constant interest and exchange rates it is possible to substitute (6), (6*) into (18), (18*) to yield

$$\Delta B_{1t}^1 + e\Delta B_{2t}^1 = b_1(Y_{D1t}, W_{1(t-1)}, r_t, t_{1t}, e) - \frac{\sum_{n=0}^{t-1} r_n \Delta B_{1t}^1}{r_t} - \frac{e\sum_{n=0}^{t-1} r_n \Delta B_{2t}^1}{r_t}, \tag{6a}$$

$$\Delta B^2_{2t} + \frac{1}{e}\,\Delta B^2_{1t} = b_2(Y_{D2t}, W_{2(t-1)}, r_t, t_{2t}, e) - \frac{\sum_{n=0}^{t-1} r_n \Delta B^2_{2t}}{r_t} - \frac{\frac{1}{e}\sum_{n=0}^{t-1} r_n \Delta B^2_{1t}}{r_t}. \qquad \text{(6a*)}$$

Now using (6a), (9), (15) and (18) and their starred counterparts it is possible to eliminate the variables $\Delta B^1_{1t}, \Delta B^1_{2t}, \Delta B^2_{2t}, \Delta B^2_{1t}$ from the model as they are of no direct interest, or in Tinbergen's terms they are irrelevant (Tinbergen, 1952). Similarly, making use of the assumption that all markets clear and all demands are satisfied and using equations (17) it is possible to remove all the irrelevant variables from the model. This results in the following system of eight equations.

$$G_{1t} + \sum_{n=0}^{t-1} r_n \Delta B_{1n} - \bar{T}_{1t} - t_1\left(Y_1, \sum_{n=0}^{t-1} r_n \Delta B^1_{1n}, e\sum_{n=0}^{t-1} r_n \Delta B^1_{2n}\right) - \Delta B_{1t} - \Delta H_{1t} = 0, \qquad \text{(1b)}$$

$$L_1(\alpha_1) - L_{1(t-1)} - \Delta H_{1t} - \Delta R_{1t} = 0, \qquad \text{(2b)}$$

$$\Delta R_{1t} - em_2(\alpha_2) + m_1(\alpha_1) + \Delta B_{1t} - b_1(\alpha_1) + \frac{\sum_{n=0}^{t-1} r_n \Delta B^1_{1n}}{r_t} + e\,\frac{\sum_{n=0}^{t-1} r_n \Delta B^1_{2n}}{r_t} - e\sum_{n=0}^{t-1} r_n \Delta B^1_{2n} + \sum_{n=0}^{t-1} r_n \Delta B^2_{1n} = 0, \qquad \text{(3b)}$$

$$Y_{1t} - c_1(\alpha_1) - G_{1t} - em_2(\alpha_2) = 0, \qquad \text{(4b)}$$

$$G_{2t} + \sum_{n=0}^{t-1} r_n \Delta B_{2n} - \bar{T}_{2t} - t_2\left(Y_2, \sum_{n=0}^{t-1} r_n \Delta B^2_{2n}, \frac{1}{e}\sum_{n=0}^{t-1} r_n \Delta B^2_{1n}\right) - \Delta B_{2t} - \Delta H_{2t} = 0 \qquad \text{(1b*)}$$

$$L_2(\alpha_2) - L_{2(t-1)} - \Delta H_{2t} + \frac{1}{e}\,\Delta R_{1t} = 0, \qquad \text{(2b*)}$$

$$-\frac{1}{e}\Delta R_{1t} - \frac{1}{e} m_1(\alpha_1) + m_2(\alpha_2) + \Delta B_{2t} - b_2(\alpha_2) + \frac{\sum_{n=0}^{t-1} r_n \Delta B_{2n}^2}{r_t} +$$

$$+ \frac{\sum_{n=0}^{t-1} r_n \Delta B_{1n}^2}{er_t} - \frac{1}{e}\sum_{n=0}^{t-1} r_n \Delta B_{1n}^2 + \sum_{n=0}^{t-1} r_n \Delta B_{2n}^1 = 0, \qquad (3b^*)$$

$$Y_{2t} - c_2(\alpha_1) - G_{2t} - \frac{1}{e} m_1(\alpha_2) = 0, \qquad (4b^*)$$

where $(\alpha_1) = \left(Y_{1t}, \sum_{n=0}^{t-1} B_{1n}^1, e\sum_{n=0}^{t-1} r_n \Delta B_{2n}^1, \bar{T}_{1t}, t_{1t}, L_{1(t-1)}, \frac{\sum_{n=0}^{t-1} r_n \Delta B_{1n}^1}{r_{t-1}}, e\frac{\sum_{n=0}^{t-1} r_n \Delta B_{2n}^1}{r_{t-1}}, r_t, t_{1t}, e \right)$

and $(\alpha_2) = \left(Y_{2t}, \sum_{n=0}^{t-1} \Delta B_{2n}^2, \frac{1}{e}\sum_{n=0}^{t-1} r_n \Delta B_{1n}^2, \bar{T}_{2t}, t_{2t}, L_{2(t-1)}, \frac{\sum_{n=0}^{t-1} r_n \Delta B_{2n}^2}{r_{t-1}}, \frac{\sum_{n=0}^{t-1} r_n \Delta B_{1n}^2}{er_{t-1}}, r_t, t_{2t}, e \right).$

On totally differentiating and taking a linear approximation the above eight equations yield a system of the form $AU + Z = 0$ where A is an (8×10) matrix of parameters, U is a (10×1) vector of changes in instruments, and Z is an (8×1) vector of constants. There are an infinite number of possible solutions to such a system, which has two degrees of freedom. Each government may use up one degree of freedom in arbitrarily choosing the value of one of its instruments, and then the system will yield a unique solution for the eight remaining instruments.

If the two countries agreed to monetary union they would reach agreement with one another upon the levels of ΔH_{1t} and ΔH_{2t}, which would reduce the size of U from (10×1) to (8×1) so that no degrees of freedom would be left in the system, which would then determine uniquely the values of the remaining eight instruments.

2. *The Foreign Country*

$$G + \sum_{n=0}^{t-1} r_n \Delta B_{2t} \equiv T + \Delta B + \Delta H, \tag{1*}$$

$$L_{2(t-1)} + \frac{\sum_{n=0}^{t-1} r_n \Delta B_{2n}^2}{r_{t-1}} + \frac{\frac{1}{e}\sum_{n=0}^{t-1} r_n \Delta B_{1n}^2}{r_{t-1}} + Y_{D2t}$$

$$\equiv L + \frac{\sum_{n=0}^{t} r_n \Delta B_{2n}^2}{r_t} + \frac{1}{e}\sum_{n=0}^{t} r_n \Delta B_{1n}^2 + C + M, \tag{2*}$$

$$C = c_2(Y_D, W_{2(t-1)}, r_t, t, e), \tag{3*}$$

$$M = m_2(Y_D, W_{2(t-1)}, r_t, t, e), \tag{4*}$$

$$L_t^2 = l_2(Y_D, W_{2(t-1)}, r_t, t, e), \tag{5*}$$

$$B_t^2 = b_2(Y_D, W_{2(t-1)}, r_t, t, e), \tag{6*}$$

$$\Delta L \equiv \Delta H + \Delta R, \tag{7*}$$

$$\Delta R \equiv X - M + F, \tag{8*}$$

$$F \equiv \Delta B_{2t}^1 - \frac{1}{e}\Delta B_{1t}^2 + \frac{1}{e}\sum_{n=0}^{t-1} r_n \Delta B_{1n}^2 - \sum_{n=0}^{t-1} r_n \Delta B_{2n}^1, \tag{9*}$$

$$Y_D \equiv Y_2 + \sum_{n=0}^{t-1} r_n \Delta B_{2n}^2 + \frac{1}{e}\sum_{n=0}^{t-1} r_n \Delta B_{1n}^2 - T + \frac{\sum_{n=0}^{t-1} r_n \Delta B_{2n}^2}{r_t} -$$

$$- \frac{\sum_{n=0}^{t-1} r_n \Delta B_{2n}^2}{r_{t-1}} + \frac{\frac{1}{e}\sum_{n=0}^{t-1} r_n \Delta B_{1n}^2}{r_t} - \frac{\frac{1}{e}\sum_{n=0}^{t-1} r_n \Delta B_{1n}^2}{r_{t-1}} \tag{10*}$$

$$T = \bar{T} + t_2\left(Y, \sum_{n=0}^{t-1} r_n \Delta B_{2n}^2, \frac{1}{e}\sum_{n=0}^{t-1} r_n \Delta B_{1n}^2\right), \tag{11*}$$

$$W \equiv L + \frac{\sum_{n=0}^{t} r_n \Delta B_{2n}^2}{r_t} + \frac{\frac{1}{e}\sum_{n=0}^{t} r_n \Delta B_{1n}^2}{r_t}, \tag{12*}$$

$$\Delta L_{2t} \equiv L_{2t} - L_{2(t-1)}, \tag{13*}$$

$$\Delta W_{2t} \equiv W_{2t} - W_{2(t-1)}, \tag{14*}$$

$$\Delta B = \Delta B^1 + \Delta B^2, \tag{15*}$$

$$Y \equiv C + G + X, \tag{16*}$$

$$\left.\begin{aligned} X_{1t} &= eM_{2t}, \\ M_{1t} &= eX_{2t}, \\ F_{1t} &= -eF_{2t}, \end{aligned}\right\} \tag{17*}$$

$$\Delta R_{1t} = -e\Delta R_{2t},$$

$$\Delta B_t^2 = \Delta B_{2t}^2 + \frac{1}{e}\,\Delta B_{1t}^2, \tag{18*}$$

$$\Delta B_{2t}^2 + \frac{1}{e}\,\Delta B_{1t}^2 = b_2(Y_{2Dt}, W_{2(t-1)}, r_t, t_{2t}, e) - \frac{\sum_{n=0}^{t-1} r_n \Delta B_{2t}^2}{r_t} - \frac{\frac{1}{e}\sum_{n=0}^{t-1} r_n \Delta B_{1t}^2}{r_t}. \tag{6a*}$$

3. *Summary of Notation used in the Algebraic Approach*

B = the coupon value of the bond-stock,
C = consumption,
F = net inflow of capital arising out of net bond purchase and net interest payments,
G = government spending,
H = domestically produced component of the money stock,
L = money stock,
M = imports,
R = reserves of foreign currency,
T = taxes,
W = wealth,
X = exports,
r = interest rate,
e = exchange rate (the domestic currency price of foreign currency).

Notes

1. See, e.g. Johnson (1972), who writes that 'deficits and surpluses represent phases of stock adjustment in the money market and not equilibrium flows

and should not be treated in an analytical framework that treats them as equilibrium phenomena', or Shone (1978), who writes that the Keynesian model 'would imply that a situation where $X \neq M$ can be repeated period after period ... On the other hand, the monetary approach would see the disequilibrium purely as a temporary phenomenon. As stock-adjustments take place the deficits/surpluses will diminish ... so the disequilibrium on the balance of payments will disappear'.

2. This definition of bonds leads to non-linearities when considering wealth effects since the value of the outstanding bond stock changes with changes in the interest rate. Such difficulties could have been avoided by following Turnovsky and defining bonds as fixed-value, variable rate deposits, but are here avoided by considering a fixed interest rate as one of the policy targets. For simplicity inter-government bond sales will be ignored. Also note that joining an Economic Community and agreeing to give up a proportion of taxes to a federal budget etc. will affect the form of the government budget constraints.
3. For simplicity the role of expectations is ignored, or else they are assumed to be static.
4. Notice that equations (15) and (15*) together imply that the total supply of new bonds equals the total demand for new bonds.
5. The traditional discussion about monetary union relates to the optimal currency area and centres around the need for perfect labour mobility. Whilst the EEC favours removing obstacles to labour mobility it remains the case that labour is not yet perfectly mobile, and also governments may wish to limit the emigration of labour from their countries. The above model fits the case of Keynesian unemployment with immobile labour and does not rely upon arguments about labour mobility.

CHAPTER 7

Techniques of Collaboration I: Monetary Policy

Rules of Monetary Co-operation

It has been accepted for well over a century that there is a need for some form of international monetary co-operation. This minimal degree of co-operation, it has been conventionally assumed, can but be achieved by an explicit or implicit set of rules of the game. These would constrain nations to agree to some policy action that would ensure some sort of stability. A much analysed rule is to maintain fixed exchange rates. The discipline thereby imposed on a country would ensure that its actions were both predictable by and not inimical to the interests of other countries. The element of predictability was especially important, a recognition of the forces recently recognized in the game theoretic models of international relations (Brams, 1975).

A long series of such 'rules of the game' have evolved over the last century. The first was the classical gold standard (1876–1914) and the associated Latin Monetary Union. The next major set of rules was the post First World War gold exchange standard. Another similar system emerged after the Second World War with the Bretton Woods system. All of these were based on rules concerning exchange rates. None were conspicuously successful, not even when reinforced by a sophisticated institutional framework, e.g. the IMF in the Bretton Woods system. In the 1970s and 1980s there has been a search for new rules of the game. This has occurred for three reasons. The first is the breakdown of Bretton Woods and its obvious failings. The other reasons have stemmed from the growth of Eurocurrency markets. This has made a 'fixed' exchange rate system impossible to operate and has also meant that it is no longer necessary for a country to deflate when it has a balance of payments deficit, reviving a truism since Gresham enunciated this principle four centuries ago (Gowland (1979), Chaps. 2 and 3; Crockett (1979)).

One favourite candidate has been 'alignment of monetary policies', defined as each country setting the same growth rate for its domestic money supply. There has been much discussion in the academic literature both of the need for co-ordination of monetary and fiscal policy as a prelude to monetary integration and of the inadequacies of such co-ordination, see the studies by Dosser and Hitiris elsewhere in this volume and the references cited therein. A clear consensus has emerged amongst practitioners of monetary policy, both Central Bankers and political leaders. This is that if the various member states of the EEC can reach agreement to align their monetary policies, then exchange rates and interest rates will move towards levels that will foster greater convergence and remove barriers towards further political and economic integration. At its strongest, it is argued that this alignment of monetary policy will produce similar growth and inflation in each member country, equilibrium in balance of payments and a common movement of their exchange rates. The appeal of this is clear, especially as it leaves member states total autonomy to pursue all other policies except in so far as the monetary targets constrain them. Thus alignment seems to provide an attractive means of avoiding the dilemmas posed in Chapters 5 and 6. The objective of this chapter is to investigate the consequences of alignment to see whether it does provide such an escape route. In particular the consequences of different techniques of monetary control and debt management structures and policies are analysed.

Present Policies Towards Alignment of Monetary Policies

Alignment has been an objective of the EEC for some years, both as an end in itself and as a sufficient and necessary condition for the workings of the European Monetary System. In addition to the pursuit of alignment by the multi-purpose EEC, a specific international association has adopted a similar objective, the Bank for International Settlements.

In fact this policy of a common monetary target has a much wider appeal. Besides the various communiqués of the BIS meetings of Central Bank Governors which have indicated that they would like to move towards such a goal, it was explicitly endorsed at the first three Big Six Summits (Rambouillet, Puerto Rico and London), if the press reports of statements by highly placed sources are to be believed. There are many merits of such an alignment of monetary policy but the purpose of this paper is to analyse and challenge the hopes placed upon it especially in the context of any European Monetary System.

Difficulties in Achieving Alignment

There are a number of distinct points that cast doubt upon the exaggerated claims made for this alignment of monetary policies.

(*a*) Common growth of nominal income may produce very different combinations of output and inflation in the different member States depending on expectations, the relative natural rates of unemployment and past history. The magnitude and nature of the problem can be gauged from Chapters 3–6.

(*b*) Common growth in income and prices may not be sufficient to produce balance of payments equilibrium. This is also dependent on the structure of trade and price elasticities. Houthakker and Magee (1976) demonstrates the problem.

(*c*) There is no reason why common monetary growth should ensure common growth in nominal income and equal interest rates. It assumes, *inter alia*, that each European country has a demand for money function with the same price, output and interest rate elasticities. In fact the empirical work suggests marked differences between the demand-for-money functions in the different countries (Hamburger, 1978).

Furthermore, it is not clear that the desired equal rate of money supply growth could be combined with capital mobility. The money supply, interest rates, capital flows and exchange rates are interdependent and it is not clear that the common money supply growth constellation is a feasible point. It is also not clear what, if any, freedom of fiscal policy is permitted by this policy. The constraints might even compel deharmonization of tax rates and social security provisions, for example. All of these are assumed away in this chapter but are considered elsewhere in Chapter 6. In this chapter, it is assumed that a combination of exchange control, official intervention in foreign exchange markets and manipulation of the forward discount avoids all these problems. It is obviously slightly bizarre to have to assume optimal control within a European monetary system but this will make it possible to focus on some crucial problems within the ambit of monetary policy and debt management. Moreover it is clear that the EEC is prepared to use exchange control to reinforce the EMS however much of a contradiction of ends and means this seems to outsiders.

The crucial problems upon which attention is focused in this chapter are problems of money *supply*; especially to different regimes of monetary control and to different techniques of debt management and structures of bond market.

However, there are some interesting questions that will be considered first. One is imply that the whole role of monetary targets has been the subject of much scrutiny (Gowland (1978, 1981); Richardson (1978); Foot (1981)). Sceptics, especially Volcker

(1976) and Foot have questioned their role and have argued convincingly that a monetary target is not a monetary policy. *Ipso facto*, a common monetary target is not a common monetary policy. Nevertheless, a common monetary target could be a strong constraint on the individual authorities and could be regarded as a reasonable substitute for a common monetary policy, if it were clear what this comment means.

A more serious problem in practice is finding and agreeing upon an appropriate definition of the money supply. One particular problem concerns the inclusion of foreign-owned demand deposits (currently included by the Commission in its definition of Money (L_1) but excluded by the UK and France in their definitions) and foreign currency deposits owned by residents especially where 'foreign' means fellow community members. Both of these will become more and more akin to money if any EMS is successful especially if it evolves towards a monetary union. Different institutional structures cause problems of both an analytical and practical nature. For example, no institution in any other country corresponds to the Credit Foncier in France. It is not clear, and cannot even in principle be established, what change in any existing financial aggregate in any other member would correspond to an increase in Credit Foncier deposits. Similarly the absence of a large-scale Giro in the UK and Ireland and the consequent different nature of, say, the 'Big Four' in Britain compared with the German 'D' banks causes analytically insurmountable problems in defining the appropriate European monetary aggregate. Different institutional structures obviously affect the underlying nature of the demand-for-money, a widely recognized point (Goodhart, 1976). However, more seriously, they also affect how economic agents regard those assets which are similar. If, as is broadly true, a UK building society account is more liquid than a Länderbank savings account, this not merely affects behaviour in itself, it also influences how those holders who also hold the comparable 'Big 4' and 'D' bank time deposits regard these latter assets. Thus, when considering the impact of alignment of monetary policy, this sort of issue moves from the arcane area of the theory of the impact of economic structures on behaviour to one of immediate practical relevance.

Alternative Techniques of Monetary Control

It is necessary to consider initially what techniques of monetary control would be available to the various monetary authorities within the minimal constraints imposed by an agreement to observe a common monetary target. Then, in this section I consider what would happen if different countries used different techniques or combinations of techniques to achieve the same (agreed) rate of change in their money supply. Finally, this analysis is related to the current practice of monetary policy in the nine member States of the EEC.

The Money Supply (M) will be defined as equal to all bank Deposits (D) and non-bank private sector holdings of currency (C). This is approximately the UK £$M3$ or $M3$, the German $M2$ and the narrower of the EEC Commission definitions ($L1$):

$$M \equiv D + C. \tag{1}$$

However, bank deposits (D) are bank liabilities (BL) and for the purpose of this analysis, all bank liabilities are assumed to be deposits and bank liabilities are by definition equal to bank assets (BA):

$$D \equiv BL \equiv BA. \tag{2}$$

In the closed economy analyses of the techniques of monetary control contained in Gowland (1978) and Gowland (1979), bank assets are taken to consist of their loads to the public sector (bLG) and to the private sector (bLp). Techniques of control are analysed in an open economy in Gowland (1981) but in the case of policy within the EEC, this is clearly no longer adequate. Two additional categories of bank assets will accordingly be included in the analysis:

(i) net claims on economic agents in partner countries (Op)
(ii) net claims on other overseas agents (Or)

Clearly Op and Or can be either positive or negative.

$$BA = bLG + bLp + Op + Or, \tag{3}$$

so by substitution:

$$M = Cp + bLg + bLp + Op + Or. \tag{4}$$

It will be more convenient to consider this relationship in first difference form, where ΔM is the change in the money supply implied by the agreed monetary target:

$$\Delta M = \Delta D + \Delta Cp, \tag{5}$$

$$= \Delta Cp + \Delta bLG + \Delta bLp + \Delta Op + \Delta Or. \tag{6}$$

The public sector borrowing requirement (PSBR, here P) can be financed by borrowing from the non-bank private sector in the form of either currency (Cp) or such non-monetary forms as bonds, non-marketable government debt, municipal securities and Treasury Bills. For the purposes of monetary control, it does not matter how the private sector holds such claims on the public sector. Thus there is no loss of generality in regarding all these as equivalent and in amalgamating all non-bank private sector finance of the PSBR under the portmanteau variable ΔPLG. The overseas sector can provide finance to the public sector only if the reserves fall, that is if the total currency flow (T) is negative (Gowland, 1981). In fact, transactions with the overseas sector can add to the public sector's financing problem. Thus the next item in the public sector's financing identity is $\pm T$. The identity is, of course, balanced by finance from the banking system which includes any bank holdings of currency.

$$P = \Delta Cp + \Delta pLg \pm T + \Delta bLg. \qquad (7)$$

This can be rearranged as:

$$\Delta bLg = P - \Delta Cp + \Delta pLg \pm T. \qquad (8)$$

(8) can be substituted into (6) to give the second basic equation in the analysis of monetary control:

$$\Delta M = P + \Delta bLp - \Delta pLg \pm T + \Delta Op + \Delta Or \qquad (9)$$

The other crucial equation is (5) above:

$$\Delta M = \Delta D + \Delta Cp. \qquad (5)$$

By analysis of the right-hand sides of the two equations, it is possible to identify and enumerate all the possible methods of controlling the monetary aggregate. If the *modus operandi* initially involves changing one of the aggregates in (9), the policy works through the asset side of the banking sector's balance sheet and thus the supply side of the monetary system, to change the money supply. Clearly any policy which changes an aggregate in either (5) or (9) must change an aggregate in the other. The possible ways of controlling the money supply are:

(*a*) *Price effects on currency holdings (Cp)*. Any economic variable can be controlled either by influencing its price or by some quality control, such as rationing. The basic methods of controlling the money supply work by either price or quantity effects on one of the identified variables. In the case of currency holdings, a price effect would have to either alter the cost of holding currency or increase the net return on alternative assets. For various reasons such policies have never been advocated by any prominent central banker or monetary economist. Its main advocate was Gesell in the 1920s who proposed a scheme whereby notes had to be stamped to maintain their value. The authorities were to charge a fee for the stamps. His plan was subject to rigorous academic analysis in Gaitskell (1931) by a future British Chancellor and Leader of the Opposition and was referred to in rather patronizing terms by Keynes in an appendix to *The General Theory*. While both Keynes and Gaitskell saw possible merits in the scheme as a reflationary device, the objections to it were overwhelming. In particular, the schemes have been attacked as impractical. More seriously, the principal substitute for currency is bank deposits, so influencing the quantity of currency is unlikely to change the money supply; merely its allocation between currency and bank deposits. Hence, this method of control is unlikely ever to be used (Gowland, 1981).

(*b*) *Quantity controls on currency holdings (Cp)*. The reasons which make control of the money supply by price effects advanced in (*a*) above also apply to quantity controls with, if anything, even greater force.

(*c*) *Price effects on bank deposits (D)*. This policy involves raising interest rates on alternative assets to reduce holdings of bank deposits, or vice versa. It is the favourite of text book writers but has never in practice been a major tool of monetary management.

(*d*) *Quantity effects on bank deposits (D)*. The rationing of bank deposits has been used as a major tool of monetary control in the UK since 1974 in the form of the supplementary special deposits scheme to control 'IBELs' (interest bearing bank deposits), or 'corset' as it is sometimes inelegantly termed.

(*e*) *Altering the PSBR for monetary purposes*. Clearly any alteration in the PSBR will influence the money supply whether achieved by tax changes, sales or purchases of assets or changes in expenditure. Nevertheless, using the PSBR for monetary purposes, involves sacrificing a separate fiscal policy and only the UK has been willing to use it in this way.

(*f*) *As price effects on bank lending (bLp).* This policy was the centrepiece of the 'new approach' to 'competition and credit control' in the UK, 1971–73, and has been used again in 1979–81. With this scheme interest rates are varied so as to fix the demand for loans (bank assets) at a level which will ensure the desired growth of money supply (bank liabilities).

(*g*) *Quantity controls on bank loans (bLp).* These are used in France as the major means of controlling money and were used in the UK from 1952–71.

(*h*) *Price effects on private lending to the public sector (pLG).* This has been a major device of monetary policy in the UK since 1974, see the next section of this chapter.

(*j*) *Quantity effects on private lending to the public sector (pLG).* 'Forced loans' are regarded with great disfavour in the Anglo-Saxon world but are a major device of monetary control elsewhere. In particular, devices to compel purchases of government bonds by various institutions are used by every member of the EEC except the UK and are of major importance in Belgium and Italy.

(*k*) *Price effects on the 'overseas items' (T, Op and Or).* All policies which operated on one of these items would involve a deliberate worsening of the overall account of balance of payments for monetary purposes when the money supply was growing too quickly. They seem unlikely to be adopted by any member country, except in special circumstances such as the UK *de facto* revaluation in November 1977. In any case use of this device would normally be destabilizing since the country with the lowest growth of money supply would have to improve what would already be a healthy balance of payments. Finally, if the monetary theory of the balance of payments is correct then the policy could not work anyway.

(*l*) *Quantity effects on the overseas items (T, Ord Op).* These would take the form of

(1) Import controls, for example, to reduce *T* and so increase the rate of growth of money,
(2) Exchange controls on *Or* or *Op,* for example, to deter inflows to reduce the rate of growth of money. These are currently employed by Germany (the *bardepot*) and Holland inside the EEC and Switzerland outside it.

Within a European monetary system, only controls on *Or* could be permitted. In fact exchange controls might be necessary within the EEC, but still seem to involve a confusion of means and ends. A European monetary system relying on exchange control surely cannot be either a stable or a desirable system in practice.

This completes the examination of the basic methods of controlling the money supply but there are three more complex methods which all seek to reduce the efficiency of banking so as to reduce the quantity of funds intermediated by the banks and hence make it possible to control the money supply:

(*m*) *A tax on banking*.

(*n*) *Restrictions on bank interest rates*. These could take the form of maxima on bank deposits, or minima on bank loans. In practice only the former have been used, for example, Regulation Q in the US and briefly in the UK (1973–74), but not for reasons of monetary control.

(*p*) *Portfolio constraints on banks*. This is a very widely used method of controlling the money supply, in the form of a reserve ratio, and is used in Belgium, Luxemburg, Holland and Germany within the EEC (and, of course, by the US). In this form bank lending to the public sector is broken down into two groups of assets. The first subset consists of reserve assets (R), the remainder of non-reserve assets. The banks are constrained to ensure that their holdings of R are at least equal to some specified percentage of their deposits.

$$M = D + C,$$

$$\frac{R}{D} \geqslant x.$$

Next it is assumed that profit maximizing banks will minimize reserves so:

$$D = \frac{R}{x}$$

Currency holdings are assumed to be a constant percentage of M (in Gowland, 1981, this assumption is dropped).

$$C = eM,$$

$$M = \frac{R}{x} + eM,$$

$$= \frac{R}{x(1-e)}.$$

Thus M can be changed by altering either R or the minimum reserve ratio x.

Monetary Control and the European Monetary System

These thirteen types of control can be combined into an almost infinite number of regimes of monetary management. The problem for analysis here is, does it matter? Goodhart (1976) and Bank of England (1980) argued that it does not, as any system of monetary control will ultimately produce the same mapping of interest rates to money supply. In Gowland (1981) it is shown that the result depends on a number of highly restrictive assumptions, in particular

(1) Perfect certainty,
(2) Perfect competition in banking.

If these are dropped there is no longer a unique mapping from money to interest rates or vice versa. In particular, see Gowland (1981),

(*a*) Interest rates will be lowest for a given money supply if quantity controls are used.
(*b*) they will be lower if a reserve ratio is used, than if price effects used.

The implications of these results for a European Monetary System are clear and important. Different countries are likely to try and achieve the same rate of growth of money supply in different ways. The techniques of control currently used by the member states are given above in the list of techniques. It is clear that none of the nine use broadly comparable techniques, except, of course, Belgium and Luxemburg which have formed a *de facto* monetary union since 1921 in the general sense rather than the technical means used in Chapter 6. It is possible to conclude in particular that France's and Italy's interest rates would be the lowest, that Holland's would be highest followed by Denmark and Belgium and Germany. UK and Irish rates would be in the middle.

There are two reasons why such a constellation of rates has to be regarded as unstable. It is not clear, firstly if it is consistent with any viable pattern of forward exchange rates, since it implies that the lira would be at a premium compared to the mark in the forward market. Central bank intervention is unlikely to achieve this. More importantly it would set off two massive capital movements that would probably mean that a common monetary target is non-feasible. The first would be arbitrage movements between the various Euro-markets and the respective domestic money market. For example, a higher rate in the domestic mark market than the Euromark would seem to be implied; thus one would expect a large inflow of Euro-funds into Germany. This would increase the German money supply both directly and indirectly, by reducing German interest rates (and thus cutting bank holdings of free reserves as they accommodate a higher demand for credit). Hence one would expect a divergence of European money supplies. This would be reinforced by flow of funds between member countries seeking higher returns in the high-interest rate countries. These flows would be lessened, however, as (*a*) all the domestic money markets are small compared to the Euro-markets; (*b*) one might be able to restrict such movements by judicious management of forward rates to make covered arbitrage unprofitable (Keynes' solution to the same problem with the gold exchange standard (1925)). The European Co-operation Fund and the member-state central banks might not be able to offer the necessarily infinitely elastic supply of forward cover, if only for the reasons cited above. There would not be a problem if the exchange rates were permanently fixed, as Keynes assumed. If alterations are possible, as is the case under all the variants of European Monetary System so far envisaged, the potential loss would make even the CAP seem cheap.

Thus, common monetary targets would imply a pattern of domestic interest rates. They would not be equal. Hence, they would induce capital movements (which would probably occur under any natural convergence of economies) that would in turn render common monetary growth impossible.

Debt Management in a European Monetary System

The aim of the section is to show that different debt management policies change the impact of money supply growth. One can express this argument either in terms of the effect on the demand for money in monetarist analysis or one may use Tobin's model. For analytic convenience the latter is used in this paper but it should be stressed that the two are equivalent.

The size of the national debt is not a policy in the strict sense but is relevant to the issue here, in view of the marked differences of the size of the national debt in different European countries, especially between the very large size of the UK debt and the rest. The type of the national debt is interesting in various ways but is a relatively unexplored issue.

It seems that the larger the size of government bonds in private sector portfolios, the greater the leverage of monetary policy. This is largely a theoretical issue but has some relevance to any depression in which confidence is destroyed – say 1974 in Europe. If agreement had been reached on common expansion of money, UK growth of output would have been faster – and so would inflationary pressure.

The effect on the impact of a change in the money supply of different sizes of the national debt is ambiguous, even for an unconstrained equilibrium case where all markets are cleared by price. Setting up a three asset simplified form of Tobin's model:

$$\text{Demand-for-Money } (M) = a - br^D$$

$$\text{Demand-for-real assets } (R) = f + gr^r - hr^D$$

where r^r is the rate of return on real assets, and r^D the rate of return on bank deposits. The impact of a change in monetary policy is shown by the change in the quantity of R demanded at a constant r^r when M changes. This will be satisfied by either an increase in the price of existing real assets or an increase in their quantity – i.e. a change in output or prices. The relevant (comparative static) multiplier

$$\frac{\partial R}{\partial M} = \frac{gd}{be} - \frac{h}{b}.$$

As $N/(N + M + R)$ rises one would expect h and b to fall. Thus the effect is ambiguous. Nevertheless as R is much larger than M, one would expect the change in b to be larger. Hence one might expect $h/1$ to be lower and thus $\partial R/\partial M$ to be larger.

A special feature of UK debt management is that it is unfettered by legal constraints. Unlike the US and several EEC countries there is no legal nor even political constraint on the size of the national debt. Nor is there a legal maximum on the rate of interest, as in Italy. This is only important in so far as it makes it easier for the UK authorities to achieve any target.

Of much more importance is the absence of legal constraints compelling people and authorities to purchase government bonds, with the trivial exception of part of building society reserves. The UK has abstained from using such measures to increase the demand for its securities since the Trustee Act of 1961. The merits of such constraints are considered elsewhere (Gowland, 1978, 1981). Of more immediate relevance is that in Belgium, Italy and Germany a considerable proportion of the demand for government bonds comes from those legally compelled to hold them. It is not straightforward to calculate the effect of this on monetary policy since the holders might like to hold either bank debt or private sector debt and real assets instead of the government debt they are forced to hold. The result depends on whether more of their portfolios are switched from bank debt or the alternative assets. As short-term public debt is a good substitute for bank debt, then the latter – that is, displacement away from private debt and real assets – is likely to prevail, so German debt management means that for the same money growth its policy stance is more restrictive. Similarly as interest rates are artificially restricted by this means, aligned interest rates plus the constraint will mean that the policy stance and effects are more restrictive.

The UK pegged the price of bonds until 1971 and then abandoned the practice. Italy, and to some extent, France, still intervene very heavily to stabilize the price of their government bonds. This means that, as was argued above, the whole of the public sector debt had been liquidized. Thus, so long as bond sales are being used as an instrument of monetary policy or the national debt is growing, then an x per cent increase in M – any M – means that Italy and France are pursuing a more expansionist policy than in the UK or Germany. Bond-pegging will become harder – or at least more expensive – as markets are more integrated. Problems will also arise when arbitrage of interest movements are out of phase.

Both the 'Duke of York' tactics discussed in Gowland (1978, 1981) and bond-pegging mean that bonds markets in France, Italy and the UK are not 'efficient' or 'rational' in the technical sense. It is not very clear what the implications are beyond those discussed above, since unfortunately the area of debt management has been neglected in the burgeoning mass of literature on rational and efficient markets. A union between countries with 'rational' and 'irrational' markets is even harder to analyse. Certainly there might be a necessity for exchange control. On the whole, it seems reasonable to assume that rational markets have higher interest rates. Thus the 'irrational' partners would perhaps have the lower effective rates under an EM alignment. This might cut the demand-for-money for a given income and therefore increase the level of income for a given level (or growth) of income, i.e. be inflationary. Alternatively, it might raise the opportunity cost of purchase for capital goods and consumer durables. This issue is a variant of the problem of interpreting the implications of structural shifts in the demand-for-money which has been so contentious in both the UK and US.

The next distinction is once more between the UK and the rest of the EEC. It is that the UK authorities encourage (*a*) short period holdings of gilt-edged securities, (*b*) speculative purchases of gilt-edged securities. The two are clearly related but separate theoretical issues. The average turnover in long-dated gilt-edged securities exceeds 80 per cent in the UK. This is in part an institutional feature as well as having been encouraged by official policy, especially by their dealing policy which by assuming short period maximization has encouraged it. Unambiguously this increases liquidity compared to the text-book idea of a bond and to continental European practice. Thus a common money supply target could produce more inflation/growth in the UK.

On the other hand, the 'speculative' issue is anything but clear. The use of speculative instruments as instruments of debt management raises some interesting issues of monetary theory. In its purest form such instruments would be 'lotteries' as issued in eighteenth-century Britain or 'premium bonds'. However, the encouragement of speculative purchases of gilt-edged and the use of part-paid stocks is similar in principle and raises some more additional problems.

There are two relatively straightforward aspects to the issues. One is that the uncertainty about the return is obviously greater with such a security. Thus, on conventional theoretical grounds, it has more of a deflationary effect on behaviour than a text-book bond. However, one might argue that a holder of such a security is relatively risk loving, in some sense, and so his psychic wealth rises with the purchase of such a security. Furthermore, if one holds money supply growth constant, as one does by alignment, this might not imply comparable sales of debt (even if every other feature of the economies were identical) and certainly could involve a different effect on the cost of capital. At this point, the precise formulation of the model matters, a theoretical believer, in Hume's '100 Channels' could not accept the monetarist case of Tobin's general equilibrium framework. In any case, it is unnecessary to resolve all the complexities of this problem as the effect depends on 'distributional' effects. Leijonhufvud has pointed out that ignoring such effects by assumption is one of the weaknesses of the post Keynesian orthodoxy. If assets are switched such that *A* (the UK 'speculator') holds bonds rather than equities and liquid assets and *B* (the German risk neutral or risk averse investor) holds the latter rather than having been induced to hold bonds. Is the effect of the difference 'inflationary' or not?

How is the result affected by holding the money supply constant so the real rate of return on capital would vary? It seems that there is no clear-cut answer. Further tax yields must be affected by any switch so the money supply equality strictly implies different fiscal policy, in other words the budget constraint is relevant – the gravamen of Chapter 6.

The other seemingly straightforward effect is on the expected holding period of the purchaser of the bonds. As a 'speculative instrument' (or a sale induced by the hope of short-term gains) must be held for a shorter period, then the effect within a portfolio balance model of monetary policy is clearly expansionary. Ironically either a text-book Keynesian concentrating on credit, or a naive monetarist would not care. (A more sophisticated monetarist would let the demand-for-money or velocity of circulation be dependent on the nature of government bonds.) If the same holder is induced to hold bonds by the prospect of capital gain rather than interest, then the result is clear-cut except for the tax effect (if gains are taxed at a lower rate, and in any case the distribution over time of the payment of taxes on an equivalent Net Present Value varies) but otherwise distributional effects once more matter.

The analysis of speculative instruments of debt management must concentrate on wealth effects, indeed it is the prospect of these which dominate the decision to purchase. However, this leads to some intriguing paradoxes. In this world, wealth effects are more powerful than in the text-book model (the marginal propensity to spend out of wealth is likely to be much higher, perhaps 0.2 instead of 0.01). Thus the case for stable interest rates is very much strengthened, since the theoretical case for stability of interest rates depends so heavily on wealth effects. However, to generate such sales the authorities need volatile interest rates.

Furthermore, the greater are wealth effects, the more potentially unstable is the impact of monetary policy. Yet, the case for partly paid issues is to increase the stability of monetary growth. Furthermore a step towards EMU which is destabilizing is almost contradictory. In conclusion, I think one can say that while this issue has been ignored in the literature, it should not have been. No firm conclusions can be reached about the implications for European monetary alignment except that the combination of debt management relying heavily on speculative purchasing and that relying on conservative (or coerced) purchases is potentially explosive. It must be emphasized that there are no pejorative overtones to 'speculation' merely the argument that it is 'different'.

Text-book models rarely consider the effect of the existence of a market in bonds on the behaviour of asset holders. The principal exception is the size of the brokerage fee in the Tobin–Baumol demand-for-money model. However, this concerns the demand-for-bonds (and money) rather than the effect on the holder once he has bought it and is of more use as a psychological cost anyway. The sale of non-marketable debt will reduce the demand for other assets and goods more than the sale of marketable debt in normal assumptions about behaviour. The lower the cost of reselling bonds and the greater the certainty about price, the less is the impact of selling it (if the cost of sale were zero and the certainty of the price total, then it would be money). This leads to an interesting problem. A 'gilt' is highly marketable, one is relatively certain about its price tomorrow and its eventual (maturity) price but very uncertain about its price in a month's time. How does one weigh these factors to judge its effect on behaviour? *Inter alia*, it is necessary knowledge for the setting of monetary targets and as part of the (structural) background to monetary policy. A non-marketable asset can be used as security for borrowing but this implies a very high transactions cost (and in practice can be encashed at say, six months' notice or by paying a penalty in terms of foregone interest). Can/should one treat the two as identical in their effects? If not, whether the PSBR is financed by sales of national savings or gilts matters (as it does for distributional reasons). If a money supply target is set and achieved by varying the quantity of marketable debt sold, then the policy may minimize variability in monetary growth but not the impact on asset holders' willingness to purchase other assets or goods.

The UK's public sector debt is more marketable than, say, France's. Does this imply, as the argument above would suggest, that *ceteris paribus* the UK money supply should grow more slowly than the French one? The issue seems relevant both to monetary alignment and to EM union if this is ever revived and is eventually the theoretical version of the authorities' argument that the special nature of the gilts market must be taken into account when harmonizing policy.

Obviously, marketability increases the underlying demand for bonds but so do higher interest rates or greater liquidity (either by price-pegging or short maturity). The authorities' need to choose the optimal degree of marketability by trading off an increase in their sales (for any given pattern of rates) against reduced effectiveness of monetary policy.

Not too contentiously, one can rank the EEC countries by marketability: UK, Germany, Holland, Ireland, Belgium, Denmark, France, Italy. The influences are marked and therefore so are the effects.

One of the most strikingly different features of UK debt management is the UK system of tap issues whereby bonds are issued in large tranches, most of which is bought by the authorities using either departmental balances or the funds of the National Debt Commissioners. The authorities then state a price for such (tap stock) and gradually release the securities on to the market. As additional exotica, the price of such bonds is nearly always above market level; it is still regarded as 'spitting on the flag' to lead the market. Hence, the tap price is not the dealing price for tap stocks. The margin return, the official price and the price at which official sales take place is widely regarded as a signal manipulated by the authorities to influence behaviour. In France, the old-boy network of *Inspecteur de Finance* and official pressure ensures that issues are fully subscribed. The Bundesbank has a system that is closer in effect though not form to the US tender system. These peculiarities are not necessarily deflationary or inflationary in themselves but are bound to produce different phasings of monetary growth within the year in each country. Such variations may be without direct economic effect but must put pressure on the maintenance of exchange rates and interest rates. In such circumstances, there might be speculation to flows that stabilize the system. Equally, however, it might destabilize it and produce even greater variability. The whole issue is another example of the well-trodden problem of knife-edge speculation, widely discussed in commodity and foreign exchange markets.

Monetary Union as Substitute for Economic Integration

In this chapter, consideration has been given to a number of problems that would arise if an attempt were made to implement an alignment of monetary policies. The attempt would either fail to achieve even the *pari passu* monetary growth at which it aimed or would produce such divergence in economic performance that instability would result. Thus the rigidity induced by alignment would not solve any of the problems that have been revealed by the failures of Bretton Woods and the EMU. In brief, monetary policy cannot provide a short cut to economic integration. The necessary co-operation probably has to be achieved either by *ad hoc* discussions like the 'Big Six' summits or by BIS meetings. Any move to an EMS is likely to inflict heavy cuts on some participants. Real income transfers may be necessary to compensate the losers.

CHAPTER 8

Techniques of Collaboration II: Real Income Transfers

Income Redistribution between Community Member States

Real income transfers in the Community at present are largely implicit, and receive justification, if at all, only in terms of the respective programme, in the Common Agricultural Policy or the Regional Fund. But in the Federal models[1] (and to a minor extent, as part of the introduction of the European Monetary System) the idea of explicit transfers has been introduced. The motives for such appear to be either political – persuading certain member states to join EMS – or historical, for example, the MacDougall Committee (EEC, 1977a) making the Community develop like other federal entities. Whilst recognizing that such motives as these, the political and historical, may demand income transfers, we shall look more at the economic case, in an attempt to clarify the mish-mash of motives and arguments for income transfers that is often presented.[2]

Income Transfers, Trade and Factor Mobility

In Chapter 3 the variety of concept as to what the Community is, or should become from an economic point of view, has been elaborated. Ideas range from a market-orientated single economy with unrestricted trade and factor flows and a relatively small central budget, to an economic union with a large budget and centrally-implemented economic and social policy. The choice in model can produce a range of results from the elimination of any case for income transfers to an argument for substantial flows.

A 'pure' Customs Union model itself should in theory tend to equalize earnings of similar factors in different regions: a region exports products intensive in the abundant factor of that region, thus raising its relative price, and in the limit equalizes earnings of like factors (the 'factor price equalization theorem'). There are many reasons why in practice this tendency is limited. But it is strengthened by factor movement itself (the Common Market of the Treaty of

Rome itself), from low remuneration to high remuneration areas, again raising the relatively low remuneration of a factor in relative abundance in a region. Naturally, the process is retarded by institutional obstacles to movement, including linguistic and social attitudes.

This concept would imply that no income transfer superstructure would be required but for the obstacles to trade and factor mobility which are present. Since these are irremovable, many would dismiss this approach as naive, and some equalization is desirable as a social policy (see Chapter 12).

But against the view that this essentially market process cannot be made to work, some would argue that it is in fact working more than we envisage. This occurs when we re-interpret remuneration to mean equalization of factor pecuniary *and* non-pecuniary rewards. Labour may only flow from Ireland to the Ruhr when its reward in the latter is twice that in its existing location, such are the non-pecuniary advantages of present location – quality of life and all that. For the Community to now subsidize living in Ireland by hiking earnings above one-half of those of the Ruhr would be folly.

Again, we have to be careful that we are comparing suitable wage rates in two areas. If the hours, intensity and conditions of work are twice as onerous in one region, the 'comparable' wage rates have to be suitably deflated.

But of course, this only relates to redistribution between supplies of the same kind of labour. Even if a grade of labour *is* receiving equal pecuniary (with or without the addition of non-pecuniary) rewards in different regions, a redistribution may be desired between different kinds of suppliers of labour, i.e. the inter-regional comparison may need to be in terms of an income class distribution not a factor classification.

But this would only be viable in so far as the specificity of skills prevented switches of supply to the subsidized types of labour (and typically the poorer groups would present the least resistance to this). And it would require a common Community-wide policy to prevent its negation by factor movements to those particular nations practising such income supplementation. Such centralization of policy is alien to the economy of the Treaty of Rome, whilst factor mobility is not.

Thus such a view of the EEC, based on total pecuniary and non-pecuniary reward, goes a long way toward eliminating arguments for income transfers.[3] It is also clear that such a combination of conditions is quite dominant and exchange rate and monetary developments make no difference to the argument. However, the problem obviously arises that factor mobility may be realized for one factor, capital, but not labour. This is the most relevant model, currently closest to reality.

In the limit, the remuneration of capital is equalized throughout the Community, *ceteris paribus* (Woolley, 1974). Thus there is no case for transfers between owners of capital. But owners of the factor labour do not move in response to differences in pecuniary and non-pecuniary rewards. Against the argument that 'poverty' is thus self-imposed are those pertaining to private moving costs, specificity of skills especially of older people, the additional social or public costs, if any, of new extensions of social infrastructure in industrial or congested areas compared with existing areas, which might make it worthwhile to subsidize employees to stay put, and so on. Policies which facilitate capital movements, for example in the exchange rate and monetary field, exacerbate this dilemma: the real income gains from an improved use of capital, accompanied by a worsening in the regional unevenness in real wages.

Thus it is noteworthy that concomitant with interest in the development of monetary union, the other side of the equation, income redistribution programmes, have received considerable attention in the 'federal' models (EEC 1977a), Forte (1979)).

Efficiency Arguments for Income Transfers

Within the context of a Customs and Monetary Union model with restricted factor mobility (capital only), the well-worn distinction between efficiency and equity can be utilized. The former depends on Pareto-concepts, although whether Kaldor-like *potential* redistribution (that *could* make some-one better off and no-one potentially worse off) would suffice rather than proceeding with actual redistribution is a doubtful point in this context.

To begin with, we have to clear the ground in the following way. If there is a differential between two regions, e.g. between the semi-skilled daily wage rate in the Ruhr and Ireland (also more zero wages in Ireland due to unemployment), this may, as noted previously, reflect either (*a*) differences in non-pecuniary advantages, or (*b*) differences in hours of work, and intensity of work, i.e. different choices between effort and leisure. As we have suggested, then, there is no economic case for transfers.

So let us make *ceteris paribus* assumptions on non-pecuniary advantages, and hours and intensity of work. Then assume the wage rate is still twice as high in the Ruhr. This reflects equilibrium in each separated labour market, due to supply in each and demand based on labour marginal productivity.

If the market integrated (*ceteris paribus* on non-pecuniary advantages, same effort/leisure preference set and ignoring removal costs), labour would flow from Ireland to Ruhr, from low or zero marginal product uses to high, until the wage rate was equalized; total Community aggregate production would increase as the average marginal product of labour would rise. Now assume labour does not flow. We take £1 per day (or 1 unit of account) away from a Ruhr worker and pay this to the Irish. Can this increase real Community product or its growth? The loss in production in the Ruhr depends on the worker's position on his effort/leisure curve; it may reduce or increase marginal productivity. Conversely, the effect is uncertain in Ireland, depending on the use of the funds: they might be used for consumption (and hence affect the Irish worker's effort/leisure position), investment in re-training, and so on. So the effect is uncertain. But this inconclusive efficiency is confined to private costs, public sector costs must now be introduced.

If labour did move from low to high productivity and higher remuneration areas, yielding a potential increase in real Community product, nevertheless attendant extra social costs may outweigh these benefits. High productivity in prosperous areas may arise from external economies due to a heavy concentration of firms, but these may provide just the same conditions that give rise to high infra-structure costs from congestion. The comparison to be made lies between the operation of existing infra-structure, albeit out-of-date, in the old area, with expanded transportation, education, health and social services in the prosperous area. But marginal additions to services (as part of general real income growth) in the old areas could still be more costly. Again, there is no *a priori* answer.

One of the very reasons for high private productivity in the congested area may arise from incorrect pricing to firms of cost-reducing public expenditure, i.e. an implicit transfer is in process from the depressed area to the prosperous. However, this is only a 'who pays' issue; whether or not firms in part pay or the public purse pays, there may be an extra resource cost of infrastructure per worker in the congested area. This resource cost has to be set against the potential gain in real Community product. If it exceeds that gain, a case may exist for subsidizing labour in the low wage area so as to prevent its movement, thus income transfers may be justified from an efficiency angle.

Again, as in the preceding discussion, the matter could only be decided empirically; there is no *a priori* case for income transfers from one region to another on efficiency grounds, although there are various actual situations where they could be justified on cost grounds.

Equity Grounds for Income Transfers

The superior wage-rate in the separated Ruhr labour market (*ceteris paribus*) results from supply and demand considerations. The demand is a function of product price (if a tradable item, constant throughout the European Community except for transport costs) and prices of co-operating factors. With mobile capital, the price of that factor should also be constant. It is the effect of environmental factors (natural resources, man-made resources, concentration of firms) that enhances the marginal product and hence wage of labour, called by Biehl (1978) the fixed resource environment. The question is: should this extra labour remuneration in the favoured areas (capital remuneration is in theory equalized) be shared out within the Community? There are two possible lines of argument that it should – a strong and a weak.

The strong is based on the fact that the relatively high remuneration arises, at least in part, from the existence of the Community, i.e. that *extra* gains are reaped in a region from its fixed resource environment due to the Community – an economic rent in fact, 'rents' always having been fair game for redistribution.

On the output side, the product price of the product in which the prosperous area has a comparative environment advantage, may have been raised by the large market afforded by the Community. On the input side, the supply price of co-operating factors may have been lowered as a result of a reduction in obstacles in the capital market. Thus the Community 'rent' earned by labour in the prosperous area may well have been heightened, *and* partly at the expense of other regions, whose previous earnings, related to their fixed resource environment, may have been compromised by the replacement of restricted product and capital markets by open ones. If all this can be proven, an equity case may be upheld for re-distributing Community 'rents', if the member states can so agree.

The weak equity argument is the only *a priori* one: that sufficient social and political homogeneity exists in the Community so that other people's welfare enters into one's own welfare function, as it does within a family and to some extent does so within a region or nation-state. As regards the manifestation of this in public provision of merit goods – education, health, social security and housing (see Chapter 12) – MacDougall answered 'No' to the question as to whether sufficient 'political homogeneity' existed to justify Community public provision. On the other hand, it can be said that there must be a difference in kind between nations *within* the Community and those outside, something of common purpose and mutual assistance. Of course, sufficient homogeneity would be required of the Community to will the financial means.

The Historical Approach: Arguments by Analogy

The MacDougall Committee based their analysis on a Fiscal Federal model, as an extension of a Customs Union model with growing monetary unification and budgetary harmonization. Considerable resource transfers between member states are envisaged, either implicitly as part of tax/Community public expenditure programmes or explicitly as income subsidies.

Three stages of federal and economic integration are envisaged:

(*a*) Federation with a large Community public sector, 20–25 per cent GDP;
(*b*) Federation with a small Community public sector, 5–7 per cent GDP;
(*c*) Pre-federal integration, with a Community public sector, 2–2½ per cent GDP.

The Report works within a framework alternatively of (*b*) and (*c*). Since Community public expenditure is currently under 1 per cent of total Community Gross National Product, a transfer of 2 to 6 per cent of this aggregate from member states to the Community is sought.

Their case for real income transfers does not closely correspond with the presentation in this paper. There is little or no reference to efficiency arguments as here interpreted. There is correspondence only with the weak equity argument, that of social and political cohesion. Nearly all the weight is put, in the MacDougall Report, on historical analogy: that successful federations do coincide with the existence of policies therein to reduce income disparities in their various parts. This is called the 'macro' approach – 'from the top looking down'; there is also a 'micro' approach, which is based on a Public Goods analysis.

The Macroeconomic Approach from Other Federations

This 'macro' approach, in fact, reduces to a Community function of 'the reduction of difference in average living standards between regions' with a dynamic element that 'when the fortunes of different regions diverge over short periods, these differences are compensated through the tax and expenditure function of the public sector' (EEC, 1977a).

This entirely normative goal is justified by reference to what some other federations do. It is not a unique feature of federation, since one of many alternative concepts of federation is the institutionalization of *differences* in units of the federation.

The type of federation envisaged by the Report implies a big transfer system through a complex inter-regional grant system. However, accepting this concept of federation, problems obtain about the indicator for income redistribution, and the measurement of the redistributional effects in the MacDougall scheme.

The MacDougall Committee calculated the range of per capita income differentials in different regions within eight countries of the Community and estimated that 40 per cent of this was equalized through the national public finance systems. Whilst fully recognizing the variability of the equalizing power of different tax-expenditure programmes, the pre-federal Community Budget of around 2–2½ per cent Community Gross National Products that they envisaged might reduce inequalities by 10 per cent.

The proposition has already met several criticisms. The relevant 'regions' are difficult to define, and in any case, the comparison made was with individual per capita incomes whilst the fiscal redistributive package of the pre-federal Community, working mainly through the expenditure side, was largely a straight member state budget equalization scheme with no clear connexion with individual incomes in particular regions.

These criticisms have been fully covered elsewhere (Denton, 1978). We might add one more of a similar type. Since some of the Community budget based on 2–2½ per cent of Community Gross Product is said to be a transfer *from* Member-State budgets, has the 40 per cent equalizing power of those budgets now been reduced, so that the Community budget's 10 per cent power is partially a replacement, not a new element?

The 'indicator' used to demonstrate the need for transfers and their effectiveness is simply Gross National Product per head. This falls into the trap discussed earlier of ignoring different choices on work/leisure curves, non-pecuniary advantages of location, intensity and quality of work, and so on.

The other dubious quantitative aspect is the Report's proposition that a 10 billion unit of account budgetary package will reduce inequalities in living standards (measured by Gross National Product per head) between member states by about 10 per cent. But the policy has to aim at a moving target. The dynamics of the inter-state income distribution are, in fact, interrelated with the budgetary policy and the associated development of economic and monetary union. If an expanded Community budget were acceptable it would probably be as a counter-part to monetary unification and capital market integration, which would themselves be accentuating industrial concentration and income disparities. Thus an increasing transfer through the budget may therefore only represent a stand-still in inter-state income distribution. In one way, such large and growing budgetary transfers again calls the MacDougall federal system into doubt as unrealistic or undesirable; other policy developments particularly labour mobility may be preferable.

The Public Goods Approach to Redistribution

This represents the microeconomic approach of the MacDougall Committee (see also Dosser, 1973). In the case of 'social goods', these are provided by a public authority for reasons of externalities, economies of scale in provision etc., but, whichever level of authority should provide same, there is no necessary redistributive element – taxes can be raised with appropriate incidence. With 'merit goods', redistribution is more likely to arise. If standards of public health and welfare provision are to be as high in areas of low fiscal capacity as in rich areas, a need for cross-border subsidization is likely to be present.

The MacDougall Committee try to determine at what level – Community or member state – different kinds of public good should be provided. Three criteria are used: economies of scale, externalities or spillovers, and political homogeneity. Three categories of public sector functions are so evaluated: external relations, defence and law and order; social and welfare services; and economic services.

In some sub-cases, e.g. co-ordination of trade and aid, market regulation, advanced technological research, structural and cyclical policies, the Community level scores quite well in the MacDougall evaluation. The criteria used, however, are very slippery ones, for example, how do you measure political homogeneity? Besides mild pressure for upwards devolution, there exists in some countries stronger pressure for downward devolution. It is not difficult, by application of the criteria, to strip away far more public service function from the member-state level to devolve downward than upward, particularly as the big spenders of education, health, social security and housing would in part go downward on the grounds of low economies of scale and high political homogeneity in the region or city. If there were to be a 'general post' of existing member-state expenditure functions, few would go upwards, far more downward.

Thus the Public Goods arguments relate strictly only to the level of authority to provide the service, not to redistribution of income flowing from those particular tax-expenditure programmes. And where intra-Community redistribution is most likely to arise, in the case of merit goods, we see that the case for Community provision – Community-wide standards in welfare services – is at its weakest.

Sharing the Economic Rent for Political Stability

Forte (1979) is acutely aware that the factor mobility model (strictly, the one-factor mobility model) which will be given impetus by Economic and Monetary Union, will exacerbate regional inequalities of various kinds (both of 'pull' deprivation, and 'push' congestion). Community budgetary instruments, he considers, must be used to correct these.

The principal justification seems to be, implicitly at any rate, a version of the 'rent' theory, sharing the real income gains of developments arising from monetary union. Forte says that monetary union is a socio-political pact whereby all lose their monetary autonomy to gain the economic benefits of monetary union. The weaker, with lower incomes, higher unemployment and less rigorous fiscal and monetary policies will benefit from greater fiscal and monetary soundness and from fiscal (meaning, income) support. Financial convergence has to be inter-dependent with income and employment convergence, it is said.

When we examine the Forte scheme within its own terms of reference, the same questions of measuring divergence of economic status between regions of stages, and the effects of corrective instruments, applies as in the case of MacDougall (as examined in Chapters 3 and 4). The measurements are certainly much more sophisticated than the simple GDP per head of MacDougall. Three real sector indices are developed; employment as a percentage of the labour force, investment as a percentage of GNP, per capital GDP deflated by purchasing power parities – and three monetary indices – the growth rate of labour cost in national currencies, consumer goods price index, growth of money supply. Each index is measured by the coefficient of variance (ratio of mean square deviation to arithmetic mean) and each set of three simply averaged into one index.

Whilst the money composite, and the most important real index (per capita GDP) were showing divergence even before the establishment of EMS, Forte has estimated the convergence force of three types of fiscal transfers, amounting to an extra 0.8 per cent of Community GDP (the existing Community budget brought up to the MacDougall pre-federal level of 2–2½ per cent by the addition of 1.2 per cent, of which 0.6 per cent represents new fiscal transfer expenditure added to the present 0.2 per cent spent in the Regional and Social Funds). The fiscal transfers are of three types: fiscal incentives for industrialization (normally 50 per cent grants towards investment costs), public expenditure on public infrastructure, and re-training type subsidies to human capital. Regional employment creation and additions to GDP are thus calculated. The general result is that a contribution of 0.8 per cent of Community GDP spent on these three tasks could increase per capital Gross National Product in the weaker regions from 79 to 81 per cent of average Community levels, hence decreasing the differential by about 10 per cent. It will be recalled that this is similar to the figure at which MacDougall aimed with its Community Budget of 2–2½ per cent.

What has happened is that Forte has excluded the non-distributive part of such a new budget (0.6 per cent) and sharpened the redistributive power of another part; the nondescript inter-state fiscal transfers have largely disappeared. However, several of the conceptual problems revealed in our brief analysis of earlier sections appear to remain. Whilst the 'neo-classical' model of factor mobility is mentioned to emphasize the deleterious effect on regions of moves towards Monetary Union, the appropriate model – which gives rise to all the trouble – of greater capital and enterprise mobility with fixed labour mobility, is still not worked out (e.g. measures to induce labour to move may be the most cost-effective of all).

Further, Forte is still redistributing, as far as one can see, to those with high non-pecuniary rewards from those with high pecuniary rewards arising from high effort, or lower quality of life, with his use of per capital Gross National Product differentials.

Relatedly, 'push finance' (pushing firms out by proper charging for public infra-structure or, going even further, fiscal penalties) applied to congested areas is ignored or subordinated to 'pull finance' (finance for depressed areas), which has difficult budgetary implications – how to raise the required revenues.

Finally, the dynamics. The Forte Report is cogniscent of the two sides of the equation – EMU exacerbates divergence whilst the Community budget has hardly begun to assist pre-EMU inequalities – and admits that the quantum of redistributive power in MacDougall and in its own scheme (both in the pre-federal state of the budget) is 'unlikely to provide an effective base for monetary union'. It hazards that a budget of 3 per cent of Community GDP employed entirely to promote convergence of income (i.e. as compared with 0.8 per cent to be used in the pre-federal budget) would solve most of the regional problems arising from monetary union.

This estimate offers many hostages to fortune. Reflecting on it throws several points we have made into sharp relief. On the one hand, it is again undynamic, implying there is an end of the process, and it may be a considerable *underestimate* in the long run as the capital and money markets completely integrate, but labour remains immobile. But on the other hand, such a thought emphasizes the nonsense of greater and greater effort to reduce the differentials of per capita income for those choosing low-intensity work modes in congenial environments.

Income Transfers for Stabilization Policy

Some years ago, short-term conjunctional policy would have provided an additional economic case for transfers of tax finance from one region into expenditure in another part of the Community. This would have been in the context of a Customs Union model with tax harmonization, and without monetary union.

Now several factors combine to make little of such a transfer operation:

(*a*) The increased trade integration in the Community has increased leakage effects from one member state to another and lessened the effect of public expenditure boosts in any one;

(*b*) Confidence in tax-expenditure measures to control inflation and unemployment is seriously weakened (and was never as strong in other member states compared with the UK);

(*c*) As the European economy moves towards monetary union, any regional fiscal action can be easily neutralized or counteracted by the free flows of short-term capital across national boundaries, so national money supply policy cannot be used to back up or enforce additions to or reductions from net public expenditure in an area.

But even so, the use of current or proposed taxes and expenditures for these purposes is still discussed and needs attention.

On the tax side, the question which arises is whether the nascent Community tax system, a sales tax, the VAT, is suitable for variation as a stabilization instrument. Certainly it is a novel situation, since, looking at other federations, a federal *income* tax is normally expected to play this part. A recent authority has claimed that it can, in the context of a model lacking full monetary union (Oates, 1977).

Such an answer cannot be given by any full-blooded monetarist, since national authorities retain control, and can adjust as they wish, national money supplies. Even adopting a more Keynesian approach, and putting this aside, the prospective Community adjustment of spending in member states by variation of VAT rates would meet counteracting adjustment of national exchange rates (still present with no monetary union) if not of money supplies. A deflationary fiscal policy may, with fairly simple assumptions, lead to an inflationary exchange rate adjustment.

This is not all. Again, in a Keynesian world, it is increasingly unrealistic to expect to cut private consumption by a VAT – increase in view of retaliatory wage-adjustment. In the limit, the real wage, and hence real consumption is constant (given no money or tax illusions), through sales tax variations (see Dernberg, 1974).

Longer-run problems in the use of the VAT as Community tax are serious. Given an initially agreed division of revenues between the Community and national levels of government, the near-to-unity tax elasticity of the VAT compared with the above-unity elasticity of (for example) the UK tax system as a whole constantly redistributes revenue back to the national level in proportionate terms, given some real GNP growth and/or inflation.

The Community would constantly have to gain acceptance for increases in the VAT *rate*, to keep constant relative shares with national tax revenues. Further, *rate* adjustments will also be required when the VAT is used in an attempt at adjusting member-state domestic expenditure, there being no 'built-in stability' in this tax, compared with a federal income tax. All in all, it seems most unfortunate that the Community is hooked on to this particular and unique form of federal tax. This is recognized to some extent in the MacDougall Report, but not as seriously as it should be.

Of course, economic activity could also be influenced in member states or regions if expenditures can be so organized. Existing programmes, for example, the Common Agricultural Policy, would not seem capable of such short-term adjustments. But labour-oriented expenditures, unemployment benefits, retraining schemes, could be. This is of the nature of short-term boosts to demand in an area: it has to meet the general objections to conjunctural policy of the day noted at the beginning of this section, and cannot, of course, be long-term without getting us back to all the difficulties about economic justification for permanent real income transfers which we have discussed.

The Weak Case for Transfers in the Current EEC

Neither the Customs Union nor Common Market models of the economic development of the Community would appear to hold much place for income transfers between parts of the Community. It is the capital-mobile, labour-immobile Customs/Monetary Union model which raises the issue most acutely, and may demand an enlarged Federal budget with income transfers as a concomitant. There may be economic efficiency arguments for transfers, but this empirical question has not been worked out by recent working groups. They dwell on the equity arguments, but the analogies of the USA, Canada and Australia must surely present the constitutional history and the social and political homogeneity to substantiate a case for transfers which an enlarged EEC does not. Further, and curiously, those federations do exhibit free labour movement. This is actually a check on one-eyed redistribution (on the basis of money GDP per head), since if transfers are made *to* an area of high quality of life and great potential (but presently low) GDP per head, the flow of labour there will erode the tax base of the payer regions and create a corrective mechanism

It may be that recent transfers, such as those made to Italy and Ireland on joining the EMS, must be seen as purely political acts in the power game between ten loosely-connected states. But if so, the economic analysis going under the head of federal finance, into which the MacDougall and Forte Reports must be classed, is not to be applied. If it is, its application to the Community seems more complex and difficult to make than has been claimed.

Transfers are going on in the Community, but implicitly; this is evident from the studies in Part III, the major redistribution being via the Common Agricultural Policy.

Notes

1. The major example is the MacDougall Report (EEC, 1977a).
2. For another ascetic view on the issue, see de Grauwe and Peeters (1978).
3. There is, of course, no call for income redistribution through fiscal means in the Treaty of Rome itself.

PART III

Microeconomic Case Studies in European Collaboration

CHAPTER 9

The Common Agricultural Policy

This chapter evaluates the general objectives of agricultural policy, and of the CAP in particular, using economic criteria. Given the objectives of the CAP, and taking into consideration the operation of the CAP, we consider whether the objectives could have been pursued more effectively by other policies.

Intervention in agriculture is justified when private actions do not lead to a social optimum. Using the possible objectives of agricultural policies as a guide to the reasons for intervention, it is possible to evaluate the need for intervention by considering why private actions may not lead to an optimal outcome. In assessing the case for intervention we consider the costs of intervention which are borne by the non-agricultural sector, as well as the benefits from intervention.

The main objectives of the CAP as outlined in Article 39 of the Treaty of Rome are:

(*a*) To increase agricultural productivity . . .
(*b*) To ensure a fair standard of living for the agricultural community . . .
(*c*) To stabilize markets;
(*d*) To assure the availability of supplies;
(*e*) To ensure that supplies reach consumers at reasonable prices.

A 'fair standard of living' was not defined by the Treaty. In directive 72/159/EEC on modernizing farms it is defined as an income comparable with the earnings of a non-agricultural worker in the same region. This directive is one of a number of directives which have been agreed since the Treaty of Rome: these are aimed at improving the structure of agricultural production and marketing (see EEC (1979c), pp. 17–20). In discussing the CAP we shall concentrate mainly on the five objectives above. The structural directives are of little practical significance simply because the amount of funds allocated to this section of the CAP is very small.

The Case for Intervention in Agriculture: The National Level

The case for state intervention in agriculture is based on two observations: agricultural incomes are below the average of other sectors, and agricultural production is inherently unstable. Furthermore, it is argued that intervention is desirable to increase agricultural production thereby increasing self-sufficiency and improving the balance of payments, and also to increase agricultural productivity. Finally references are made to consumer welfare.

Agricultural Incomes

Income support is probably the main reason for state intervention in agriculture. It is generally accepted that agricultural incomes are below average, although the disparity is difficult to measure (see Hill and Ingersent (1977), pp. 100–2). One way of obtaining an indication of average incomes in other sectors is to compare the percentage of national output accounted for by agricultural production, with the percentage of the labour force employed in agriculture (Ritson (1973), p. 96). The necessary data is shown in Table 9.1. This approach suggests that in the Community agricultural incomes vary from about one half of average incomes upwards. The low values for Germany and Italy may be because of the high incidence of part-time farming in those countries.

An alternative estimate can be derived by comparing the average gross hourly earnings in industry and agriculture. The data shown in Table 9.1 show that wage rates in agriculture are below those in industry. This is consistent with the hypothesis that income levels in agriculture are below those in industry, but is not conclusive proof because the average number of hours worked in industry is less than in agriculture. Further caveats are that estimates of agricultural earnings may be lower than industrial earnings because there are psychic rewards from working in agriculture or payments in kind, and earnings figures exclude increases in wealth from increases in the value of land. Accepting the hypothesis that income levels are lower in agriculture, what is the cause of the disparity?

One view maintains that the existence of relatively low farm incomes is due to four characteristics of the agricultural sector, namely, an inelastic demand for agricultural products with respect to prices and income, rapid technical progress, a competitive industry, and labour immobility (Metcalf (1969), p. 117). In this market situation labour-saving technical progress is forced on individual farmers because of the atomistic structure of the industry. Falls in

TABLE 9.1
The Importance of Agriculture and Estimates of Relative Earnings

	1978			1968			1976		
	Agriculture as % of GNP (a)	Agricultural employment as % of total (b)	Ratio (a) ÷ (b)	Agriculture as % of GNP (c)	Agricultural employment as % of total (d)	Ratio (c) ÷ (d)	Average gross male hourly rate in agriculture (e)	Average gross male hourly rate in industry (f)	Ratio (e) ÷ (f)
BE	—	3.2	—	4.9	5.6	0.88	123	173	0.71
DE	5.8	8.8	0.66	7.5	12.8	0.59	27.0	34.6†	0.78
FR	4.8	9.1	0.53	7.5	15.7	0.48	11.3	14.7	0.77
GE	2.5	6.5	0.38	4.4	9.9	0.44	8.4	11.2	0.75
IR	17.1	22.2	0.77	18.8	29.4	0.64	89	—	—
IT	7.8	15.5	0.50	10.7	23.0	0.46	1474	1631*	0.90
LU	3.2	5.6	0.57	4.6	10.2	0.45	132	188	0.70
NE	4.5	6.2	0.73	6.9	7.9	0.87	9.8	11.3	0.87
UK	2.3	2.7	0.85	—	3.5	—	99	150	0.66
EC	4.1	8.0	0.51	—	12.0	—	—	—	—

Sources: Cols. (a), (b), (c), (d), EEC (1980), *The Agricultural Situation in the Community: 1979 Report*, Brussels; col. (e), 'Earnings in Agriculture: 1976', *Eurostat*, Statistical Office of European Communities, 1977; col. (f), 'Hourly Earnings, Hours of Work, Oct-1976', *Eurostat*, Statistical Office of European Communities, 2-1977.

Notes: BE, DE, FR, GE, IR, IT, LU, NE, UK, EC denote Belgium, Denmark, France, Germany, Ireland, Italy, Luxemburg, Netherlands, United Kingdom, and the European Community, respectively.

* October 1975 figure.

† Figure for all workers (male and female).

the prices of agricultural products cause a fall in the gross income of the sector because of the inelastic demand, and workers remain in agriculture at low relative wages. If technical progress continues, and the number of people in agriculture does not fall, the low relative wage continues. The obvious defect with this argument is that it does not explain why agricultural workers are less likely to move than workers in other sectors. The explanation may be the existence of rewards other than wages.

An alternative explanation is that farm wages are low because labour productivity is low, wages in the non-agricultural sector being higher because of a skill differential. Such a differential might be due to educational facilities being below average in rural areas. If this explanation of the disparity is correct, and taxes are levied on the non-agricultural sector to finance income subsidies to agriculture, this results in misallocation of labour towards agriculture.

There is no economic reason why two workers doing different jobs should necessarily receive the same income. The wages of non-agricultural workers represent the opportunity cost of workers *of the same quality* in the agricultural sector. If, because of a factor market distortion such as imperfect information, agricultural workers do not move out of agriculture in sufficient numbers for earnings to be equalized, the appropriate policy is to remove the distortion by providing information, not to subsidize incomes in agriculture. Furthermore, if incomes in agriculture are increased at the expense of non-agricultural incomes, this will tend to maintain or increase the supply of labour in agriculture. Therefore, attempting to cure the problem may prolong its causes. Even if the aim of economic policy is income equality *per se* (for political reasons), a general policy of income redistribution from the rich to the poor is called for (e.g. through taxes), not income support in one sector.

There are many explanations of the disparity between agricultural and non-agricultural earnings (see Hill and Ingersent (1977), pp. 106–16; and Josling (1974), pp. 231–2). The causes of the disparity cannot be ignored because they determine whether there is a case for intervention, and if so, what form the intervention should take. However, the observation that incomes in one sector are below those in another sector is not of itself an economic justification for government intervention to improve earnings.

Instability

Governments might also intervene to increase market stability. Agricultural production is prone to fluctuations caused by the weather, and by animal and plant diseases. Instability of agricultural output may be accompanied by price and/or farm income instability, which can be the justification for government intervention. When producers' plans are based on expected prices, and unstable market prices are used to predict future prices, producers plans will not be realized if their predictions are inaccurate. For some products the time lapse between the decision to produce and the sale of the product by the farmer is considerable, which makes prediction difficult.

Market instability alone is not a valid argument for state intervention, because the existence of instability does not imply that in the absence of intervention agricultural resources will be allocated inefficiently. There are many ways in which farmers can reduce the potential market instability they face, for example, by diversification of production, or private storage. Stabilization implies smoothing around a trend, and there is no obvious reason to suppose that an official agency can predict the trend better than farmers themselves. Also, it is not clear which groups (consumers or producers) lose and gain from stabilization, or if on balance society as a whole gains or loses when the cost of operating the stabilization policy is included (see Colman, 1978). A further argument against stabilization is that domestic stability may be increased at the expense of international stability. Free trade in agricultural products will produce a more stable international solution than restricted trade, because through trade each country's disturbance is spread over a wider area. A single country can achieve a greater degree of domestic stability than on world markets by restricting trade, but this will destabilize the world market. The theoretical case for or against stabilization is weak, and in practice stabilization schemes have been price support schemes. Thus one may be sceptical about the importance of this objective relative to that of income support (see Josling, 1979).

Self-sufficiency

Self-sufficiency can be measured by the ratio of domestic production to domestic consumption. In principle there are two basic methods of increasing self-sufficiency: lower imports or higher domestic production. The costs associated with these two methods are likely to be different, and thus one would not be indifferent between them. Also, the costs of achieving self-sufficiency are related to the product concerned. For example, an import ban, or subsidies to domestic production, could give the UK complete self-sufficiency in peaches! The case for increased self-sufficiency has two elements: a security argument and a balance of payments argument.

Agricultural policies may be used to increase self-sufficiency, and thus to guarantee the security of supply as insurance against the possibility that supplies of imports are disrupted. One view maintains that there is a strong case of attempting to guarantee the 'minimum nutritional needs of the population' (Ritson, 1980). Failure to meet this level would be so costly, that even if there is a very small probability of supplies being disrupted, this level should be guaranteed. However, the case for increasing the security of supply beyond this level is weak. The benefit is the ability to adjust gradually to changes in world markets, which may be accomplished by other policies – for example food stocks. Also, as self-supply increases, the probability of disruptions because of short-falls in domestic supply increases.

The balance of payments argument for increased domestic production is that it reduces the need for imports of food, and 'improves' the balance of payments. The overall effect on the balance depends on how the increase in agricultural production is achieved. To the extent that production in other sectors is adversely affected by the policy of increasing agricultural production (as by the taxes levied to finance agricultural subsidies), other imported goods may replace agricultural imports. Even if one concluded that agricultural expansion causes a net improvement in the balance of payments, this is not a justification for intervention in this sector: intervention in another sector might be more effective. Finally, the loss of welfare from financing an expansion of agriculture as a way of improving the balance of payments, is likely to be greater than the costs of adjustment induced by a flexible exchange rate. Agricultural expansion may improve the balance of payments, but this does not imply that agricultural expansion should be used to improve the balance of payments when less costly alternatives exist.

Increased Productivity

At first sight the objective of increased productivity seems an attractive reason for intervention, but again it is necessary to consider whether there is a case for a policy favouring agriculture at the expense of other sectors. Productivity can be measured by the number of units of output per unit of input, the units may be units of value or quantity. Taking productivity measured in value, farmers acting independently attempt to minimize the cost of inputs in relation to the value of output, and choose the combination of inputs according to their relative costs and contributions to output. There is no reason to suppose that the government can perform this activity better than farmers, or that agriculture is likely to be less efficient than other sectors. On the contrary farmers are more likely to maximize profits because the divorce between ownership and control in other sectors is not typical of agricultural production.

A valid case for government intervention exists when the market prices used by farmers do not reflect social values. For example, the private cost of using an insecticide does not include the damage to the environment, so that the private measure of productivity differs from society's. Similarly the case for intervention to increase productivity measured in physical units can be based on a disparity between private and social values. Without such a disparity intervention is unnecessary, however even if some disparities do exist it is unlikely that a policy aimed at increasing productivity in agriculture generally is called for. Environmental considerations may lead one to favour a *less* intensive use of resources (for example, see Shoard (1980)).

Consumer's Interests

The case for intervention in agriculture (in the form in which it usually takes place) on behalf of consumers is particularly weak when one considers the alternative. In the absence of intervention consumers would be able to buy at world prices, and it is difficult to see how consumers are better off in a system where domestic production is subsidized in some way at their expense – for example, by tariffs or through subsidies financed by taxes. World markets may be less stable than domestic markets which are protected, but if the choice is between unstable low average prices and stable high prices there is no reason to suppose consumers would choose stable high prices. Also, free access to world markets gives a diversity of choice which is not available from domestic supplies.

Thus, the case for state intervention in agriculture for economic reasons is weak. The arguments for intervention break down when the costs to other sectors of state intervention in agriculture, or the possibility of intervention in other sectors, are considered.

The Case for Intervention in Agriculture: The Community Level

The need for a common agricultural policy can be explained by the inclusion of agriculture in the customs union, and the consequences of that inclusion. Agriculture was included to satisfy national interests, and (perhaps) because it was expected that free trade in agricultural products would be beneficial. A common agricultural policy was thought to be necessary to avoid distortions of relative competitiveness and maintain free trade in other sectors, and because of agriculture's importance within the member states.

National Interests and Industrial Policy

One explanation of the inclusion of agriculture stresses the view that the Treaty of Rome reflects the national interests of the signatories (Swan (1973), pp. 116–17). Germany was more efficient in industrial production than France, whereas France was more efficient in agricultural production. If both countries were to gain from the Treaty, free trade in agricultural products was a necessary accompaniment of free trade in industrial products. The second explanation is that agriculture was considered to be an area where free trade would bring about a 'better division of labour' and lead to higher living standards for producers and consumers (EEC (1975c), p. 7). An alternative interpretation of events is that each of the Six envisaged a common policy would be developed satisfying their national objectives and there would be an increased level of trade (rather than free trade and the adjustment of their agriculture sectors to foreign competition, albeit from other Community members). Certainly with hindsight the alternative interpretation is attractive.

If one assumes that national governments require agriculture to be supported for one of the reasons discussed above, in the absence of a Community agricultural policy which satisfies the minimum requirements of the members, one would expect national policies to be pursued. These policies may affect relative industrial competitiveness, thus it can be argued that a common policy is necessary to prevent distortions in other sectors (for example, EEC (1975c), para. 8; Swan (1973), p. 117). This argument implicitly assumes that a common policy is neutral in its effects on relative industrial competitiveness. As the degree of self-sufficiency and the nature of agricultural production differs between countries, a common policy is unlikely to benefit all members equally, and therefore will not be neutral. If a common policy is not neutral, then the desirability of a common policy over a set of national policies is not proven.

A related justification for a common policy is that it is necessary for the maintenance of free trade. Without a common policy, it is argued that governments would take measures to protect their own agriculture which could adversely affect other members. If such a situation existed: 'There is a danger that such action in one sector would quickly extend to other parts of the economy and undermine the whole basis of the Community.' (EEC (1977b), p. 4). Since 1969 a significant part of trade between members has been subject to tariffs in the form of monetary compensatory amounts (MCAs). The common market *has* survived. The little evidence we have shows that members have not based their industrial policy on the CAP precedent of restricted trade. Therefore, the argument that a common agricultural policy is necessary to maintain free trade in other sectors appears incorrect.

The Importance of Agriculture

The importance of the agricultural sector is sometimes cited as a justification for a common policy. Although there is no doubt that agriculture is important (see Table 9.1), government intervention is surely not justified simply by importance? Intervention in one sector (rather than another) is justified when the characteristics of the sector are such that private actions do not bring a socially optimal allocation of resources. Size alone is not necessarily a cause of sub-optimality, so that importance cannot be used as a reason for intervention.

Common Interests

A common policy might be desirable if the Nine shared common objectives, and attach equal weights to them. Table 9.2 shows that

TABLE 9.2
Member's Interests in Agricultural Support

	*National average earnings**	*Average farm size (hectares 1978)*†	*% of food imports from EEC (1978)*	*% of food exports to EEC (1978)*	*Food as a % of household consumption (1977)*
BE	14188	14.8	0.67‡	0.81‡	19.7
DE	12333	23.9	0.30	0.64	18.8
FR	11240	25.9	0.44	0.67	19.7
GE	12911	14.6	0.49	0.67	15.8
IR	6977	20.5§	0.66	0.86	24.0
IT	7797	7.8§	0.47	0.66	30.5
LU	14152	25.9	—	—	19.8
NE	14913	15.2	0.41	0.78	17.8
UK	6420	66.0	0.36	0.52	18.5
EC	10066	17.2§	0.46	0.70	17.9

Sources: EEC (1980), *The Agricultural Situation in the Community: 1979 Report*, Brussels.
* 'Remuneration of wage and salary earners in EUA'.
† Farms in excess of one hectare.
‡ BE and LU.
§ 1975.

this is unlikely to be the case. Average earnings differ considerably across the Community and a common policy which supports agricultural incomes to a similar extent will not equalize agricultural and non-agricultural incomes. Farm size differs, and one would expect the problems of agriculture and the need for intervention also to differ. The importance of non-EEC markets varies, so that a common policy towards external markets will not be in the interests of all members. Finally the proportion of household expenditure on food varies, so that one would expect the importance attached to agricultural objectives to vary.

The Case for a Common Fisheries Policy

The case for a common fisheries policy is strong and is different from that of agriculture. The special characteristics of the industry are that fish stocks are potentially exhaustible but also regenerate if allowed to, and fish migrate between the areas controlled by different countries (see EEC (1978d)). The sea is common property, therefore although it is in the collective interest of the industry to conserve stocks, each individual fisherman has little incentive to refrain from catching as much as possible. A balance between depletion and regeneration must be achieved, and this requires government action. One country acting alone cannot conserve fish stocks because fish migrate between country areas, e.g. restrictions may be necessary on fishing a spawning ground in one area, to ensure supplies of mature fish in another area. These problems are not limited to the Community waters, and require an international fisheries policy. Hopefully the evolution of a Community policy will not hamper the development of a more general policy.

One possible policy is for a private or official organization to fix quotas for fishing in certain areas. A crucial determinant of the effects of the policy is how the quotas are allocated, and to whom. If the objective is to ensure that the most efficient boats exploit the limited resources, the quotas should be auctioned. The group allowed to bid for the quotas should be as large as possible to encourage efficiency (i.e. free entry), but political and economic objectives may restrict the group to fishermen within the Community, or even within certain member states.

The Operation of the CAP: The Policy Instruments

The CAP operates mainly through two mechanisms. First, the Community market is protected from low (and high) world food prices through a variable levy which raises (reduces) the price of imports to the 'threshold price', a price fixed in relation to the desired market price for the product. Second, a minimum price is guaranteed to producers for their produce. If there is surplus production at the chosen intervention price, intervention agencies buy up the excess supply, the agencies sell their stocks when the market price rises.

Levies

The system of variable levies is a variable tariff system. The height of the tariff varies according to the world price. In the case of cereals the levy is fixed to equal the difference between the lowest c.i.f. offers on world markets and the 'threshold price'. The threshold price varies with intervention prices so that a decision to raise intervention prices raises the levy on imports and increases protection.

The desirability of a tariff relative to other alternative instruments is a common topic in international trade (for example see Bhagwati (1971)). If one assumes that the objective is to subsidize domestic producers it can be shown that a subsidy is less costly than a tariff for a given increase in domestic output. If the objective is to decrease the volume of imports, a tariff is less costly than a subsidy for a given reduction in imports. This result has been used by some economists to argue that the policy of a variable levy is an inefficient method of achieving income support (see for example El-Agraa (1980)). Alternatively, one could argue that the objective of self-sufficiency has been the dominant objective and that a tariff is an efficient way of reducing imports and achieving that objective. However, it is probably more realistic to assume that income support is the dominant objective.

A tariff which raises the consumer price of a good for the purpose of supporting production, can be thought of as a tax on consumers of the good, which is used to raise revenue for a production subsidy. The existence of tariff revenue indicates that the consumption tax is greater than is necessary to finance the production subsidy (Corden (1974), p. 44). A tax on the consumption of a product distorts consumer choices, and there may be other ways of financing the agricultural subsidy which cause less distortion, for example, through general taxation. Also, the proportion of income spent on food increases as income falls, so that taxes on food are regressive, and this may conflict with income distribution objectives. A further argument against income support through prices is that higher prices increase the return to *all* agricultural inputs, and clearly this is not an effective way of raising the return to one input, labour.

Finally, and perhaps most important of all, price support through tariffs conceals the true cost of agricultural income support. For the Community as a whole Morris (1980) estimated that the CAP raised agricultural incomes in 1978 by about £14.3 billion, or £1,700 for each person employed. There is little doubt that direct income subsidies of this size from government funds would not be acceptable. This is not an argument in favour of price support rather than direct subsidies however, as the financing of the subsidy to agriculture by maintained prices (which are in effect food taxes) is even worse. On the contrary, the analysis suggests that the present level of income support survives because the true costs of income support are hidden.

Intervention Buying

The mechanism of intervention buying is used to achieve the objective of price stability by balancing fluctuations in demand and supply around a chosen price. It is possible to envisage an intervention price being chosen so that average intervention stocks are stable and low. When there is excess supply at the intervention price intervention stocks are increased, and when there is excess demand stocks are reduced. An intervention system which operates in this way provides market price stability, but not income support or even income stability (when supply fluctuates). If a higher intervention price is chosen purchases of surplus production exceed sales of stocks on average, and stocks increase. An element of income support exists because market demand is augmented by the demand of the intervention agency as stocks increase, which tends to increase the price level. Similarly if the average level of an intervention stock is only kept constant by sales of stock to foreign markets at subsidized prices, the average price level will be higher than when the stock is sold on the Community market. The famous example is the sale of butter to the USSR in 1973 which cost £150 million in export subsidies (see Swan (1978), p. 180). Subsidized exports are a continuing feature of the CAP (see EEC, 1979c), which shows that the intervention system is being used for income support. The cost of income support through intervention consists of two elements: consumers pay higher prices for food, and taxes are levied to finance the disposal of surpluses.

The CAP is organized on the basis of a common price level which reflects the principle of market unity. In practice the common price level was abandoned when the rates of exchange used for converting support prices fixed in units of account into national curencies – the 'green' rates – diverged from market rates in 1969. In 1968 the green rates of exchange were such that when country *A*'s intervention price was converted into country *B*'s using market exchange rates, country *A*'s intervention price equalled country *B*'s. When France devalued in 1969 a rise in French intervention prices was unacceptable, but at the devalued market exchange rate French intervention prices were below those in the rest of the Community. To prevent trade taking place simply to exploit the higher intervention price in the rest of the Community (as with French sales of wheat to German intervention agencies), monetary compensatory amounts (MCAs) were introduced. These are tariffs and subsidies which equalize intervention prices. In the example given, MCAs took the form of tariffs applied to French exports and subsidies to imports. When Germany revalued a similar problem arose in reverse, and exports (imports) were subsidized (taxed). Irving and Fearn (1978) examine the evolution and effects of MCAs in more detail. MCAs reflect the desire of member governments for different intervention prices (the fact that intervention prices are equal when expressed in units of account is irrelevant because trade takes place in national currencies, not units of account).

If we assume that the objective of the CAP is income support, will common prices bring a common level of support? Provided that the costs of all inputs used in agricultural production are the same in different countries, the same nominal income will result if the efficiency of their use is the same. However, if the objective is relative income equality between sectors, this will not be achieved unless in addition all non-farm incomes are equal, which they are not (see Table 9.2). Therefore, the policy of common prices will not lead to the attainment of a common level of income support.

The Results of the CAP

For ease of exposition the performance of the CAP will be assessed by considering the effect of the CAP on each of the objectives in the following order: prices, self-sufficiency (quantities), productivity, market stability, and incomes. Finally, the financial cost of the CAP will be examined. Any exercise of this nature is somewhat speculative because one cannot be sure what would have happened without the CAP.

Prices

Ideally one would like to be able to compare the present Community prices with the world prices that would prevail in the absence of the CAP. If we use existing world prices, these may underestimate the prices that would exist in the absence of the CAP to the extent that there would be a significant increase in imports of food from third countries. In Table 9.3 we have used the lowest third country offer price, the lowest price at which the Community was offered imports. A further qualification is necessary because the lowest offer price may underestimate existing world prices (for example, if most trade is conducted at higher prices, the offer prices may be for small quantities of surplus supply on world markets). Subject to these qualifications which are unlikely to change the result significantly, the figures in Table 9.3 support the hypothesis that the operation of the CAP

TABLE 9.3
Prices of Agricultural Products

	EC entry price EUA/100 kg (a)	*Third country offer price EUA/100 kg (b)*	*(a) ÷ (b) as %*
Common wheat			
1973/74	14.34	18.06	79
1974/75	15.70	14.64	107
1978/79	20.23	10.50	193
1979/80	20.72	12.69	163
Barley			
1973/74	12.91	13.44	96
1974/75	14.29	13.40	107
1978/79	18.40	8.19	225
1979/80	18.86	11.71	161
Beef and veal			
1973/74	103.04	93.71	110
1974/75	115.47	71.07	162
1978/79	152.29	76.47	199
1979/80	154.58	75.63	204
Pigmeat			
1973	103.75	79.30	131
1974	115.62	106.47	109
1978	129.56	83.47	155
1979	139.07	91.36	152
Butter			
1973/74	232.52	72.63	320
1974/75	236.58	74.76	316
1978/79	309.17	76.71	403
1979/80	309.90	75.39	411
Skimmed milk			
1973/74	93.80	60.11	156
1974/75	113.98	81.85	139
1978/79	135.23	29.52	458
1979/80	135.54	35.77	379

Source: EEC (1980), *The Agricultural Situation in the Community: 1980 Report*, Brussels.

leads to prices substantially above world prices. This general conclusion is consistent with other work on the CAP (for example Bacon *et al.* (1978); and Morris (1980)). Whether or not CAP prices can be called reasonable in terms of objective (*e*) is inevitably a subjective question. If a price above the lowest price at which supplies are available is defined as unreasonable, clearly the CAP does not lead to reasonable prices.

Self-sufficiency

Turning to the objective of greater self-sufficiency the objective has been achieved over a range of commodities as shown in Table 9.4. The policy of limiting imports and increasing Community prices does not guarantee that demand equals supply in the Community market, because the price is not free to fluctuate and clear the market. The

TABLE 9.4
Degrees of Self-Sufficiency

	EC	*BE-LU*	*DE*	*FR*	*GE*	*IR*	*IT*	*NE*	*UK*
Wheat									
1968/69	94	59	103	154	86	68	95	54	45
1974/75	106	60	131	192	95	50	89	48	61
1977/78	105	72	139	185	98	59	78	62	65
Barley									
1968/69	103	64	103	158	80	97	22	89	99
1974/75	104	60	104	169	86	98	33	72	100
1977/78	106	71	113	163	84	118	35	57	107
Sugar									
1968/69	82	148	124	117	89	94	93	101	34
1974/75	95	181	151	158	103	109	66	128	29
1977/78	117	208	190	183	123	121	91	153	37
Beef and veal									
1968	90	89	252	109	87	590	63	109	61
1975	95	95	313	119	95	580	59	130	77
1979	97	93	315	106	98	578	61	129	74
Pigmeat									
1968	100	130	495	85	95	162	88	171	58
1975	99	174	389	86	87	130	72	208	65
1978	100	169	357	84	88	144	76	224	63
Butter									
1968	91	110	332	119	104	198	67	298	10
1975	100	280	317	111	126	222	57	443	15
1978	111	110	273	112	133	283	70	481	38
Skimmed milk									
1968	140	187	128	183	146	426	—	48	91
1975	135	132	184	148	195	764	1	94	151
1978	110	127	130	111	179	703	13	53	153

Sources: EEC, *The Agricultural Situation in the Community*, Brussels, various issues.

result has been that at times supply has exceeded demand in some sectors, and the surplus production has been taken into intervention. The continuing surplus in the milk sector is the most notorious example. If one examines Tables 9.3 and 9.5 together, it is not surprising that the sectors with the highest prices relative to world prices have the largest surpluses relative to production. Part of the tendency for stocks to accumulate may be explained by the intervention system (as well as the price of course). Public storage is likely to lead to higher stocks and costs than private storage, because the intervention agency does not have the same incentive to reduce stocks as farmers do when farmers retain ownership of the stocks (private storage could even be subsidized if necessary).

TABLE 9.5
Percentage of EEC Production in Stocks

	1973/74	*1974/75*	*1975/76*	*1976/77*	*1977/78*	*1978/79*	*1979/80*
Durum wheat	–	0.2	9.4	6.5	0.8	4.0	3.5
Common wheat	3.2	5.8	4.4	2.4	1.4	2.3	4.9
Barley	1.7	1.7	0.8	0.2	0.3	0.1	0.5
Rye	5.5	8.9	7.0	6.7	9.5	12.0	12.0
Tobacco	2.1	2.3	3.8	10.5	6.9	6.8*	8.0*
Butter	5.6	2.8	6.9	8.2	8.7	14.7	14.4
Skimmed milk	6.8	23.8	59.4	43.0	38.0	22.8	7.4
Meat (beef)	0.5	4.4	4.7	4.7	6.7	4.0	4.5

Sources: EEC (1980 and 1981), *The Agricultural Situation in the Community: 1979 Report* (and the *1980 Report*), Brussels.
* Provisional.

Productivity

Agricultural production in the Community has not grown as fast as industrial production since 1973 (Table 9.6). This has been reflected in a falling percentage of GNP accounted for by agriculture. The agricultural labour force declined over this period, and labour productivity increased in consequence. Average yields have also risen, and the average size of farm has increased, while utilized agricultural land has fallen. The CAP includes measures which tend to reduce the quantity of labour employed in agriculture, such as modernization aid and help for giving up farming, whereas price support maintains labour in agriculture. It is not possible to say for certain what the net effect of the CAP has been. However, given that market support accounts for over 90 per cent of agricultural spending, the increase in productivity which has taken place could have been greater if fewer marginal farms had been supported in production.

TABLE 9.6
Average Annual Growth Rates Between 1973 and 1978

	GNP volume (all sectors)	*Agricultural final production 1975 prices*	*Agricultural yields per hectare**	*Labour productivity* in agriculture*	*Employment in agriculture, forestry and fisheries*	*Utilized agricultural land*
BE	2.2	−0.3	0.7	3.4	−3.6	−1.1
DE	1.7	2.7	3.1	4.0	−1.2	−0.4
FR	3.0	0.0	0.2	3.7	−3.6	−0.2
GE	1.9	1.5	2.3	5.6	−3.9	−0.8
IR	3.7	3.3	3.3	6.1	−2.6	−0.1
IT	2.1	1.8	1.8	4.4	−2.4	0.1
LU	0.7	−0.6	−0.3	3.5	−3.9	−0.3
NE	2.7	3.7	4.3	5.5	−1.7	−0.1
UK	1.2	−2.1	−1.8†	0.4†	−2.0	−0.4
EC	2.2	−0.7	−0.4	2.3	−2.9	−0.6

Sources: EEC, *The Agricultural Situation in the Community*, Brussels, various issues.
* Based on final production.
† 1976/73.

Market Stability

The CAP has been successful in achieving market stability. 'Between 1968 and 1974 . . . the monthly variation in market prices during the year was much less than on the world market or even of the United States market. While the monthly prices for common wheat varied by only 3% in the EEC, this figure was 11% on the world market and 13% in the United States.' (EEC (1975c), p. 17). Assuming this conclusion still holds, the benefit of this greater stability must be set against the higher consumer prices and surpluses which have developed as a result of the policies which promote stability. Also, Community stability may have been achieved at the cost of destabilizing world markets.

Incomes

The data in Table 9.1 suggest that farm incomes are below average. However, the data are not accurate enough to allow one to say whether farm incomes are now nearer average incomes than ten years ago. The figures shown in Table 9.7 suggest that the disparity between farm wages and average incomes has not reduced significantly. Given that income support is the objective of price support which *has* raised prices, why has there not been an improvement in agriculture's relative position? One explanation is that higher prices lead to an increase in the price of the fixed factor of production – land –

TABLE 9.7
Changes in Earnings and Value of Agricultural Land

	Average annual change in per capita remuneration of wage and salary earners		*Average annual change in farm wages*		*Value of land*
	1978/68	*1978/73*	*1978/68*	*1978/73*	*1978/73*
BE	12.3	13.4	12.7	14.7	12.9
DE	11.8	12.2	—	13.2	21.2
FR	13.1	15.1	15.9	17.3	12.6
GE	9.9	7.9	9.4	9.1	11.7*
IR	18.1	20.3	16.3	17.5	—
IT	17.6	20.0	22.1	27.8	—
LU	11.2	12.5	—	—	—
NE	12.2	11.0	—	12.3	30.2
UK	14.5	17.8	14.6	17.7	11.4†

Sources: EEC (1980 and 1981), *The Agricultural Situation in the Community: 1979 Report*, (and the *1980 Report*), Brussels.
* 1978/74 (calculated by the author).
† Average of figures for England, Wales and Scotland.

and an increase in purchases of inputs from other sectors (Josling (1973), pp. 268–9). The value of land has certainly risen (see Table 9.7).

Financial Aspects

The financial cost of the CAP is not an indication of the true cost of the CAP mainly because it excludes the cost to consumers in the form of higher prices. However, the financial cost *is* significant, with over two-thirds of the overall budget of the Community spent on agriculture (Table 9.8). In consequence the distribution of Community spending across members has largely been determined by the distribution of agricultural spending. A major criticism of the CAP is

TABLE 9.8
Agriculture and the Budget

	*1976**	*1977**	*1978**	*1979†*	*1980†*
EEC budget	8252	8898	12152	14447	15683
FEOGA	6051	6757	9123	10747	11857
FEOGA guarantee section	5721	6586	8657	10384	11486
Guarantee expenditure in milk sector	2115	2504	4015	4460	4930
GEOGA guidance section	325	166	460	356	359

Source: EEC Dairy Facts and Figures 1980, Thames Ditton, Surrey, Milk Marketing Board.
* Expenditure.
† Appropriations.

the transfer of resources it causes between members of the Community: receipts are determined by the degree of surplus production in the member countries (see Godley, 1980).

A second criticism of the financial aspects of the CAP is that the funds allocated to market support (through the guarantee section) account for more than 90 per cent of the funds allocated to agriculture. This occurs because price levels are set on the basis of the existing market structure, and not on the basis of an efficient desired structure, so that Community funds are channelled to supporting the status quo – that is, to some extent the incentive to improve agricultural efficiency is removed by support. The solution to this problem is simply to cut guarantee expenditure. Some increase in expenditure in the guidance section (socio-structural expenditure) may be desirable, but part of the case for guidance expenditure is artificial and occurs because of excessive guarantee expenditure. For example, Directive 72/160/EEC encouraging the cessation of farming is 'needed' because of support which discourages the cessation of farming! Finally, the proportion of guarantee expenditure going to the milk sector is significant. This expenditure is mainly for export subsidies or intervention activities, and reflects the imbalance between demand and supply described earlier.

Reform

Whether the CAP should be reformed, and if so how, depends on the reasons for intervention in agriculture. In the preceding discussion it was shown that there is little economic justification for state intervention in agriculture, or for a common agricultural policy. However, it may be unrealistic to propose that the CAP should be abandoned. Let us assume that the objectives of the CAP are given in the short run, and consider ways in which the objectives might be achieved more efficiently.

Our evaluation of the CAP based on the stated objectives led to the conclusion that the major defects of the CAP are that food prices are maintained above world prices (which may be unreasonable for consumers), supply and demand do not always balance, and farm incomes continue to be below average. Prices are high under the CAP because they are used for income support. If the CAP were reformed to include a system of direct income subsidies high consumer prices would be unnecessary and the desired level of income in agriculture could be guaranteed – for example by a negative income tax for farmers. Also, if prices were not used for income support they could be allowed to fluctuate to equate demand and supply. The incentive to farmers to increase productivity would continue because the farms with the lowest costs would enjoy the highest profits. Finally, if market stability is important this system does not preclude intervention to stabilize prices around the trend.

A reform of the CAP to shift the burden of income support from prices to direct income subsidies has been suggested before (e.g. Riemsdijk (1973); Koester and Tangermann (1977)). The *true* cost of achieving a given level of income support through direct subsidies financed from general taxation is less than the cost of supporting incomes through prices. Why then has the reform not been implemented? The reasons are probably that it would involve a large increase in government/Community expenditure, and if the cost of agricultural support were visible, support on the present scale would not be politically acceptable.

This may explain the present financing of farm support, but it does not justify it. If agricultural incomes are to be increased at the expense of incomes in other sectors, then it is desirable that the system chosen involves the least cost, and that the cost is clear. These considerations lead to the conclusion that if the objective is to support incomes, then the appropriate policy is to intervene directly to increase incomes.

In the long run the desirability of the objective of income support is questionable. As the Commission (EEC, 1975c) has stated: 'Income subsidy implies that optimum use is not being made of the labour factor in the farms considered. It can therefore only be justified economically as a provisional solution pending the modernization of farms or the retraining of farmers for other types of economic activity' (p. 26). If agriculture is to adjust so that incomes do not need support, short-run policies should at least be consistent with this long-run objective. Income subsidies tend to maintain the quantity of labour in the sector, therefore subsidies must be of limited duration. For example, income subsidies could be reduced in stages over a period, say, of ten years. The exact details of the period of transition from price support to direct income support, and the duration of direct income support are less important. The agreement of the Community members that such a move is desirable in principle must first be obtained.

Conclusions

The main conclusion which can be drawn from our assessment of the CAP is that there is little, if any, justification for supporting agriculture at the expense of other sectors. Even if intervention in agriculture is desirable, the case for a common Community policy is weak. Finally if intervention is to continue at Community level the CAP is not the best policy. The objectives could be achieved more efficiently through direct income support. A similar critical appraisal can be applied to European technology policy.

CHAPTER 10

Defence and Advanced Technology

The Policy Issues

Advanced technology industries are of continuing concern to European governments. Examples include aerospace, computers, microelectronics and medical equipment (for example, scanners). Such industries are believed to be the determinants of the EEC's future international competitiveness. Inevitably, questions arise as to whether the EEC needs a policy towards advanced technology and the appropriate form of any policy. Advocates of a common technology policy (CTP) point to the amount of effort which the EEC has devoted to technically backward and declining sectors such as agriculture, coal and steel. Moreover, in the absence of an EEC policy, member and non-member nations have established a number of international collaborative ventures, especially in the aerospace sector. Policy makers need to know whether such joint projects have been successful. In this context, aerospace is an illuminating case study since it combines advanced technology, defence and international collaboration. Indeed, it will be shown that defence industries embrace some of the high technology sectors, whilst others have benefited from technical spin-offs resulting from weapons programmes. At the outset, the economic logic of state intervention in technology is assessed. Consideration is then given to the implication for EEC policy resulting from the relationship between technology and defence. Aerospace is analysed as an example of the EEC's efforts to formulate both an advanced technology and an industrial policy.

Technology and Policy

Prosperity and military power are believed to be associated with technology. Since 1945, European governments have become worried by the increasing technological domination of the USA in their domestic and world markets. Between 1957 and 1966, US R and D expenditure was over three times greater than in the whole of industrial Western Europe; but this was an over-estimate of the 'technology gap'. Adjusting the figures by an R and D exchange rate suggested that in 1963–64, Western Europe would have to double its R and D expenditure to reach US levels (i.e. divide US expenditures by 1.75: OECD (1970), p. 116). Much of the difference was attributable to American expenditure on defence, space and nuclear R and D, particularly in the aerospace, electrical and electronic industries. However, such international comparisons conceal the extent of duplication and ignore the productivity of research inputs. Further evidence based on a study of 73 product groups showed that by 1971, the USA had a strong and increasing comparative advantage in research-intensive products, namely aircraft, chemicals, electrical machinery and power equipment, office machinery, pharmaceuticals, photographic supplies and scientific instruments (Balassa, 1977). Throughout the period 1953–71, aircraft manufacture continued to occupy first place in the US comparative advantage scale. In addition to worries about American technological domination, the EEC has to adjust to a new international division of labour. By the late 1970s, it was apparent that both labour-intensive and capital-intensive industries were developing in regions outside of the major industrial nations. In this changing world market, the European Commission believed that the future competitiveness of European industry will depend partly on the adaptability of its economies and on its ability to mobilize new technologies (EEC (1978b), p. 18). Its chosen technologies include aerospace, computers, electronics, nuclear power, telecommunications and new sources of energy. But why does the EEC need a policy towards advanced technology?

Does Economic Analysis Offer Any Policy Guidelines?

Technology markets involve the creation and exchange of information and knowledge, much of which is embodied initially in human beings (stocks and flows of human capital). Firms use patents to establish property rights in their marketable ideas. Exchange then occurs through the sale of products embodying the new technology or the marketing of licences or, indirectly, through take-overs, the poaching of valuable scientists or even industrial espionage (theft). However, socially desirable exchange might be impeded by imperfections and public goods – externalities. Indeed, it has been argued that competitive markets will under-invest in invention and research due to risks and uncertainty, the costs of establishing property rights in marketable ideas (cf. patents) and increasing returns in the use of information (Arrow, 1962). Such arguments are often used to justify state subsidies for R and D, particularly for activities which generate technological 'fall-out' so providing a general stimulus to innovation throughout the economy. But the analysis and associated proposals for subsidy policy have been criticized, much depending on the interpretation of market failure in a world of scarcity and transactions costs. For example, it has been shown that free enterprise economies are likely to result in a 'correct' (efficient) adjustment to risk and uncertainty once it is recognized that such adjustments are not costless (Demsetz, 1969). And even if the market failure analysis is accepted, it is far from clear that this provides the rationale for current EEC policy towards advanced technology. A market-improving policy would be restricted to the removal of significant externalities and imperfections in product and factor markets. Using such criteria, it is illuminating to consider some of the arguments for an EEC technology policy. These embrace the technology gap, and a concern with the employment consequences of the changing international division of labour.

Politicians, Bureaucrats and the Technology Gap

The argument about the technology gap between the EEC and the USA tends to be emotional special pleading, lacking both analysis and supporting microeconomic evidence. Theory suggests that nations will have different comparative advantages in capital, labour and technology. Innovation might improve a country's relative advantage, at least in the short run, until rivals copy or introduce a superior idea (Johnson, 1975). In the circumstances, any technology gap indicates that opportunities are available for mutually-advantageous international trade and exchange. After all, the EEC seems unconcerned about the West Indies' technological domination in banana production! However, market failure might arise if the opportunities for worthwhile international trade are not being exploited due to, say, tariffs and government procurement policies which favour domestic suppliers. This suggests a case for reduced tariff barriers and for creating a common market in the procurement of government goods and services. Instead, it usually leads to a further argument for an EEC technology policy involving supply-side intervention based on the need to emulate the scale of US firms and their large home market.

Apparently, an EEC technology policy is required in those high technology industries which involve substantial set-up or entry costs and a large market to spread fixed R and D outlays and to obtain production economies (cf. infant industry protection). Without an EEC policy, the belief is that European nations will continue to 'suffer' from 'too many' competing national projects leading to 'duplication' of costly R and D with firms restricted to a series of 'fragmented' domestic markets (Layton (1969); Foch (1970)). An obvious solution seems to be supply-side intervention to create European, rather than national, high technology industries. Such arguments cannot be accepted uncritically. Questions arise about the operation of capital markets, state involvement on the supply-side and the optimality of EEC solutions. Properly-functioning capital markets will provide finance for the substantial 'set-up' costs required in high technology, so long as projects are expected to be profitable. The fact that private capital markets 'fail' to supply funds for technically attractive ventures such as space exploration and supersonic airliners might be an indication that markets are working properly and making clear commercial judgements based on expected profitability. Moreover, mergers or other forms of co-operation between private companies would enable European firms to achieve the minimum scale required for high technology R and D without state intervention. Here, there might be a role for the EEC in harmonizing company law and reducing any major barriers to the creation of a European capital market. More often, of course, high technology projects involve national governments and the standard arguments about nationalism (for example, security; independence, especially from the USA). Increasingly, though, nations are finding that independent technology is costly, which leads to the inevitable search for lower cost solutions without resorting to the extreme of trading on the basis of comparative advantage. Some form of international collaboration allows the sharing of costly R and D and its associated risks. However, it does not follow that the optimal solution will be confined to EEC members. Mutually-advantageous agreements might involve all European nations and others (for example, USA and Japan), or even a sub-set of the EEC. Examples of European, as distinct from EEC, solutions include the European Space Agency and the Independent European Programme Group which consists of the European members of NATO together with France. Within the EEC, the worry is that European collaborative solutions determined by governments will lead to a technological version of the CAP, with protection of domestic industries. Such solutions are likely to favour producers rather than consumers and taxpayers, with work allocated by bargaining between Ministers and officials, further influenced by lobbying from interest groups of scientists and technologists. Companies involved in state-supported collaborative ventures will have every incentive to seek further income from EEC agencies rather than by developing their competitive ability (Pavitt, 1976). This suggests an alternative explanation of the extent and form of EEC technology policy involving the economics of the political market place.

High technology is attractive to interest groups of scientists and engineers with an obvious monetary and intellectual interest in expanding the frontiers of knowledge at the taxpayer's expense. Such groups, which are likely to benefit from a ministry's increased spending, will have every incentive to support the bureaucracy with a major budgetary involvement in advanced technology. In aiming to raise their budgets, departments will exaggerate the demand for their preferred policy and under-estimate its costs. Bureaux with an interest in technology (e.g. defence, education, science) can stress its substantial social benefits. References will be made to the need to keep a nation in the forefront of technology, to copy its major rivals so as to avoid 'undue' dependence on foreign technology, to the valuable (but difficult to quantify) spin-off and fall-out for the rest of the economy, and to a new technological revolution which will provide the next generation of highly-paid jobs. Vote-sensitive politicians might be attracted by such alleged benefits, particularly if state support for new technology shows that a government is involved in 'solving' a nation's economic problems. Understandably, bureaucracies and interest groups will be enthusiastic about social benefits, but relatively silent on the reliability of a project's cost estimates. High technology and defence work provide many examples of cost estimates which were substantially less than actual expenditures (Hartley and Cubitt, 1977). Once started, state-supported research projects are difficult to stop. Agents and interest groups in the political market place have an interest in continuation and the costs are borne by the taxpayer. Certainly this is a plausible explanation of behaviour at the national and EEC levels. In the latter, the constitutional and electoral arrangements are likely to allow substantial (greater?) opportunities for discretionary behaviour by bureaucrats and Ministers. The bargaining environment will encourage officials and Ministers to seek the support of interest groups of experts. Profitable opportunities can then be appropriated by successful lobbying, as reflected in the allocation of monopoly rights, lucrative (non-competitive) contracts, tariff protection and subsidies.

Employment and the Changing International Division of Labour

The changing international division of labour is also used as an argument for an EEC technology policy. Claims are made that

Europe will be increasingly unable to compete with low wage countries in established manufactured products. Examples are given of the rising European imports of cars, motor cycles, radios and TVs, with adverse employment consequences for domestic suppliers. It is then concluded that the future competitiveness of Europe depends upon greater specialization in high technology products. However, the argument is subject to two major reservations concerning methodology and evidence. First, it confuses the technical issues concerned with the causes of any market failure and the policy issues involving the selection of the appropriate solution. For example, changing comparative advantage suggests that there might be opportunities for public policies to correct any significant failures in the EEC's market *adjustment* mechanisms (e.g. finance for human investments). If so, some additional criteria are required for the choice of an EEC technology policy as the appropriate solution. Nor can uncertainty be ignored since today's advanced technology might be tomorrow's industrial archaeology. In which case, the major policy issue concerns the choice of the most appropriate economic framework and incentive system for coping with, and adjusting to, change under uncertainty. In this context, it is not at all obvious that governments and bureaucrats guided by interest groups have a comparative advantage in predicting accurately the future. Second, the case for an EEC technology policy cannot ignore the empirical validity of the employment argument. Evidence is required on the employment effects of the changing international division of labour.

Usually, emphasis is placed on the job losses of rising EEC imports from developing nations to the neglect of any favourable employment effects of higher EEC exports to these countries. Estimates show that for the EEC, the average number of jobs for $1m. of output is a gain of 18.5 for exports to, and a loss of 28.4 for imports from, the developing nations (1976 prices, see Balassa (1979)). Much depends on the assumptions about the increase in manufactured trade between developed and developing regions. Estimates based on the projected expansion of world trade for 1976–86 show no net employment effects for the OECD nations as well as a continuing shift of labour from low to high-skill occupations. For the OECD nations, job losses are likely amongst unskilled and semi-skilled production workers and in clothing, electrical machinery and equipment, furniture, leather, rubber and plastic products, and textiles. Employment gains in the developed countries are expected in chemicals, instruments, printing, publishing and especially in non-electrical machinery and transportation equipment (Balassa, 1979). In other words, the evidence on the employment effects of the changing international division of labour does not provide convincing support for an EEC technology policy. On the contrary, it reinforces the argument for policies to correct any failures in market adjustment, including the operation of human capital markets (for example, training and skill acquisition, see Hartley, 1977a). There are, however, further arguments for some form of EEC technology policy, resulting from the relationship between national governments and domestic weapons industries.

Technology, Defence and the EEC

European nations prefer to maintain some form of domestic defence industry, its size depending upon the government's objective function and the relative efficiency of its weapons contractors. Such industries are believed to contribute to security of supply, weapons designed for national requirements and a degree of independence in technology and foreign policy. The nature of military demand with its emphasis on the technical superiority of weapons (the arms race) means that defence industries embrace some of the high technology sectors, particularly aerospace, electronics, engineering, machine tools and nuclear power. Clearly, the EEC's involvement in advanced technology cannot ignore defence markets. Nations are willing to incur higher weapons' costs to obtain the alleged benefits of domestic defence industries. For example, involvement in the F16 co-production programme will cost the European nations 18 per cent more than if they had purchased the aircraft directly off-the-shelf from the USA. Similarly, a 10 per cent cost premium was estimated for 25 per cent European industrial collaboration in the NATO AWACs programme.

Inefficiency in European Defence Industries

Critics claim that European armaments industries are highly inefficient due to 'unnecessary' duplication of costly R and D and short production runs for small domestic markets. The result is a 'waste' of R and D resources, a 'fragmented' industrial base, relatively high weapons' costs due to small volumes which, in turn, reduce the quantities which can be acquired from a given defence budget (Tucker, 1976). An EEC solution has been advocated through the creation of a European Armaments Procurement Agency which would aim to establish a common market in military equipment, associated with the formation of a 'jointly organized, re-structured and co-ordinated' European armaments industry as part of the Community's common industrial policy (Klepsch-Normanton, 1978). The elimination of waste and duplication inherent in Europe's overlapping national R and D armaments industries and the achievement of scale economies in production are expected to result in a more efficient allocation of resources. Such gains do, of course, assume standardization of European military equipment. Studies have estimated that within NATO as a whole, the wastes due to excessive product differentiation in weapons procurement might be some $6–11 billion per annum (1975 prices, see Callaghan (1975)). Alternative estimates suggest that if NATO weapons' standardization leads to scale economies, learning and the gains from free trade in defence equipment, it could result in unit cost savings in the region of 20–30 per cent (Hartley, 1981c). Such estimated savings have also reinforced both NATO and US support for the creation of a common European defence production effort as part of a broader policy objective of standardizing weapons in the Atlantic Alliance and promoting a two-way transatlantic trade in military equipment. And yet, European governments continue to maintain national weapons industries with their inevitable cost penalties. Rather than conclude that nations are irrational, short-sighted and ill-informed, it is more useful to analyse why they appear willing to sacrifice the apparently massive gains from standardization and a NATO free trade area in weapons.

Applying the self-interest postulate to both economic and political behaviour suggests that national weapons' industries are believed to be worthwhile in terms of their alleged benefits. Such benefits might embrace broader policy objectives than a narrow concern with defence equipment (for example, votes, technology, jobs). Distributional factors might also be dominant. Individual nations might believe that the potential gainers from a NATO free trade area in weapons might not compensate the potential losers, particularly in the absence of a legally-enforceable international agreement about the distribution of gains and losses. The fear is that US industry will be the gainers and that the Europeans will incur substantial adjustment costs, especially in their labour markets. The numbers are not trivial with direct employment in the British, French and West German defence industries exceeding 650,000 in 1980. There are also fears of a US monopoly of weapons with higher prices for equipment and spares. Moreover, nations might have different weapons demands reflecting diversity in their views about the optimal defence requirements for *their* country: they might be willing to pay a premium for such equipment. These and other arguments for supporting national weapons industries have been most clearly specified for the European aerospace sector. This is a classic example of an industry which involves governments, defence and advanced technology.

EEC Aerospace Policy

The Treaty establishing the EEC made no specific reference to aerospace nor to industrial policy. However, aerospace is one of the few industries where the Commission has made specific policy proposals (Nobbs, 1979). Whilst these have been restricted to civil aircraft, it is recognized that the industry's dependence on defence business means that military markets cannot be ignored. Given the original Treaty and its exclusion of military affairs, it would be a fascinating exercise to explain why the Commission became involved in industrial policy and its choice of aerospace.

The development of a common aerospace policy is based on the industry's 'importance' to the Community. It is a major source of employment, especially of highly-skilled labour requiring 'sophisticated technologies' which are believed to be so vital for the future economic development of the Community. In 1978 EEC employment in aerospace exceeded 400,000 with the UK and France accounting for 75 per cent of the total. Aerospace R and D is also viewed as a major source of scientific invention and technological innovation across a wide range of products. Indeed, the Commission regards aerospace as one of the 'commanding height technologies' (Nobbs, 1979). Finally, Europe's capacity to contribute to its own defence 'must depend in a large measure upon the strength of its aircraft industry' (EEC (1975a), p. 7). Persuasive though such arguments appear, they by no means constitute an overwhelming case for an EEC policy. Opportunity costs and evidence cannot be ignored. Would some of the resources currently employed in aerospace make a greater contribution towards technology, jobs and, ultimately, human satisfaction, if they were used elsewhere in the EEC? For example, since all economic activity creates employment, evidence is required to show that aerospace results in *more* jobs, or *more* technology, than the next-best alternative (Hartley, 1974). What would be the size of the industry without state support: would such a market solution be large enough for policy makers? Nor is it sufficient to argue that competitive markets will under-invest in R and D. Even if such arguments are accepted, they do not necessarily constitute a case for EEC support of the aerospace industry. Some additional criteria are required for the choice of aerospace rather than other sectors in the EEC (including basic research). Furthermore, since politicians and bureaucrats have no special competence and expertise for involvement in the aerospace industry and for the 'correct' choice of projects, there is considerable potential for *government failure* (cf. market failure).

EEC policy starts from the proposition that the aerospace industries of member countries are 'too small and too fragmented' to be able to compete with the USA. An indication of the differences between America and Europe in the scale of civil aircraft output is shown in Table 10.1. Typically, US production runs are three times greater than for European projects. EEC policy aims to intervene on both the demand and supply sides of the market (see Chapter 11). Proposals have been made for establishing common markets for civil and military aerospace products and for expanding collaboration between European firms so as to promote 'rationalization' and avoid the 'wastes of duplication'. Collaboration through joint projects involving EEC members is the preferred solution. But what are the likely costs of joint projects? Aerospace experience with international collaboration is worthy of detailed examination both in its own right and as a possible model for other European advanced technology sectors.

TABLE 10.1
European and US Civil Aircraft Output

European Company	*No. ordered*	*US Company*	*No. ordered*
Aerospatiale Caravelle	280	Boeing:	
		707	962
Airbus:		727	1,811
A300	227	737	851
A3100	79	747	559
British Aerospace:			
1-11	230		
Trident	117	Lockheed Tri-Star	238
HS 748	351		
Viscount	440	McDonnell Douglas:	
Fokker:		DC 8	556
F27	517	DC 9	1,069
F28	169	DC 10	361

Source: World airliner census, *Flight International*, London, 27 December 1980.
Note: Figures are based on orders at December 1980. In some cases (for example, Caravelle, Trident, Viscount) production has been completed.

The Economics of Joint European Aircraft Projects

Europe has substantial experience of government-supported collaboration in advanced technology aerospace work, particularly in the military sphere. Aircraft examples include the Anglo-French Jaguar, Concorde airliner and helicopter 'package'; the French-

German Alpha Jet trainer; the UK-German-Italian Tornado; the UK-Italian helicopter agreement and the French-German-UK-Dutch-Spanish participation in the civil Airbus. Other joint European projects have embraced missiles and space in such forms as the UK-French Martel, the French-German Roland, together with the French-German-UK Euromissile Dynamics Group and the European Space Agency.

It has been claimed that a nation's involvement in joint European aerospace projects results in cost savings. Compared with an independent venture, a joint project was reputed to result in two sets of savings. First, the sharing of R and D costs. Second, scale economies from the longer production runs associated with the pooling of orders. Little published evidence exists on the magnitude of cost savings from joint projects. This section provides some tentative estimates, using published data and simplifying, but plausible, assumptions. Two questions are considered. First, under what circumstances (assumptions), do cost savings result? Second, how large are such savings?

Methodology

The economic analysis of joint European aerospace projects raises a fundamental methodological issue, namely, the counter-factual. In the absence of a joint venture, what would have been the policy choices of each of the participants? Consider the three nation Tornado aircraft, with a planned output exceeding 800 units. This is a multi-role combat aircraft (MRCA) involving two international organizations, namely NAMMA and Panavia. NAMMA is the NATO MRCA Management Agency which represents the partner governments or customers with their requirements for 385 aircraft for the UK (220 of the strike version and 165 of the air defence variant or ADV), 324 for West Germany and 100 for Italy. Panavia is the main contractor for the development and manufacture of the aircraft and its partner companies are British Aerospace in the UK, Messerschmitt-Bölkow-Blohm or MBB in Germany and Aeritalia in Italy (participation of 42.5, 42.5 and 15 per cent, respectively). Engines are produced on a similar basis by Turbo-Union whose partner companies are Rolls Royce, MTU and Fiat. Without this joint project, would the UK have built an identical aircraft, using the same contractors and procurement policy and purchasing the same quantity; and would the project have been affected by domestic economic conditions? One British view is that a UK only project would have been cancelled (cf. TSR-2). Indeed, a reduced probability of cancellation is often presented as one of the major 'benefits' (to whom?) of collaboration! For simplicity, it can be assumed that an independent national venture would have been identical to the joint project, receiving the same domestic order (for example, 385 units for the RAF). Even so, this is a restricted analysis of cost 'savings'. It excludes comparisons with the savings which could be achieved by purchasing from the least cost suppliers within world markets (cf. trade diversion and trade creation). Nor is it claimed that cost savings are the only element in collaborative European projects. Other elements cannot be ignored, namely, the concern of European governments with the acquisition of advanced technology and a collective desire for military and political independence from the USA. To the UK, some joint projects have been regarded as part of the entry costs to the EEC. Such objectives mean that collaborative European projects involve wider policy aims than the acquisition of aircraft and produce group benefits which might not be available to any nation acting independently (at reasonable cost). In other words, the nature of the benefits might differ between collaborative and independent ventures. A further methodological difficulty arises from the limited population of European aerospace projects. The small numbers have also involved different projects, various partners and alternative forms of organization, all of which reduce the opportunities for reliable generalizations. Moreover, if a learning process operates, experience on some of the earlier ventures is likely to give a misleading impression of the costs of collaboration. Solving international differences in language, measurement, managerial practices and national pride can be viewed as investments which will be reflected in savings on *future* projects (Heath, 1979).

Alternative Views on Joint Aerospace Projects

Ceteris paribus, joint ventures are believed to result in cost savings for each member of the club. But other things are rarely equal. On joint military aircraft, each nation might require modifications, so raising research and development (R and D) expenditure and possibly reducing the economies from a long run of one type. Nations will demand their 'fair' share of each sector of advanced technology and production work. As a result, development and production on collaborative projects will tend to be allocated on equity, rather than efficiency, criteria. Not surprisingly, there are mixed views on collaborative ventures. These views will be presented as generalizations, although in some instances, the arguments can best be illustrated with specific examples. Where necessary, references will be made to the three nation Tornado-combat aircraft and comparisons will be made between the joint venture and an identical UK only programme (Angus, 1979).

Interviews with European and US aerospace firms suggested three schools of thought on the value of joint European projects. Each is distinguished by its beliefs about the effects of collaboration on total R and D and unit production costs compared with a national venture. School I, the enthusiastic supporters of joint projects argue that they result in substantial gains to a country (Heath, 1979). School II claims that there are some relative inefficiencies, but none the less, net gains to participation. School III is extremely critical and claims that there are major inefficiencies and net losses from participation. The economist has the task of identifying and critically analysing the different views and, where possible, assessing their predictive accuracy. In the absence of empirical verification, the analyst can contribute by clarifying some of the issues in the controversy (Walker (1974); Greenwood (1975); Saul (1975)).

The Supporters of European Collaboration

The supporters of collaboration (School I) maintain that compared with a national project there is little, if any, increase in *total* R and D outlays and that unit production costs are lower. This school argues that *total* R and D costs on a joint project are about the same as for a national venture and they ask the critics to identify the sources of extra R and D expenditure. Consider the following possibilities which critics claim are characteristic of collaborative programmes:

(*i*) *Duplicate organisations*. Usually, there appear to be duplicate organizations for procuring, managing and building a joint aircraft project. For example, critics refer to the creation of a separate procurement organization and a new company (NAMMA and Panavia, respectively) for the three nation Tornado. It is then alleged that the individual governments and the partner companies of Panavia also become involved in the same problems at the same time. But appearances are deceptive and the supporters of collaboration argue persuasively that many of the tasks performed by the international organizations represent *net* additions to output (that is, wages reflect marginal productivity which is positive). In other words, the international agencies on collaborative ventures are defended as undertaking tasks which would be required for a national project, as well as providing the necessary co-ordination between partner nations and partner industries. One view is that without NAMMA and Panavia, there would be greater co-ordination problems. Each organization reflects the previous experience on joint ventures (for example, Concorde, Jaguar). Also, the international organizations are managing a large-scale project which exceeds the recent experience of a European nation's aircraft industry and procurement authorities. If, say, the UK were undertaking the Tornado project at a scale of output exceeding 800 units, a correspondingly greater organizational input would be required. Moreover, since NAMMA is devoted to Tornado only, it claims to be exploiting the gains from specialization.

(*ii*) *Duplication of R and D work, including duplicate flight test centres and too many (costly) development aircraft.* On the Tornado project, it is claimed that there is little, if any, duplication of R and D tasks. For example, there is said to be no duplication of jigs, tools and testing. Apparently each firm specializes in solving an agreed and clearly-specified problem, thereby avoiding substantial overlap. The existence of three flight test centres is 'explained' by the scale of the Tornado development effort, with each centre specializing on particular aspects of flight testing and operating in different climates.

(*iii*) *Extra travelling costs, including the value of travelling time.* Supporters claim that these are trivial when related to the total R and D budget (possibly 3 per cent of development: Heath (1979)). Indeed, the advocates of European collaboration make the point that American firms incur travelling and transport costs between suppliers and procurement agencies in the geographically larger US market. European distances between the UK, West Germany and Italy are much less than in the USA.

In total, the supporters of collaboration maintain that if there are any extra R and D costs they are under 20 per cent; and even this is regarded as 'too high'. Some suggest that the collaboration premium could be 'very little' and has been falling with greater experience of joint programmes. Moreover, the point is made that there are possibilities of substitution between R and D and production, so that development expenditures might reduce subsequent production outlays. Some also argue that the total R and D cost of the Tornado could be *less* than a UK only venture. Such a result could arise if, as is claimed, Tornado resulted in better selection procedures; greater competition in technical ideas using the knowledge available in three nations rather than one; more competition for work (for example, UK firms are not automatically entitled to contracts) and less 'gold plating'. On balance, this school can be represented by the view that the R and D costs of joint projects are the same as for a national venture. Thus, on the Tornado where the UK's share of total R and D is 42.5 per cent, Britain apparently 'benefits' by financing under 50 per cent of the bill.

It is also claimed that unit production costs are lower, mainly due to the economies of scale and learning associated with longer production runs. On the Tornado, each nation specializes in manufacturing parts for *all* 809 operational aircraft, so obtaining the available learning economies. West Germany manufactures all centre fuselages, the UK produces the front and rear fuselages and Italy is responsible for the wings. A large planned order, already announced, allows firms to tool-up for a greater scale of output and adopt capital intensive methods, which further reduces unit costs. A large order also means more competition from components firms, so resulting in lower prices. In other words, the Tornado allows European aircraft firms to approach the US scale of output. Assuming a *given* 90 per cent unit production cost curve, the Tornado project could result in unit cost savings (manufacturing) of about 10 per cent for the UK, 15 per cent for West Germany and almost 30 per cent for Italy.[1] However, this is a 'best case' estimate and usually there are policy constraints on the extent to which all potential economies are realized. Nations prefer to maintain a 'total capability' rather than specialize according to comparative advantage. In the production of Tornado, this has resulted in multiplication of final assembly, with each nation assembling and testing its own aircraft. Critics claim that this raises unit production costs and is a source of inefficiency.

An analytical framework is required to clarify some of the cost concepts used in the comparative assessment of joint and national ventures. A crucial issue is whether joint projects are relatively inefficient, resulting in costs additional to those which would have been incurred by one nation only after standardizing for output. Joint projects *cannot* be condemned because they incur costs: there are no costless projects (nor policies). The *appearance* of 'duplicate' organizations and travelling 'burdens' (which are readily observable) cannot *per se* be presented as conclusive evidence of relative inefficiency in joint ventures. A collaborative project would be relatively inefficient if it used higher cost methods of development and production for a *given* output. Figure 10.1 presents a simple analytical framework for clarifying the issues. It compares the three nation Tornado with a UK-only programme.

In Figure 10.1 the least-cost method of producing any output is shown by the total cost curve, TC_1 and the corresponding long-run

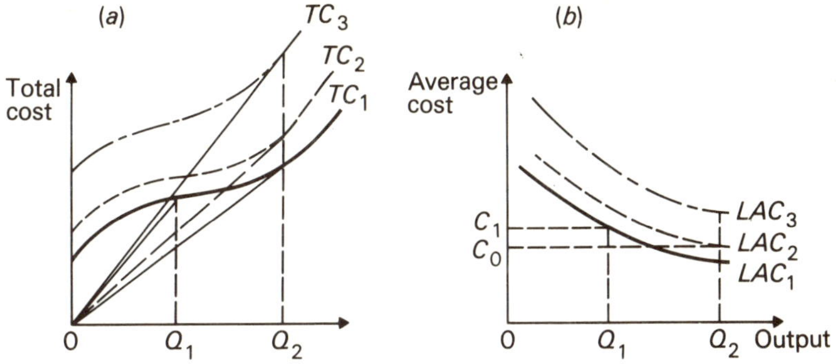

Figure 10.1

Note: TC_1, TC_2, TC_3 show three different total cost curves, with LAC_1, LAC_2, LAC_3 being the corresponding long-run average cost curves. For simplicity, costs embrace R and D and production. Output Q_1 reflects a UK-only buy whilst Q_2 is the output of the joint project. Alternatively, it could be assumed that the US industry is the least-cost supplier, with higher cost curves for the UK and joint ventures.

average cost curve, LAC_1. Assume initially that the UK industry is technically efficient. Output level Q_1 reflects a UK only buy of 385 aircraft whilst Q_2 illustrates the Tornado production of 809 units. If the Tornado organization operates on TC_1, it is *not* inefficient, even though total costs are higher at Q_2 than Q_1 (average costs are lower at Q_2). Inefficient projects are those operating on cost curves which are above TC_1 and LAC_1. Cost curves TC_2 and LAC_2 would reflect some X-efficiency in a joint project, although its unit costs at Q_2 would be lower than for a UK firm operating at Q_1 on LAC_1 (i.e. C_0Q_2 compared with C_1Q_1). Costs TC_2 represent the views of School II, whilst a curve approximating TC_1 reflects School I. The total opponents of joint projects (School III) claim that TC_3 is a more accurate representation of the cost levels on collaborative ventures, with unit costs greater than shown by LAC_1 at Q_1. Of course, predictions about relative costs depend on the empirical validity of the assumption that the UK industry is technically efficient (TC_1).[2] This is an unrealistic assumption in view of the British government's traditional preference for UK military aircraft suppliers, non-competitive bidding and cost-based defence contracts (Hartley (1974); Hartley and Corcoran (1975)). In other words, there is a danger that nirvana or ideal (but never achieved) UK cost levels will be compared with actual costs for joint projects, ignoring completely the realized costs on British ventures. Ultimately, the relative positions and slopes of the different cost curves shown in Figure 10.1 is an empirical matter.

The Middle View on European Collaboration

Not everyone accepts that joint projects provide participants with the major cost savings suggested by the ideal case. There is a view, probably a majority, which believes that R and D costs are substantially greater than on a national venture (School II). Typically, joint projects are reputed to increase R and D expenditures by 30–40 per cent, with some estimates in the range 50–70 per cent. One 'rule' states that on international work, total R and D costs are likely to be multiplied by the square root of the number of nations involved, with total development time scales approximated by the cube root of the number of participants. However, such 'rules' are no more than tentative hypotheses, lacking an underlying analytical framework and empirical support. Generalizations are especially difficult in view of the small size and diversity of the population of collaborative ventures. And, if the supporters of joint projects are 'correct', a collaboration premium of 20 per cent or less appears to refute the 'square root rule'.[3]

For the 'middle view', most estimates of the collaboration premium in development are substantially less than 2.0. Given Britain's 42.5 per cent share of Tornado development work, it will 'save' on R and D expenditure so long as a joint project costs under twice a UK-only venture. For example, if the cost of a UK-only Tornado were 100, the square root 'rule' suggests that the Panavia Tornado should cost 170, with Britain's share at 72. Within this school, there is general agreement that the administrative and organizational costs of international work are major sources of extra costs. Inefficient partners, together with each nation's preference for an independent capability and a share of advanced technology further increase development costs. On production work, it was generally felt that joint projects resulted in higher unit costs for a *given output*. Estimates of *X*-inefficiency ranged from as little as an extra 1–2 per cent for aero-engines to typically 5 per cent for airframe manufacture. But, it was suggested that the inefficiency premium could be substantially higher. Examples were given where the unit production costs of a joint venture with an output of 400 units might be the same as the unit costs of producing 200 in one nation! This implies an inefficiency premium of some 10 per cent (assuming a 90 per cent unit cost curve). Inevitably, difficulties arise in obtaining reliable data in this area. Interviews can give misleading results, with the respondents providing answers based on different output assumptions. Generally, it was believed that production inefficiencies arose from duplication in final assembly, from higher administration costs, organization problems and transport costs involving suppliers in two or three partner nations. Nor can equal partners be treated like sub-contractors and subjected to the same penalties and sanctions which would be applied for 'poor performance' by suppliers. Not all these items are sources of *major* inefficiencies. For example, final assembly accounts for some 20 per cent (± 10 per cent) of total production outlays and duplicate assembly lines might raise unit production costs by as little as 2 per cent. In total, the 'middle view' argues that joint projects result in production inefficiencies such that the cost savings represented by the best case or least cost solution are unlikely to be fully realized. Instead, a joint project with twice the output of a national programme might result in savings in unit production costs of between 5 per cent and zero (i.e. 90 per cent unit cost curve and inefficiency premiums of 5 and 10 per cent, respectively). In the zero case, the 'savings' on joint projects are confined to R and D.

In the absence of evidence, some of these views about R and D and production costs can be evaluated by returning to basic principles. Consider the hypothesis that joint ventures result in higher R and D costs. Any project, such as Tornado, requires the solution to a set of technical problems which remain *given* whether the aircraft is an independent national or an international venture. Of course, there is the hypothesis that joint ventures will aim for greater advances in the state of the art. However, where there are a *given* set of technical problems, there will be alternative solutions. Will *ex ante* decision-making and problem-solving under uncertainty be 'superior' (lower cost) for a national compared with an international venture? There is a presumption that the formation of a new international organization for procurement, development and production will be a costlier method of solving given problems than using an established organization with clear management-organizational 'guidelines' and previous experience of working with each other. New international organizations for procurement and development will inevitably incur 'set-up' and learning costs. Some indirect support for this presumption can be obtained from UK evidence on the performance of newly-merged firms. Studies show that take-overs and mergers can involve substantial adjustment costs with adverse effects on efficiency and profitability (Meeks, 1977). Since these effects arise where private firms influenced by commercial criteria can select their partners, they are more likely to be present in international projects where governments determine the major contractors. In addition, joint ventures involve substantial search costs, which are frequently ignored. Governments have to find partner nations with similar operational requirements and time-scales. How many man-years are involved in the search, information, negotiation, bargaining and legal transactions required before two or more nations agree to combine? Two to three years is not unknown, and such search and transactions costs could further raise the expenditures on joint projects compared with 'doing-it-yourself'. Thus, the formation of a new international company and procurement organization to solve complex technical problems is likely to increase transactions costs or the costs of doing business. In other words, there is *prima facie* support for the view that total R and D costs on joint projects will exceed those for a national or UK-only aircraft. Significantly, for the UK, the procurement and development of joint aerospace projects has involved a variety of partner nations, companies and international arrangements. Such variety can reflect experimentation or the benefits of learning and experience from previous projects, or the influence of budget-maximizing bureaucracies. Whatever the explanation, one short-term result of this variety might be higher costs associated with new searching and new learning as different partner nations, procurement agencies and companies have to adjust and familiarize themselves with the basic techniques of 'doing business with strangers'. Costs are likely to be higher if some firms are selected by governments rather than by commercial criteria. Once again, though, care has to be taken to avoid comparing *actual* joint projects with some 'ideal' but never realized UK procurement and contractor organization. The relevant comparison must be between *actual* ventures (for example: Tornado and US F111; French-German Alpha Jet and UK Hawk). Even so, the general conclusion suggests higher R and D costs on joint projects. On Tornado, an extra 20–40 per cent has been suggested. Such estimates are not necessarily unfavourable to Tornado since they are below the square root 'rule'. Moreover, the costs of forming new project-specific collaborative companies and procurement organizations has led to the view that a European aerospace industry should be developed around *established* collaborative arrangements. On this view, Airbus Industrie, Euromissile and Panavia seem to be the obvious basis for a *European* military and civil aircraft and missile industry. Such a solution would, of course, satisfy the preferences of bureaucrats and producer groups associated with the existing organizations, but the outcome is likely to be technically and allocatively inefficient.

Some of the beliefs of the 'middle view' (School II) about the production costs of joint projects are equally disturbing. Such beliefs raise two possibilities. First, since they are based on interviews, they could be wrong, reflecting bias or ignorance. For example, how do we interpret the views of firms that have lost work as a result of joint projects or of those that have never experienced international collaboration? Second, these beliefs could be valid, in which case we need to know why scale and learning economies are not being realized. A critical evaluation and evidence is required, so that policy makers can be aware of the logical and empirical validity of these views. Consider the possibility that higher administration costs on joint projects reflect inefficiencies rather than the costs of managing a large output in an international organization (see Figure 10.1). Why does inefficiency exist? It could reflect inexperience (ignorance) in that the joint European procurement agencies and contractors lack the experience of large-scale US type of operations. Or, inefficiency arises where there are political constraints on the allocation of work by comparative advantage. Such constraints result from a desire for an 'equitable' sharing of the work between club members and associated limitations on new entrants from outside the partner nations. Sometimes, the runner-up in a competition has to be given a reward! Also, in this context, it has to be remembered that the allocation of production work is *planned and agreed* at an early stage in a project's life cycle and will reflect each nation's estimated orders and ruling exchange rates. Any subsequent *major* re-allocation of work to reflect changing comparative advantages due to unforeseen variations in national resource endowments, inflation and exchange rates, can be costly. For example, in the 1970s, during the development of the Tornado, West Germany had to adjust to changing exchange rates and higher salaries by adopting advanced, capital-intensive production technology which reduced man hours on its share of the work and enabled the country to remain 'reasonably' competitive on project unit costs. Alternatively, inefficiency is likely where international procurement agencies and joint companies in non-competitive markets are more concerned with pursuing objectives other than maximum profits. And if the inefficiency is worth eliminating (improving efficiency is not costless), is the more appropriate policy to change the organization of procurement and contracting for international ventures (but what is the 'ideal' organization?) or to introduce more competition into procurement? The US aircraft industry provides some relevant evidence. American firms usually produce over 800 units, which is the Tornado output, with runs of 3,000–5,000 not unknown (for example: Phantom; F5). Their success in competing in both the US and world markets suggests that managerial diseconomies are not a necessary feature of large-scale output. However, US firms are unanimous in emphasizing that the competitive nature of their aircraft industry is one of its major features and a factor in its success.

The Case Against European Collaboration

One view asserts that the case for joint ventures of the Tornado-type is extremely dubious (School III). Some of the arguments were reviewed above. Apparently, joint European projects do not result in the expected cost savings: indeed for the UK it is claimed that costs could be *higher* than if it had 'gone alone'. Critics maintain that when two equal partners collaborate, each nation's R and D effort is not reduced to 50 per cent of the level required for an independent national programme. Instead, full-sized R and D teams are used in each country for two to three times longer than on a national venture. In addition, the slow decision-making process by 'over-involved' governments delays the joint companies. Delays are inevitable where all the partner nations have to be consulted before a decision can be taken. Problems also arise from differences in language, measurement, managerial practices and national pride. Where a new joint company is created, it will also lack an established reputation in export markets. The net result is reputed to be perverse, since higher costs, 'over-elaborate' technical requirements and delays are unlikely to generate competitive products in world markets. It seems that the simple sharing of R and D and economies of scale in production arguments for joint projects ignored two factors. First, the national constraints on the choice of least-cost suppliers. Each partner requires a share in *each* sector of advanced technology (that is, participation in the airframe, engine, equipment and electronics business). Indeed, nations sometimes regard joint projects as a means of establishing, protecting and sharing property rights in advanced technology: such contractual arrangements are not costless. In some cases, there are substantial learning costs (which are allocated to the joint project) as new entrants are awarded a nation's 'fair' share of the work. Moreover, partners of different experience and capability might see different problems whereas experienced partners might see fewer problems. Critics have alleged that the Tornado project resulted in a net transfer of technology from the UK to West Germany, so enabling the Germans to establish a competitive, and potentially rival, aircraft industry. Whilst West German airframe firms accept that they have derived some technical benefits, they claim that on the aircraft, including equipment, the technical flows are about 'balanced'. Such a view might be further supported by the continued *voluntary* participation of the original partners. Continuation suggests that the project is believed to be worthwhile to each participant, although partners might differ in their perceptions and valuations of the 'benefits'. Second, joint projects involve substantial transactions costs which are frequently ignored. There are the bargaining costs of two or more partner nations which have to reach decisions on the project and work sharing (horse-trading), as well as the additional costs associated with collaboration between 'partner' firms selected on 'political' rather than commercial criteria. In total, the views of this school are more consistent with an *international* economics of politics and bureaucracies explanation of joint projects. Such ventures provide discretionary power to politicians and bureacrats in each nation's political market (Hartley, 1977b). They are attractive to vote-conscious politicians as a means of 'protecting' high technology producer interest groups (such as scientists, engineers), as well as providing opportunities to these groups for satisfying their technical aspirations at the expense of the general taxpayer: hence the prediction that such projects are likely to be 'over-elaborate' and 'too complex', as each national group insists upon applying its own ideas. Joint projects also provide bureaucracies (in partner nations) with large budgets, together with opportunities for international travel, bargaining about each nation's 'fair-share' of the work and allocating contracts. Indeed, as budget-maximizers, bureaucracies have every incentive to under-estimate the costs of joint ventures: this might explain the 'myth' (there is no published evidence) that UK only projects are 'too costly' and that joint projects are the *only* method of reducing the UK's costs of developing and producing modern military and civil aircraft. Bureaucrats supported by producer groups can also over-estimate the social benefits of collaboration, especially when the alternative would be to 'buy from abroad'. In other words, the economics of politics predicts that budget-maximizing bureaucracies in partner nations, supported by scientific-technical interest groups in the form of weapons firms, have exaggerated both the R and D and production savings in joint ventures in order to persuade vote-conscious governments to undertake such work. And collaborative European ventures are attractive to governments seeking re-election. Each national government can be seen to be providing jobs for its own people, 'protecting' the balance of payments and preventing 'undue' dependence on American technology and military equipment.

Critics of joint projects (School III) have estimated that with two nations, R and D costs can be 2.6 times as great as a UK only venture; and with three countries, it has been estimated that on some items, the figure could rise to 4.4! Administrative costs, duplication and escalation of performance requirements are asserted to be the causes of these cost increases. For example, as the number of partners rises from two to three, the time taken to reach decisions may start to increase by the square of the number of participants or greater. The number of people attending meetings can be inversely proportional to the gravity of the decisions involved (Heath, 1979). Duplication in R and D emerges since each nation wants its own flight testing centre which requires more (costly) development aircraft. Finally, it is maintained that the operational requirement on a joint venture is inevitably more complex: it has to satisfy the different demands of each nation's airforce as well as the aspirations of the technical staffs amongst the partners. Table 10.2 shows one estimate of the effects of collaboration on the development costs of aircraft equipment.

TABLE 10.2
Equipment Development Costs

Item	*Non-collaborative*	*Two nations*	*Three nations*
Engineering	4	12	20
Administration	2	6	12
Prototypes	3	6	9
Test rigs and equipment	1	2	3
Total	10	26	44

Source: R. Howard, *Meeting the Requirements for Equipment from European Sources*, London, Royal Aeronautical Society Symposium on Co-operation in European Air Transport, February 1976 (ref. no. 99013 PG 430).

Do Joint European Projects Result in Cost Savings for the UK (or any partner)?

Obvious difficulties arise in choosing between the alternative views outlined above. One possibility is to calculate the estimated cost impact on joint ventures using different assumptions. An example based on the Tornado is shown in Table 10.3 where it is assumed that the UK would have developed an identical multi-role aircraft, purchasing 220 units of the strike version and 165 of the air defence variant. The estimates are based on simplifying assumptions and should be regarded as no more than illustrative orders of magnitude. The best case estimates show the upper bounds of savings, with alternative assumptions about inefficiency reducing the magnitude of any gains.

Compared with a UK-only venture, collaboration could result in maximum savings to the UK of 22 per cent or some £800m. (1976 prices), although *X*-efficiency might reduce the figure to £400m. (± £50m.). Alternatively, collaboration reduces unit costs (R and D and production) by a *maximum* of 30 per cent on the strike aircraft and 10 per cent on the air defence version; inefficiency could reduce these figures to 18 per cent and a premium of 3 per cent, respectively. It can be seen that R and D contributes at least 60 per cent of

TABLE 10.3
Cost Savings from Collaboration

		Costs to UK on joint project (£m.):				
	UK only MRCA project (£m.)	*Best case: no collaboration premium*	*Maximum savings to UK*	*Collaboration premium: Assumptions*	*Costs*	*Savings to UK*
1. *Strike version. UK buy = 220 units*						
Estimated R and D costs	845	360	485	xl.4	503	342
Estimated unit production costs	6.08	5.29	0.79	+10%	5.82	0.26
Total production bill	1338	1164	174		1280	58
Total programme costs	2183	1524	659		1783	400
2. *Air defence version. UK buy = 165*						
Estimated R and D costs	240	240	0	xl.4	336	(96)
Estimated unit production costs	7.42	6.45	0.97	+10%	7.1	0.32
Total production bill	1224	1064	160		1172	52
Total programme costs	1464	1304	160		1508	(44)

Notes: (i) All estimates are in 1976 prices and exchange rates. Savings are spread over the whole programme, say, 20 years and they are not expressed in present values. The figure in brackets shows a net increase in costs rather than savings.

(ii) The estimates are based on the following assumptions:

(*a*) For the strike version, the UK share of collaborative R and D is 42.5 per cent.

(*b*) The unit production cost of £5.29m. for the strike version (announced in *Hansard*, 21 January 1976, col. 467) is assumed to be a least-cost estimate. Alternative assumptions would change the magnitude of the savings.

(*c*) An 87½ per cent unit curve for production costs, common to both the UK only and joint venture. In fact, 90 per cent unit cost curves are more typical in the UK. A UK buy of 385 units is 47.6 per cent of the total joint output and the unit cost savings might be 13 per cent (87½ per cent unit cost curve and slightly more than a doubling of output).

(*d*) R and D for air defence version is estimated at £240m. – i.e. 20 per cent of £845m. plus an escalation factor of 1.4. Since the UK is responsible for the extra R and D costs of the ADV, it is assumed that there is no difference between R and D costs for a UK only venture and 'best case' collaboration.

(*e*) Unit production costs of the ADV are assumed to be 122 per cent of the unit costs of the strike version.

the savings, so supporting the view that the main aim of collaboration is to save money by reducing development overheads. However, such estimates are subject to at least four qualifications. First, the figures are for the UK only and do not include the savings which accrue to other partners. On the basis of each partner's share in Tornado, savings on the *project* might total some £1,900m. (1976 prices). Of course, much depends on the counter-factual. For example, it is highly unlikely that without Tornado, Italy would have undertaken the independent development of an identical aircraft for a requirement of 100 units. A more likely option would have been an off-the-shelf buy of US aircraft or participation in the European co-production programme for the F16, resulting in the acquisition of a different, but possibly, cheaper aircraft. Second, the estimated savings relate to acquisition and not to the life-cycle costs of the aircraft. Life-cycle costs (such as acquisition, training, operation, maintenance, bases and support) might be at least twice unit production costs, which suggests a doubling of the estimated maximum savings on production, or an extra £174m. saving for the UK. Alternatively, savings in operating costs due to collaboration might be confined to common training and some support, say 10 per cent, which results in extra savings to the UK of about £17m. (Nelson *et al.,* 1974). Third, the estimates relate to *collaboration only* and exclude the savings due to the development of a *multi-role* aircraft. For example, if the UK had undertaken the independent development of a specialist fighter aircraft similar to the F15, it might have incurred R and D costs of some £450m. (1976 prices). In other words, compared with the Tornado ADV, there would have been extra development expenditures of £210m, plus the loss of learning economies otherwise associated with the larger scale production of a common multi-role aircraft, possibly totalling some £290m. Thus, the UK only development of a multi-role aircraft compared with the separate domestic development of specialist strike and fighter aeroplanes could mean savings to Britain of £500m. Fourth, the estimated savings are based on a comparison between collaboration and an independent UK programme. Such an exercise is not necessarily an accurate indicator of opportunity costs, which requires comparisons based on the lowest cost source of supply: this is most likely to be the USA (cf. trade diversion and trade creation).

European and US Costs

Traditionally, productivity in the European aerospace industry (value added per employee) has been between one-third and two-thirds of that in the US industry, with the larger scale of American output explaining a substantial proportion of this differential. However, international comparisons are complicated by differences in inputs, product quality, exchange rate variations, pricing policies and differential performance between airframes, engines and avionics. At the firm level, comparisons are often based on the *best* foreign enterprises, rather than the average. In the circumstances, micro-economic studies can provide further useful insights and evidence. For example, in the UK aero-engine sector, after attempting to allow for all relevant factors, it has been estimated that currently the productivity differential between Rolls Royce and the US Pratt and Whitney Company might be in the region of 30 per cent (Rolls Royce plan to reduce this differential by 1984). Whilst volume is a major explanation of this productivity 'gap', there are other causes associated with the labour market and the utilization of manpower and plant. For engines, the US productivity advantage over the UK is attributed to such factors as the flexibility of the workforce within a plant, the willingness of workers (without union opposition) to operate more than one machine, relatively low absenteeism, higher metal removal rates, lower shift premiums, as well as intangible elements in the form of the motivation and commitment of the labour force. Interestingly, Rolls Royce engines does not appear to be at a competitive disadvantage in the vintage of its capital stock: higher productivity American companies used *older* machine tools (Rolls Royce, 1978). For the European aerospace industry as a whole, there are additional explanations of the productivity 'gap', particularly the US 'hire and fire' policy which gives their firms a higher manpower elasticity (Hartley, 1981a).

Until the mid-1970s, the US productivity advantage was offset partly by lower European labour costs (EEC, 1975a). For example, in the late 1960s, if Britain built 155 units of a subsonic jet airliner, the USA had to manufacture almost 500 to achieve the same unit costs (Ministry of Technology, 1969). However, during the 1970s changes in relative inflation and exchange rates reduced Europe's traditional competitive advantage in labour costs. In the circumstances, it has been suggested that US aircraft might be 15–30 per cent cheaper than European projects, including joint ventures. In testing such hypotheses, problems arise because nations have different policy objectives and *identical* US and joint European aircraft rarely exist within the same time-scale. Nevertheless, evidence on relative prices is available from the UK evaluation of the American F14, F15 and F16 fighters as alternatives to the Tornado ADV. By late 1975, Britain had decided that the 'difference in cost between the ADV and the possible alternatives was probably not very great' (HC 254, p. 5). The evaluation showed that the F14 was the closest substitute but it was a costly aircraft, probably 50 per cent more expensive than the Tornado; the cost of an F15 alternative seemed to be similar to the ADV but it was felt that its single crew member would be incapable of coping with the complex UK air defence tasks; and the F16 lacked the required long-range, all-weather capability, although it was a cheaper alternative. Our independent cost estimates shown in Table 10.4 support these assessments.

TABLE 10.4
Comparative Costs of US and Collaborative Aircraft

				Three-nation Tornado	
	F14	*F15*	*F16*	*ADV*	*Strike*
Unit production cost (£m.)	n.a.	6.6	3.13	6.45–7.72	5.29–6.34
Unit costs (£m.)	13.1	8.2	3.7	7.91–9.17	6.93–7.98
Domestic orders	521	749	1338	165	644
Total output (1980)	601	842	<2000	809	

Notes: (i) All figures are in 1976 prices using market exchange rate of £1 = $1.83. The F16 price is based on a European not-to-exceed price of $6.09m. (1975) and a 1975–76 European inflation rate of 10 per cent.

(ii) The lower of the Tornado cost estimates are based on January 1976 unit production costs whilst the higher figures are based on November 1976 production costs; both estimates use the same average R and D costs (best case) as shown in Table 10.3.

(iii) For the F14 and F16, domestic orders are for US Forces; for the Tornado they are the total purchases for the armed forces of the partner nations. For the F15, Japan is producing under licence an additional 92 units.

(iv) Data based on interviews with US and UK firms in 1977, and the estimates in Table 10.3.

The estimates in Table 10.4 are no more than general orders of magnitude. Independent observers encounter inevitable difficulties in ensuring that cost estimates are on a uniform price basis. Moreover, to obtain a European order, American firms might be willing to offer a competitive price based on unit production costs, with only a token contribution to R and D. Nevertheless, using the data in Table 10.4, the collaborative Tornado ADV could be some 30–40 per cent cheaper than the F14 and similarly priced to the F15, possibly 4 per cent cheaper or up to about 12 per cent more expensive; but, the strike version of the Tornado is some 3–18 per cent cheaper than the F15. Significantly, the output for the collaborative Tornado is similar to that of the F15 and larger than for the F14; and larger scale is one of the standard arguments for European collaboration compared with independent national programmes. For example, a UK only development of the Tornado ADV or an equivalent type would have been some 8 to 30 per cent more expensive than the unit cost of the F15 (see Table 10.3). In the event, the UK decision to proceed with the collaborative Tornado ADV rather than 'buy American' was taken after considering 'operational, industrial, financial and foreign exchange considerations' (HC 254, p. 5). If the F15 is a close substitute (is it?), the UK preference for the Tornado ADV at the mean of the cost estimates suggests that policy makers 'valued' these operational, industrial and other 'benefits' at a minimum of £56m. (£0.34m. × 165 aircraft); or, if the higher estimate is more accurate, the benefits would be valued at £160m. (0.97m. × 165). Such 'benefits' are equivalent to tariff rates of between 4 and 12 per cent on the F15, which are by no means penal for weapons markets. There is a further aspect of the collaborative Tornado, concerning the costs and benefits of the specified operational requirement: is it worthwhile? For example, Tables 10.3 and 10.4 show that Britain's share of collaborative R and D expenditure involves the sacrifice of 160 F16 aircraft before receiving a single operational Tornado. Total UK participation in the joint Tornado is equivalent to the sacrifice of over 760 F16s. Presumably, UK policy makers believe that a substantially smaller Tornado force will make a greater contribution to national defence (and other objectives) than similar expenditure on the F16. Without implying that a particular choice is undesirable or mistaken, such examples identify some of the trade-offs in procurement. They raise more general problems concerning military views of 'need' (operational requirements) and whether a weapon is 'needed' regardless of costs.

Conclusion: An Alternative Policy

It is not claimed that this chapter has presented a comprehensive analysis of all aspects of EEC policy towards advanced technology industries. The aim has been to examine the economic logic of EEC involvement in technology and to present a detailed analysis of one aspect, namely the cost implications of collaborative aerospace ventures. In this context, actual experience of government-promoted international collaboration provides evidence on the likely success or otherwise of such solutions for other EEC high technology sectors. However, there remain some unresolved and controversial policy issues. Collaboration cannot be assessed solely on the basis of comparative costs. Consideration has to be given to other cost–benefit implications, such as the effects on development time scales, product quality (as in committee aeroplanes), risk-sharing, profitability, exports, technology and European defence capability and unity. Alternative policy solutions cannot be ignored. Does economic theory offer any 'guidelines' for a public policy towards joint ventures?

A competitive solution provides a set of general principles which might be the basis for an alternative policy. The creation of a NATO free trade area in *both* weapons and civil goods would allow nations to specialize by comparative advantage and reap the gains from mutually advantageous international trade. Nor would resource allocation be distorted through restricting free trade to one product category, namely, military equipment. With a market solution, weapons firms would be allowed to select any partners on a commercial basis, restricting governments to the role of correcting major market deficiencies (e.g. removing trade restrictions and entry barriers to national markets). Such a proposal has some similarities to the US view of collaborative ventures.

Compared with the European approach, American aircraft firms prefer *ad hoc* international consortiums rather than the formation of new permanent international companies involving governments (such as Panavia). To the US industry, Tornado-type collaboration is an example of how *not* to proceed. They prefer a single source of design leadership, with associated risk obligations, and 'work sharing' through co-production arrangements. But, the US model has its limitations. The sales performance of American firms does not necessarily imply that inefficiency is absent and only exists in Europe. There are many instances where European aerospace equipment has competed successfully with American products. Also, the US opposition to European-type collaboration might reflect their lack of experience with such organizations. Evidence on Tornado suggests that it is competitive with the rival F14 and F15 aircraft (Table 10.4). Moreover, the American preference for a single design source is based on the implicit assumption that this will (must?) always be the United States. Nor is co-production necessarily conducive to efficiency if the work is allocated on equity criteria, which are also characteristic of European joint ventures. And, the possibility of a competitive market solution and of collaboration between European and American firms encounters all the standard arguments about nationalism. On both sides of the Atlantic, there are a set of myths about monopoly and spares pricing, about the loss of 'independence' and technology: arguments which often lack both analytical and empirical support, especially on the costs of nationalism. For example, with a NATO free market in weapons (e.g. with voters instructing governments to act as competitive buyers) the structure and organization of UK and European aerospace industries would be different. The UK would specialize, with a potential comparative advantage in electronics, ejector seats, engines, sub-assembly work, small missiles and STOL technology. But such policy options are usually criticized because of the 'fear' that the UK and Europe will become sub-contractors to the USA. Indeed, it is believed that the US will acquire a monopoly of advanced technology with the UK restricted to 'metal-bashing'. Even if this occurred – and evidence suggests that the UK has a comparative advantage in areas of aerospace technology – it has to be remembered that production work can also involve technology (for example in aircraft production technology, including organization and management, the UK is reputed to be *at least* 5 years behind the USA). Moreover, aerospace production can be relatively profitable: and firms cannot survive on the technical nature of their inputs and outputs, independently of the marketability of their outputs.

Critics of competitive solutions worry that international specialization by comparative advantage might mean that a nation's access to technology could be cut off at some time in the distant future. They accept that specialization leads to gains in the present but at a possible cost of re-creating a technological capability which could exceed the financing of a relatively expensive national weapons producer over the same period. This insurance argument assumes that current technology will be required in the future and that technical progress is evolutionary rather than revolutionary. Nor should it be forgotten that the argument concerns the cost and benefits of *alternative* methods of coping with risk and uncertainty (neither of which can be eliminated, or are worth eliminating, completely). Economists can make a major contribution to the debate by estimating the costs of options, including nationalism. For example, studies show that for some high technology weapons, nationalism could be almost 60 per cent more costly than a competitive solution (Tucker (1976), p. 38). With such orders of magnitude, voters may question whether some objectives are worthwhile. The political market is also relevant in understanding the development of industrial, competition and transport policies in the Community.

Acknowledgements

The author of Chapter 10 is grateful to NATO and Dr F. Welter for sponsoring this research as part of a NATO Research Fellowship; to the Ford Foundation and to the SSRC Public Sector Studies Group at York; to all the individuals and firms in Belgium, France, West Germany, UK and USA, who kindly assisted with the project; and to Brian Hillier and John Hutton, ISER, for comments and suggestions. The usual disclaimers apply.

Notes

1. A 90 per cent curve shows that unit costs decline by 10 per cent for each doubling in cumulative output. The cost savings are estimated by using a 90 per cent curve and comparing each partner's output with the total output of 809 units (385, 324 and 100 units): see Hartley (1969).
2. The analysis is identical if the UK industry is technically inefficient but less so that on joint projects.
3. Some of these estimates could reflect earlier experience with European collaboration, when a 30 per cent premium was regarded as typical. If the supporters of joint ventures are correct, this premium could have fallen with learning and experience to a figure of less than 20 per cent.

CHAPTER 11

Competition Policy, Industrial Policy and Transport Policy

The Policy Issues

The institutions of the European Community, the Commission and its Directorate-General, the European Court and the European Parliament, have worked actively in the fields of industrial policy, competition policy, and transport policy. This chapter cannot review all the issues raised by this regulation but it will seek to highlight the complexities of the arguments and the difficulties involved in creating a common market in goods and services. Examples will be based on two sectors, pharmaceutical products and civil aviation.

A competitive common market would result in production in areas of greatest comparative advantages, so maximizing the productivity of the community's resources. However the achievement of this ideal is fraught with difficulties. The first section illustrates the problems associated with translating the Treaty into active industrial policy by considering the activities of the pharmaceutical industry in terms of safety and efficacy, price regulation, and product liability. The second section is concerned with competition policy. This policy has many aspects to it, not the least the definition of dominant or monopoly position in the market. Both dominance, and the parallel imports of pharmaceutical products are analysed. The third section is concerned with the civil aviation market as an example of transport policy. A final section identifies common trends and argues that the nature of the political market place makes progress towards the creation of a common market slow and complex.

Industrial Policy: The Case of Pharmaceuticals

Policy makers in Directorate-General III of the European Commission are concerned with industrial policy. The civil servants in this directorate-general seek to interpret the Treaty of Rome, initiate legislation (which has to be agreed by the Commission and the Council of Ministers), and use the European court to ensure that, within their severe budget limits, the Community progresses towards the goal of a common market. The difficulties are well illustrated by the events surrounding the EEC regulation of the pharmaceutical industry. The work of Directorate-General III in creating a free market in pharmaceutical products has involved the harmonization of the rules governing the testing, manufacture and marketing of proprietary medical products, the regulation of their prices, and the arguments about product liability.

The Safety, Efficacy and Quality of Pharmaceutical Products

Directorate-General III began work on harmonizing the legislation relating to the testing, manufacturing and marketing of pharmaceuticals in 1961 after the thalidomide case had illustrated the paucity of regulation in this area. At that time five of the six member states had similar systems of regulation with regard to the safety, efficacy and quality of medicine. The exception was Germany where although some documents had to be registered formally with the government prior to the issue of a licence, there was no scrutiny by the government of these documents.

The political effects of the thalidomide case (1961) changed the policy environment. A preventive system of registration was advocated with the definition of the characteristics of the product, examination of a dossier of information from the firm by the government, and the possibility of a refusal to grant a licence to market the product, i.e. the development of detailed tests on the safety, efficacy and quality of the product. The principle rationale of these proposals was the protection of human life from potentially damaging substances. However there was little careful articulation of these objectives, or of their costs and benefits in relation to possible alternatives.

The machinery for EEC harmonization of this regulation was established by directive 1965/65 (known as 65/65). This first general directive on pharmaceuticals was passed by Council in January 1965 and by it member states agreed to introduce all the necessary legislation and administrative changes within 18 months and to apply the rules to create uniform methods of marketing control progressively over five years. After five years no drug was to be sold unless previously licensed; registrations were to be renewed every five years, and the issue of licences was to be based on uniform criteria of safety and efficacy, with uniform information shown on labels.

A companion directive controlling uniformity of manufacturing, checking, and test evidence for the issue of a licence was opposed by

Germany and, despite an amendment to exclude certain products (such as serums, vaccines, human blood, radio-active products and some others) and a proposal to delay its implementation, this opposition contributed to a lack of application of both the directives. In 1967 the Commission responded by submitting to Council a timetable for implementation by the beginning of 1970 (Collins (1975), see Vol. 2). This did not assist progress. By 1969 only France and Belgium had adjusted their national rules to allow for the implementation of the 65/65 directive by 1974. It has been argued that this lack of progress is indicative of 'the reluctance of states to give up their control over health matters and of the strength of the drug manufacturers' (Collins (1975), Vol. 2).

A new era of Community action began in 1975 when two new directives were agreed (1975/318, and 1975/319). The objective of these laws was to regulate the 'correctness of the medicine' and 'the correctness of the manufacture of medicine' respectively. The directive (75/318) on standards and certificates supplemented 65/65 and specified the characteristics of the product which had to be revealed by the manufacturer, established a uniform system for the presentation of testing data to the licensing authorities, and set out standard guidelines for the performance of tests.

The directive 75/318 set out detailed requirements concerning qualitative and quantitative particulars of a drug's constituents, toxicological and pharmacological tests (part 2), and clinical trials. For example 'as far as possible' trials will be 'double blind' and statistically sound (EEC, 1978c).

Directive 75/318 was published in the *Official Journal of the European Communities* in June, 1975 and under it member states were directed to implement any regulatory changes that were needed to comply with the directive, by November 1976. The Directive covered a wide range of preclinical and clinical tests but only in slight detail and after due consultations with the experts and the industry, it has published 17 sets of detailed guidelines. These guidelines have not been published in the *Official Journal* and their exact legal status is unclear. Also their content is disputed by some.

The directive on the correctness of manufacture (75/319) specified the authorities, obligations prior to their agreement to the manufacture and marketing of products. This legislation requires manufacturers to have the necessary premises and technical equipment, and to employ at least one qualified person if his products are to be traded freely in the Community.

In order to facilitate the eradication of inter-state inconsistencies in the application of this legislation, and hence barriers to trade, the

75/319 directive established a Committee for Proprietary Medicinal Products (CPMP) and sought to eliminate systematic inter-Community import checks on these products: the latter would be possible if there was uniform manufacture and testing rules throughout the EEC.

The CPMP was devised to obviate inconsistent decisions about marketing authorizations in the EEC. It uses a standard application form for applications for marketing authorizations (see EEC, 1978c). The Committee was empowered to publish an opinion if:

> (*a*) When a holder of an initial marketing authorization applies for its extension to at least five other markets;
> (*b*) When inconsistent decisions are taken by member states in respect of one and the same product.
> (*c*) When a member state wishes, in specific cases where the interests of the Community are concerned, to obtain the Committee's opinion before reaching a decision.
>
> (EEC (1976), p. 68.)

The Council of the European Communities has stated clearly that the present directives (65/65, 78/25 (controlling colouring ingredients), 75/318 and 75/319), are only a step towards the achievement of the EEC policy objective of free movement of proprietary medicinal products. However a time-table for the eventual achievement of free movement has been set out and the Commission was obliged to submit to Council before 22 November 1980 a proposal containing the necessary measures to eliminate the remaining barriers to the free movement of drugs in the EEC.

The Commission sees the Pharmaceutical Committee (established by Council decision 75/320) as having an important advisory role during the period prior to the attainment of the free movement objective.

This Committee is made up of senior officials (civil servants) from the member states and is required to advise the Commission on general questions in the field of proprietary medicinal products.

The effects of directives 65/65, 75/318, 75/319, 75/320 and a 1978 directive (directive 78/25) led to the creation of EEC regulations to control the colouring matters that could be added to human and veterinary medicines; the conditions necessary for marketing authorization, the nature of tests and trials, the nature of manufacture in the pharmaceutical industry and its control, the qualification of persons required to work in the industry, and the nature of labels and package leaflets, and colouring. All these new laws were aimed at harmonizing practice in these areas so that the obstacles to trade in pharmaceutical products in the EEC were reduced. In fact little harmonization of practice has taken place. The industries prefer to market in individual countries separately and have treated EEC initiatives with great caution because of their fear of the development of a restrictive (to them) 'Federal' policy like that in the USA. An intense debate about future policy, in particular the creation of new EEC regulatory devices and their imposition is likely to take place in the first half of the 1980s.

POLICY IMPLEMENTATION, OR LACK OF IT

The experience of the Commission in the period 1976–80 was meant to inform the process of determining future EEC policy. In fact CPMP has been ignored by the industry as a mechanism for the acquisition of marketing rights across member countries. The right of companies, under article 9 of directive 75/319, once a licence to market has been acquired in *A*, to notify a licensing need in another five states to CPMP and acquire marketing rights in six states, has been used in only four cases. This obligation to pursue the CPMP procedure in a minimum of five other member states has been regarded as the main obstacle to use by the industry. Article 12 of 75/319, the right of appeal to CPMP when after getting marketing rights in one state a company is refused them in another, has not been used. Article 14 which permits a member state to refer an authorization application to CPMP before it decides to grant marketing rights, has been used, in relation to the safety and efficacy of products, in some 50 cases.

Thus overall, the members of the CPMP and Directorate-General III have acquired little knowledge of the problems of harmonization in this area as a result of 75/319. They are moving into a period of a policy reform with little practical experience of the working of any form of regulation. There are at least two causes of this outcome. Firstly one of the exceptions to harmonization of free movement concerns matters which affect the 'protection of health and life of humans'. This clause in article 36 of the EEC Treaty has given member states the power to maintain their control over public health measures. Thus Germany opposed initially directive 75/319, arguing that it preferred on grounds of 'efficiency' in protecting human life, to have mutual (EEC wide) recognition of licences throughout the Community. This opposition led to explicit recognition by the Commission and the Council that 75/319 was transitional in nature and that by the early 1980s Directorate-General III would prepare another directive meeting the German's demands.

Governmental opposition to directives and EEC policy has been exercised with the active advice and encouragement of the pharmaceutical industry which has particular views about the nature of the harmonization process. The industry accepts that the creation of a free market in pharmaceutical products will be advantageous, especially because of the potential economies of scale which may arise in the filing and scrutiny of testing evidence. However its members have not used CPMP because it is, they argue, 'bureaucratic'. The meaning of this term is not always clear but one interpretation is that it is slow, prohibits dialogue between the companies and the Committee, and is rigid, particularly in regard to article 9 (the other five member state obligation). With patents of limited duration (20 years) and pre-market launch trials consuming more time and resources (7 to 12 years of the patent life), delays in the marketing launch may circumscribe a company's ability to earn profits. This makes the industry loath to be involved in additions to the regulatory process. The partcular problem of the CPMP mechanism to which the industry objects is that there is little possibility of industry–regulator dialogue. In the UK, the Medicines Division of the Department of Health and Social Security can debate issues with those seeking licences and, where necessary, involve them to provide any necessary additional evaluative evidence. This facilitates a rapid market launch and ensures that regulator and the regulated are fully informed about, and involved in, the regulatory process. The absence of this flexibility in the way CPMP works, makes the industry avoid it and seek national, rather than EEC marketing authorization.

Article 15 of the directive 75/319, requires the Council to make a decision on the new proposals the Commission will put forward in the early 1980s. Whether this will be possible to achieve is unclear. At present marketing authorizations remain the responsibility of the authorities of the member states and industry makes little use of the CPMP mechanism to get EEC marketing authorization. Any change in this outcome will depend on the result of the forthcoming negotiations where the competing camps will debate the merits of mutual recognition of national marketing licences and a supra-national regulatory body.

POLICY OPTIONS

The objectives of reform are twofold. Firstly there is a desire to limit the degree of conflicting national decisions about the manufacture and marketing of drugs by member states and to ensure that testing is cost effective. Secondly there is a wish to avoid repetition in the scrutiny of testing and other documents prior to marketing. A strong supra-national agency, equivalent to the United States Food and Drug Administration (FDA) could meet these two objectives. An EEC–FDA would have the sole right to license drugs for marketing in the Community. It would define and control pre-clinical and clinical testing and evaluate itself in a manner similar to the American FDA. The creation of such a body would require a strong political will from the member states as it involves their giving up sovereignty and, in effect, re-writing article 36 of the Rome Treaty. At present it does not seem that this option is likely to be adopted, especially because the industry fears that such a body will slow down further the processing of marketing authorization and consequently reduce the effective patent life (and profits) derived of new products. The merits of this policy option seem considerable and its political impossibility is unfortunate.

An alternative policy option is mutual recognition. A policy of mutual recognition of the issue of national licences might achieve the first objective of reform, limiting conflicting national decisions. But it may not achieve the second aim of reducing repetition of scrutiny of documentation. Success will depend on the nature of mutual recognition. The variants of this option will, no doubt, be debated vigorously by the member states. If a national licence became automatically an EEC licence, the problem of national sovereignty (and article 36 of the EEC Treaty) would again be acute. In any dispute, e.g. Britain refusing to accept a German licence, a dialogue would be necessary. Such a dialogue could take place in the CPMP with this body evaluating the acceptability of objections (by Britain, for example) to any product. However the power of any CPMP decision, and whether it would be binding on all members, would be a matter of intense debate. Despite these difficulties this is the preferred policy of the Commission.

A third policy option is a system of national licences but with the issue of national licences dependent on prior CPMP agreement with regard to the safety and efficacy of the product. This option, the compulsory EEC consultation procedure, leaves the power to issue licences with the national authority but their power can be exercised only after EEC (CPMP) agreement has been obtained.

The problems common to these options are national sovereignty (article 36 of the Rome Treaty: this together with all other articles cited in this chapter are set out in its appendix) and exceptions. The previous history of debate in this area has been that agreement is sometimes obtained by exempting some products from the scope of new directives. Clearly such exemptions change the nature of the options and make the attainment of the ultimate policy objective, free movement of pharmaceutical products within the EEC, more difficult to attain. Exemptions will require further particular directives if a competitive common market is to be achieved.

The involvement of industry in the regulatory process is a further problem. As argued earlier regulation can be used by the regulated to their own advantage. This may be a good *prima facie* case for continued exclusion of the industry from the detailed work of CPMP. However the benefits of this policy must be offset against its costs. The member states have given the industry particular rights, namely patent protection, to generate high profits and fuel, hopefully, the engine of creative innovation. A refusal to involve the industry in working of the regulatory procedures may affect its capacity to generate funds for R and D. To avoid this outcome, it might be sensible to involve the industry closely in the regulatory mechanisms but to ensure also that this process and the success of the industry in evolving new and effective therapies is carefully monitored by the regulated and the regulators. At present much of the debate about the regulatory system in member states and in Brussels is value laden and subjective. Both sides of the regulatory 'divide' are responsible for this and clear definitions of policy objectives and the evaluation of the success of these policies is required, particularly on the part of the regulators. This is happening in the USA where subjective but plausible criteria (such as novelty in therapeutic effects and originality in the chemical entity) are used to evaluate the effects of the industry and speed up the regulatory process for those few products which are novel and efficacious (Department of Health, Education and Welfare, 1979).

The first report of the CPMP boldly stated that the various directives between 1965 and 1978 had harmonized national laws and 'eliminated major obstacles to the free movement of proprietary medicinal products' (EEC, 1979b). Whilst some valuable ground work has been done, the CPMP has been circumvented by the industry and the market remains fragmented. It is clear that some substantial obstacles to the free movement of products remain and that the invention and application of rigorous legislation is a task which will continue to exercise many minds. The Commission is obliged to draft new legislation but is not certain that this new legislation will effectively harmonize the rules governing the testing, manufacture and marketing of medicaments in the European Community.

The objectives of any new rules are to increase competition and create a common market in drugs. These objectives are difficult to achieve because they affect the profits of producer groups and the interests of member governments. The power of these interest groups is formidable and progress is likely to be slow: capitalists have never liked competition!

The Regulation of Prices

On the one hand member states increase profits by giving firms in the industry patent protection. On the other hand they seek to reduce prices (and hence profits) with price regulations which may be at variance with the Treaty of Rome. The regulation of the prices and the consumption of pharmaceutical products is quite extensive within the EEC. The regulation of the consumption of drugs is a matter which is a concern of Directorate-General V (social affairs). It has also shown interest in the price-regulation policies of member countries (see Abel-Smith and Grandjeat, 1978).

It is only recently that Directorate-General III has become interested in this area. The Pharmaceutical Committee has set up a Pricing Committee which is seeking to identify and monitor the price regulatory system of the member states. This acquisition of basic information could be the first step in a policy of integrating (presumably under article 100 of the EEC Treaty which is set out in the appendix) the price regulatory systems of the Community, although the Commission denies this intention (European Parliamentary Question, 4 January 1979).

The problems to be resolved in any such policy are obvious and complex, factors which will not necessarily inhibit policy changes in the direction of EEC price control. Prices may differ between member states for a variety of reasons. The demand for products may differ substantially between, say, France and Britain, because of different prescribing habits. For example, the use of antibiotics is greater in Britain than in France where tetracyclines are used in the treatment of bacterial infections. Furthermore, prices may be deflated by the monopsony (sole buyer) power of Department of Health and Social Security and the sickness funds. Prices may also vary because of supply differences: the costs of production may vary due to the absence or presence of economies of scale (advantage of which can be taken only if demand circumstances are favourable). A further problem is that exchange rates may not reflect purchasing power and may thus deflate or inflate prices artificially. Moreover the prices of many products vary across national boundaries and indeed perhaps the prices of products should vary more within such boundaries if prices are to reflect costs and demand (Cooper, 1975). The cost of marketing a bar of Rowntree's chocolate in Shetland is not the same as in York where it is made, with the profits on the York sale financing, in part, the costs of distribution to Shetland. Casual analysis of prices may lead to erroneous conclusions and such conclusions may affect industry profits and R and D potential.

Both national and supra-national EEC price regulation may be in contravention of the EEC Treaty. Article 30 of the Treaty prohibits restrictions on imports and 'all measures having equivalent effects'. The European Federation of the Pharmaceutical Industry Associations and questions in the European Parliament have forced the Commission to investigate complaints from the industry that the Italian, British and French price regulation schemes contravene article 30 (set out in the appendix). The Commission has delivered a preliminary critical opinion to the Italian government and is investigating complaints about the French and British price regulatory system.

The pharmaceutical market is highly imperfect, largely due to barriers to trade created by governments. Government-created monopoly power (by patents), their concern about pharmaceutical export revenues and the pricing outcomes of the 'market' process may lead to prices bearing little relation to opportunity costs. However, from the points of view of the participants concerned, particularly government, high and unequal prices may be efficient outcomes. The efficiency of pricing outcomes depends on the objectives sought by policy makers and if policies distort markets by mitigating the regulatory effects of the competitive process (so that they are in contravention of the Rome Treaty), such national benefits may have to be traded off against the failure to create a common EEC-wide market in pharmaceutical products.

Product Liability

In July 1976 the Commission published a proposal for a Council directive relating to the harmonization of product liability laws of the member states of the EEC. The Commission rationalized the introduction of the directive with reference to article 100 of the EEC Treaty, arguing that because the laws of member states diverged, individuals were treated differently and in some cases were unprotected against the effects of deficient products. Furthermore, the Commission argued, differences in liability laws affecting the costs of manufacture amongst the member states and to avoid competitive advantages in countries with poor liability laws, it felt that harmonization was necessary.

In order to harmonize liability laws the directive proposed full producer liability, irrespective of fault, for a period of ten years.

The liability is for damages suffered from the product by the buyers and any other persons and the producer is defined as being any person who was involved on their own responsibility in the process of producing the defective element in the article.

The draft directive ran into considerable opposition, not the least because of its costly implication for producers, and as yet it has not been translated into law. The draft was sent to the European Parliament and to the Economic and Social Committee for comments. In April 1979, after a much delayed consideration of the draft, the European Parliament adopted by a large majority a resolution inviting the EEC commission to incorporate several radical amendments into the proposed directive. They recommended that the manufacturer should be exonerated from liability for those risks where, having been made aware of their existence, he took adequate steps to inform the public and eliminate any harmful effects. These proposed amendments caused a bitter controversy in the Commission. The commissioner for consumer affairs (Mr Burke, 1975–80) was pressured by consumer bodies to ensure the rejection of the Parliament's proposals. Viscount Davignon, the then commissioner for internal market and industrial affairs, wished to comply with the Parliament's wishes. In September 1979 the Consumer Affairs faction won and, as a result, the Commission presented the Council of Ministers with a document which, although revised, did not exclude liability for development risks, The revised draft directive (dated 26 September 1979) is inevitably controversial.

The harmonization of product liability laws is a clear example of the difficulties of translating a draft directive into law. The process begun in 1976 is still on-going and there is every reason to believe that the harmonization of Community law in this area will be delayed for some time yet. The reasons for this long delay are that legislation could severely affect industry costs and, as a result, considerable pressure is being brought to bear to ensure that its effects are mitigated. The economic regulation is the outcome of a political debate in which powerful groups struggle to shift costs onto each other, in particular consumer groups seek to acquire safer drugs at the cost of higher industrial production costs.

Overview

The resources (especially manpower) of Directorate-General III are very limited. Despite this the officials have sought to implement the spirit of the Rome Treaty in a variety of ways. However industrial policy by its very nature is contentious: potentially it can have radical effects on markets and the profits of industry. Thus it has been inevitable that the implementation of articles 30–7 of the Treaty has been difficult. This is well illustrated by the market for pharmaceutical products where government-created (by patent monopoly and other laws) monopolists and oligopolists have fought vigorously and quite successfully to maintain their positions. Little has been harmonized with regard to safety and efficacy, prices and product liability.

Competition Policy

The Commission's desired to achieve the free circulation of pharmaceutical products in the community does not manifest itself solely in Directorate-General III. Directorate-General IV (competition) is also very active in seeking to prevent the abuse of dominant positions and the use of restrictive practices. The Commission's view is that there are considerable 'distortions' in the prices of pharmaceuticals in the EEC and:

> The Commission is determined to facilitate parallel imports of medicines in order to eradicate unjustified price differences and to institute inquiries whenever there is a reason to suspect the existence of an abusive price policy on the part of enterprises enjoying a dominant position, or of agreements which aim at restricting competition.
> (Commission reply at the European Parliament, March, 1978)

This statement includes some words whose meanings are ambiguous. 'Unjustified' price differences, 'abusive' price policy, and 'dominant' position are phrases used liberally in Commission documents. The meanings of these words is being defined in the case law of the European Court although it might be argued that these definitions are legally sound but, in some cases, economically imprecise.

Since this policy statement by the Commission there has been a series of judgments by the Court of Justice aimed at suppressing many of the restrictions on parallel imports: the interest of the Court in this policy area dates back to the Centrafarm cases in 1974. This section discusses the problems of parallel imports and the associated issues of trade marks, patents and marketing authorizations. Then reference will be made to the problem of defining dominant position (a term used in articles 85 and 86 of the EEC Treaty).

The Obstacles to Parallel Imports

Parallel imports, importing into *B* where the product is high priced, products purchased in *A* at a low price (i.e. the equalizing of prices across markets), can be inhibited by a variety of government created obstacles: marketing authorizations, trade marks and patents. The legal question is whether a distributor can purchase the product in Britain from a wholesaler and market under its original trademark in the other countries after repacking it. If so the distributor can equalize prices between markets and frustrate price discrimination policies of the producer. If the importer is able to demonstrate that the manufacturer's exercise of trademark rights is intended to divide the market and create barriers to free trade (and sufficient evidence of this will be to show that the prices of the product differ between countries), then the manufacturer will be unable to prohibit the importer from applying the original trademark to the repackaged form of the product.

But does the importer have to get a marketing authorization prior to his selling the product? The product already has a marketing authorization in the country of importation, although this is issued to the manufacturer. The legal disputes in this area centre round whether the marketing authorization is granted (*a*), to the product, and is as a consequence valid for whoever sells that product, or (*b*) to the manufacturer who holds the patent. At present the answers to (*a*) and (*b*) seem to differ in the member states of the Community.

In Germany if the composition of the product is identical in Britain and Germany, the importer can make a 'distribution notification' for a product whose registration number is the same as that of the manufacturer. Further documentation (a control bulletin) is required in principle but in practice the German authorities follow the European law's ruling on the Centrafarm–Dutch authorities case (see below), and waive this requirement. As a consequence, a distributor (like Centrafarm) can sell Roche's Valium in the Common Market.

In the Netherlands, the importer is required to file details of ingredients, preparation methods, and test evidence with the Public Health Inspector. This documentation must replicate foreign evidence. The importer will be exempted from producing with each product batch a declaration of conformity with the file, following the Centrafarm–Hoffman La Roche case in 1976. The Dutch Government in 1974 complicated matters by a judgment which contravened EEC rules but since then the European Court has reduced barriers to trade and made it easier for Centrafarm to trade and equalize prices.

The French authorities would require the importer to acquire a marketing authorization. To obtain such an authorization, technical information about the product would have to be filed and the French Commission for Marketing Authorities could then only refuse a licence, following EEC law, if it could show that a refusal did not result in the partitioning of the French market and a restriction on competition. If a licence was granted the importer would then have to get his product on the list refundable under Social Security arrangements. How the Social Security authorities would deal with two examples of an identical product, one imported and one produced by a manufacturer is not clear.

Thus marketing authorizations for an importer vary from one member state to another and may not always facilitate free trade. The outcome may be complicated by *trademarks*. In the Centrafarm–Hoffman La Roche case (1976) the importer was marketing in Germany Roche's product which had been repackaged from the original British Roche packs. The European Court admitted that article 36 was relevant in principle – or that free movement should not infringe industrial property rights (patents or registered trade marks) – but that in fact, Roche's behaviour contributed to the partitioning of markets and Centrafarm's repackaging did not affect the original state of the product. Thus, provided the original state of the product is not altered, provided the new pack bears the importer's name and provided the trademark owner is notified, firms such as Centrafarm can carry out parallel importing policies.

After this decision by the Court, the outcome of the Centrafarm versus American Home Products case was awaited with interest (1975). The situation was that a product was marketed in *A* under trademark *X* and in market *B* under trademark *Y*. The legislation in country *B* gave the trademark's owner the right to oppose the sale by others of the product bearing the *Y* trademark. The legislation in country *B* also allowed the importer to sell an imported product under a trademark other than that which was registered in country *A*. The European Court had to decide whether the owner of trademark *Y* could oppose the marketing by an importer of products carrying the same trademark. The Court ruled in October 1978 that the trademark owner could oppose sales by the importer on grounds of breach of trademark if use of different trademarks in different countries was justified objectively and did not partition national markets.

So the situation is that the trademark owner (manufacturer) cannot prevent re-packaging and marketing by an importer if the trademark is unaltered and some other conditions are met. In this case, parallel imports cannot be prevented. However, if the manufacturer uses different trademarks for the same product in different countries, and if this does not artificially partition markets (for example, raise prices) the importer can be prevented from selling the product: the manufacturer can maintain his industrial property rights in each of the countries in which he markets the product.

In the Centrafarm versus Winthrop case (1974), the European Court treated trademark rights and patent rights in the same way. In the Centrafarm versus Parke-Davis case (1968), the owner of two patents for the manufacture of chloramphenicol accused Centrafarm and two other companies of manufacturing and selling the product at a lower price than the patent owner. This case was developed around articles 85 and 86 (concerning competition) of the Treaty and the European Court found that Centrafarm were guilty of infringing the Dutch Parke-Davis patents.

The Court has not ruled concerning whether products marketed in a country with no patents could freely circulate in the Community. However, in the Sterling Drug versus Centrafarm case it has accepted the doctrine of exhaustion of rights of industrial ownership resulting from first entry into circulation (that is, first point of sale). This conclusion was also given in the Centrafarm versus Winthrop case. Thus, the patent is seen as a reward for the inventor's creative effort but the patent right can be used for the first circulation of the product only, otherwise it contravenes articles 35 and 36 (free movement) of the EEC Treaty. Thus, Centrafarm was able to import and sell the Negram it has purchased in Britain in spite of the existence in the Netherlands of a patent and a trademark belonging respectively to Sterling Drug and its subsidiary Winthrop B.V.

The final obstacle which can inhibit the parallel importer is marketing authorization, issued when safety and efficacy procedures have been met. The directives 65/65, 75/318 and 75/319 were one step on the path to removing barriers to trade arising from marketing authorizations and further steps along this path will be taken in the next few years. However, the European Court of Justice in the Centrafarm–Hoffman La Roche case (1976) intervened in this area.

The particulars of the case were that Roche sold Valium in the Netherlands through one of its Swiss owned subsidiaries. In 1973 Centrafarm bought from an English source at a lower price and in packs of 500 doses. This material was repacked in the Netherlands under the name Centrafarm, and sold under the generic name Diazepam without the required authorization. Centrafarm admitted not having the necessary authorization but argued that Roche G.B. (the manufacturer) was the sole source of such documents and refused to give them up. The Court ruled that the refusal to provide a dossier was restrictive and that the Dutch legislation which required the dossier was illegal. The Court argued that the Dutch already had the dossier (from Roche), that this dossier covered Centrafarm's parallel imports, and thus these imports did not endanger public health (article 36 of the EEC Treaty).

Thus the only barriers to free circulation are marketing authorizations. The patent or trademark can be used to oppose free circulation of a product in the Community only if the product has been put into circulation:

(*a*) outside the Community,
(*b*) in a member state by an unauthorized third party,
(*c*) by a third party in a state where it is not patentable.

Centrafarm or whoever, can carry out parallel importing activities freely provided it observes these provisions.

The Commission and the Court have actively and successfully applied the competitive spirit of the Treaty in the area of parallel imports. This application has been caused in no small part by the vigorous activity of Centrafarm, a distributing company which has challenged the large producing companies successfully and contributed to the equalization of the prices of pharmaceutical products in the EEC.

Dominant Position

The rules on competition are set out in articles 85 to 90 of the Rome Treaty (see the appendix). It is article 86 which is of particular relevance in the definition of a dominant monopoly position; the associated problem with this definition is whether a firm uses such a position to 'distort competition'. The legal niceties involved in defining these terms have resulted in protracted litigation.

One course of litigation is caused by the ambiguity of the terms 'market' and 'product'. Take ampicillin, a broad spectrum antibiotic. Does the market consist of all broad spectrum antibiotics, or does it consist of all anti-bacterials, including another widely used substance like tetracycline? Or is the relevant market, the market for bananas, or the market for all fruit? If the former definition is used, United Brands can be seen to have a dominant position, but if the wider definition is used they do not. In the United Brands case (1978), the Court upheld the view of the Commission that the market was to be narrowly defined (in that case, for bananas).

More recently (1979) it was held that Hoffman La Roche had a dominant position in each of the seven markets in which it sold vitamins (A, B2, B3, B6, C, E, and H). The argument was that each of these products had specific metabolizing functions and were for this reason not interchangeable with one another and competing in separate markets (EEC, 1980a). Thus the legal position is that the existence of a market implies that there can be effective competition between the products which make it up. In other words, there is sufficient cross-substitutability for the same use between the products in the market. From the economic position it can be seen that these definitions, whilst sensible are not unambiguous: how much cross substitutability is 'sufficient', and what is 'effective' competition? Each case has to be treated on its merits in relation to legal precedents.

However the degrees of ambiguity in the EEC law are declining and where cases are detected by the under-staffed Commission, vigorous anti-trust activity is possible and likely. Hoffman La Roche (1979) were fined 300,000 EUA for abusing their dominant position in the vitamin markets: they gave preferential or exclusive supply agreements to all their industrial buyers in such a way that they obtained all their supplies from Roche. Whether this decision will reduce the large income acquired by Roche from (unpatented) vitamins only time will tell.

Like all anti-trust litigation cases those above appear to have had a demonstration effect. Many other restrictive marketing and production and agreements seem to have been abandoned, rather than, as required by the Treaty, registered with the Commission. It is possible that this effect is window dressing with restrictive agreements being driven underground into implicit and secretive forms. The capacity of the Commission to investigate such problems is limited due to its small size: it tends to react to publicized cases, or cases brought to its notice by individuals, firms, or the European Parliament. It is unfortunate that it does not have the capacity to investigate more fully the problems of dominant position and its abuse.

Transport Policy: Civil Aviation

Directorate-General VII is responsible for the application of article 70, concerned with transport, of the Rome Treaty. However to illustrate some of the problems of creating a common transport policy, this section will be concerned only with the civil aviation market, in particular air passenger transportation.

The air passenger transport market is cartelized and regulated to meet the policy objectives, usually ill defined, of governments. One objective is to 'show the flag', an attribute of foreign policy which should perhaps be financed by the Foreign Office. Another objective is related to the balance of payments, generating export revenue, although in times of loss making this may result in redistribution to foreigners. A third objective is to provide a market for domestically produced (and sometimes relatively inefficient) aircraft: a form of subsidy to the aircraft production industry which a Department of Industry might finance. Objectives such as these are rarely debated but clearly exist to prevent the managers of the companies being concerned solely with breaking even or making a designated (nationalized industry) rate of return.

Regulation, Property Rights and Competition

Since 1946 the international scheduled passenger market has been regulated by bilateral agreements (international treaties) between countries in which property rights in air space were exchanged under carefully regulated conditions (Cooper and Maynard, 1971 and 1972). Air fares are regulated by a producers' cartel, the International Air Transport Association (IATA), which meets secretly, fixes European fares by unanimous votes, and has its decisions sanctioned by the governments of the member states of the Community. Governmental protectionism is extensive, not least because many national airlines (such as British Airways) are state-owned and the public policy makers are not indifferent to the demands of pressure groups which may affect that political survival.

Until recently the behaviour of the Commission with regard to air transport has been relatively muted. However in 1979 the Commission published a memorandum in which it analysed the complexity of the market place and some policy options. In an attempt to precipitate a debate on policy systems the Commission pointed out that under the Treaty it could act on three different legal bases (EEC, 1979a):

(*a*) that based on article 70 of the Treaty (on transport),
(*b*) that based on article 100 and 235 which give general power of action,
(*c*) that based on specific chapters of the Treaty (e.g. competition and right of establishment).

Access to routes is dependent on licences issued by national authorities. Thus for a carrier (such as Laker Airways) to acquire access to a UK–France route it must get licences from the British Civil Aviation Authority and its French counterpart. Without such licences the carrier has no landing rights at home or abroad and can be prevented from entering the air space of another country. Thus the property right is exclusive and illiberally allocated.

Many international EEC routes are duopolies (i.e. there are two nominated carriers (one from each country) on the route) and these producers co-operate closely in fixing prices, schedules and most of the characteristics of the commodity. Furthermore, they share revenues and within revenue sharing agreements may have little incentive to compete for traffic. The duopolists have no incentive to differentiate their products to any great extent, they are practically identical in principle and in practice differ little (Cooper and Maynard, 1971).

Policy alternations are difficult to implement. The greater the degree of competition on a route, the lower the prices (Cooper and Maynard, 1972). However lower prices affect revenue yields and profits and some national governments are unwilling to see competition if it affects the financial results of their state airlines. Profitability depends on costs (the most inflationary item of which is fuel) and revenues with the latter highly dependent on load factors. The competition on the North Atlantic in the face of escalating fuel costs has required carriers to achieve (or fail to achieve in fact) higher and higher load factors because price increases were ruled out in 1980 by the competition: supply expanded, rapidly, in the face of demand severely affected by the economic depression. Competition in Europe could have similar outcomes with inefficient carriers being driven out of business or acquiring increased subsidies from governments.

Deregulation

It seems that the problems of deregulation is one of 'when' and 'how', rather than 'if'. The Commission has adopted a policy of trying to increase competition between airlines. However the process of applying articles 85 and 86 to this industry are quite substantial. At present these articles do not give the Commission the power to apply competition policy to airlines, as they do not cover air transport. The Commission, using article 87 which permits extensions in their fields of activity, has drafted extensions to articles 85 and 86 to air transport. If and when adopted this draft will permit the application of the rules of competition to air transport. Such an extension of competition policy seems logical as article 90 prohibits public undertakings from behaving contrary to the rules in the Treaty 'in particular those rules provided for in article 7 and articles 85 to 94'.

The Commission's intention seems clear but the path to its fulfilment is likely to be obstructed at many points. It is unlikely that all member governments will suddenly change their policies and permit greater freedom to their airspace for competing carriers. Furthermore liberalization may be inhibited by air traffic control practices which, for instance, give France a powerful position. The French, by prohibiting over-flying, could prevent, for instance, UK–Italy prices being reduced.

The unit costs of EEC carriers generally seem to be higher than some of their foreign rivals. Competition can give an impetus to the control of cost and its minimization (Davies, 1971 and 1977). Competition could offer a more differentiated product with lower quality – convenience travel being associated with lower prices as has happened on the North Atlantic (Cooper and Maynard, 1971). Inevitably greater competition will drive marginal firms out of business and will lead to the withdrawal of carriers from uneconomic routes: these effects of de-regulation have been seen in the USA following the Carter liberalization of Federal air routes. Competition, like any other policy, had costs and benefits. At present the regulation of the EEC air transport market offers protection to inefficient and efficient carriers, offers few incentives for cost minimization and product differentiation, and offers the passenger a limited choice at a high price compared to the USA.

The liberalization of air transport on the North Atlantic required a political decision, by President Carter, even though the economic case had been demonstrated to be sound many years earlier. Similarly, the de-regulation of EEC air routes requires political action, by the ten member states. The self-interest of these states and their airlines will make the process of de-regulation difficult and possibly protracted unless any two or three countries act independently, liberalize prices and schedules, and make the maintenance of the existing cartel impossible.

Conclusion

It is not easy to summarize the preceding analysis of disparate economic problems in disparate markets. The common themes linking these disparities are the policy objective of a competitive common market in goods, and the self interest of national regulators and the regulated in inhibiting the achievement of this goal.

Despite the desire of the Commission to harmonize the regulation of the safety and efficacy of medicines, the logical policy of a supranational body is unlikely to be adopted. The regulatory activity of the Commission, in particular the 1975 directives, have been ignored by the industry and the European regulators have had little impact on the national processes by which the safety and efficacy of pharmaceutical commodities is regulated.

EEC policies on the regulation of the prices of pharmaceutical products are ambiguous. On the one hand the Commission claims it is not concerned with the harmonization of price regulation systems within the EEC. However indirectly the Commission cannot avoid the problems of price regulation. Patents create high prices to generate profits, *inter alia*, to fuel the R and D process, monopsonistic (state) influences affect prices differently and national price regulation schemes may be in contravention of article 30. The influence of government in this market is extensive and unlikely to prevent EEC involvement in the processes by which national and EEC prices are fixed.

The debate about product liability laws in the EEC has been protracted and inconclusive. Consumer interest groups have sought to make producers fully liable for the effects of their products. Producers have sought to avoid full liability because of its possible effects on costs, R and D and innovatory behaviour. In time an agreed position on the trade-off between risks and benefits, and liability for the former will be evolved. Perhaps part of that liability should be borne by insurance, public or private, rather than by consumers and producers alone. The consumption of all drugs (which are poisons of one sort or another) is inherently risky and the property rights in liability for adverse side effects needs clear definition. Inevitably the definitions of such rights affects the economic position, for better or worse, of the producer. The member states of the EEC protect the pharmaceutical industry because, *inter alia*, it produces valuable export revenues and it produces, encouraged by patent protection, new clinical entities with valuable therapeutic properties. However these states also regulate the industry to ensure the production of safe and efficacious medicines, whose price is not 'excessive', and whose producers do not compete in a monopolistic manner.

The interests of the member states are mutually incompatible. For instance price regulation in the UK (the pharmaceutical prices regulation scheme – PPRS) sets prices in relation to an 'adequate' rate of return (defined by the Department of Health). Maximizing prices may be possible because of patent protection and would maximize export revenues, but this may be in violation of the PPRS. Alternatively drug economy in the NHS would reduce the sales, profits and rate of return of the drug companies, and permit, via PPRS, the raising of prices to restore rates of return. Safety and efficacy legislation raises the costs of marketing a drug, reduces the effective patent life of the commodity, reduces the rate of return to R and D, and possibly the quantity and quality of innovation. Perhaps because of the safety and efficacy legislation it is best to be second, copying (with suitable variations to give patent protection) the innovators and avoiding their mistakes.

Competition policy can clearly affect these elements of the

pharmaceutical market. The marketing activities of Centrafarm have led to some liberalization of the conditions under which parallel importing takes place. The clearer definition of 'dominant position' and the use of articles 85 and 86 of the Rome Treaty to affect the prices and profits of pharmaceutical companies may be appealing *prima facie* but, given the nature of Government regulation, may lead to adjustments in other government policies (in, for example, PPRS) which negate these effects. Competition policy pursued in isolation of the other aspects of regulation, in particular isolation of the objectives of the member states, may attract public attention but may have minimal economic effects: all markets have general not partial equilibrium characteristics.

Like the pharmaceutical industry, the civil aviation industry is highly regulated by the state and, unlike the drug industry, many of the producers are state-owned companies. The limiting factor on competition is the restricted access to air space. These property rights are limited by international agreements and their liberalization is dependent on political decision making rather than the economic logic of competitive markets.

One aspect of these policies which is pre-eminent is that the policy problems are rarely analysed as a whole and the motivations of the regulated and regulators is examined incompletely. Greater competition in the market for pharmaceuticals might follow from the abolition of patent protection which gives firms monopoly rights and may not ensure an efficient flow of R and D (Arrow (1962) and Demsetz (1969) have debated the merits of the theoretical alternatives). Greater competition in the civil aviation market might result from a decision to offer freedom of the air – in other words access to EEC routes for any carrier provided it meets safety criteria. However such policies are unlikely to be advocated by the regulators or regulated. Stigler (1971) has argued that regulation is designed and executed to favour (i.e. protect) the regulated. Whilst some subsequent writers (such as Peltzman (1976)) have argued that the regulated pursue selfish and altruistic motives, the consensus remains that government regulation can be used to protect industrial interests and inhibit the workings of the market mechanism. Politicians are interested in maintaining their political power and they are unlikely to implement policies which damage the interests of powerful industrial groups on whom their power is dependent. Those seeking to reform imperfect markets are required to demonstrate the economic benefits of their proposals in the light of these political realities. Policy reformers must analyse the effects of their proposals in the economic and the political market places.

The rules of the Treaty of Rome with regard to industrial matters, competition policy, and transport policy are clear in their general intent: the creation of free and competitive trade within the EEC. However the path towards this goal is full of obstacles created by the self-interest of consumer, producer and government interest groups. The Commission's piecemeal approach is limited by the Treaty of Rome (e.g. it does not cover civil aviation matters) and all their best endeavours in the limit can be productive only if there is a political commitment to competition within the EEC. The behaviour of groups such as the pharmaceutical industry, airlines and governments in relation to the Commission and the European Parliament indicates that this commitment is not strong in the EEC: capitalists inevitably collude to protect their interests and destroy the market mechanism. Or as Adam Smith argued over two hundred years ago:

> People of the same trade seldom meet together, even for merriment and diversion, but the conversation ends in a conspiracy against the public, or in some contrivances to raise prices.
>
> Adam Smith, *The Wealth of Nations*, Bk. I, Chap. 10, p. 117.

It also has to be accepted that policy changes involve both gainers and losers. Community social policy is an obvious mechanism for compensating potential losers from change.

Appendix

Text of Relevant Articles of the Treaty of Rome

ARTICLE 30

Quantitative restrictions on imports and all measures having equivalent effect shall, without prejudice to the following provisions, be prohibited between Member States.

ARTICLE 34

1. Quantitative restrictions on exports, and all measures having equivalent effect, shall be prohibited between Member States.

2. Member States shall, by the end of the first stage at the latest, abolish all quantitative restrictions on exports and any measures having equivalent effect which are in existence when this Treaty enters into force.

ARTICLE 35

The Member States declare their readiness to abolish quantitative restrictions on imports from and exports to other Member States more rapidly than is provided for in the preceding Articles, if their general economic situation and the situation of the economic sector concerned so permit.

To this end, the Commission shall make recommendations to the States concerned.

ARTICLE 36

The provisions of Articles 30 to 34 shall not preclude prohibitions or restrictions on imports, exports or goods in transit justified on grounds of public morality, public policy or public security; the protection of health and life of humans, animals or plants; the protection of national treasures possessing artistic, historic or archaeological value; or the protection of industrial and commercial property. Such prohibitions or restrictions shall not, however, constitute a means of arbitrary discrimination or a disguised restriction on trade between Member States.

ARTICLE 70

1. The Commission shall propose to the Council measures for the progressive coordination of the exchange policies of Member States in respect of the movement of capital between those States and third countries. For this purpose the Council shall issue directives, acting unanimously. It shall endeavour to attain the highest possible degree of liberalisation.

2. Where the measures taken in accordance with paragraph 1 do not permit the elimination of differences between the exchange rules of Member States and where such differences could lead persons resident in one of the Member States to use the freer transfer facilities within the Community which are provided for in Article 67 in order to evade the rules of one of the Member States concerning the movement of capital to or from third countries, that State may, after consulting the other Member States and the Commission, take appropriate measures to overcome these difficulties.

Should the Council find that these measures are restricting the free movement of capital within the Community to a greater extent than is required for the purpose of overcoming the difficulties, it may, acting by a qualified majority on a proposal from the Commission, decide that the State concerned shall amend or abolish these measures.

ARTICLE 85

1. The following shall be prohibited as incompatible with the common market: all agreements between undertakings, decision by associations of undertakings and concerted practices which may affect trade between Member States and which have as their objective or effect the prevention, restriction or distortion of competition within the common market, and in particular those which:

(*a*) directly or indirectly fix purchase or selling prices or any other trading conditions;
(*b*) limit or control production, markets, technical development, or investment;
(*c*) share markets or sources of supply;
(*d*) apply dissimilar conditions to equivalent transactions with other trading parties, thereby placing them at a competitive disadvantage;
(*e*) make the conclusion of contracts subject to acceptance by the other parties of supplementary obligations which, by their nature or according to commercial usage, have no connection with the subject of such contracts.

2, Any agreements or decisions prohibited pursuant to this Article shall be automatically void.

3. The provisions of paragraph 1 may, however, be declared inapplicable in the case of:

– any agreement or category of agreements between undertakings;
– any decision or category of decisions by associations of undertakings;
– any concerned practice or category of concerted practices;

which contributes to improving the production or distribution of goods or to promoting technical or economic progress, while allowing consumers a fair share of the resulting benefit, and which does not:

(*a*) impose on the undertakings concerned restrictions which are not indispensable to the attainment of these objectives;
(*b*) afford such undertakings the possibility of eliminating competition in respect of a substantial part of the products in question.

ARTICLE 86

Any abuse by one or more undertakings of a dominant position within the common market or in a substantial part of it shall be prohibited as incompatible with the common market in so far as it may affect trade between Member States.

Such abuse may, in particular, consist in:

(*a*) directly or indirectly imposing unfair purchase or selling prices or other unfair trading conditions;
(*b*) limiting production, markets or technical development to the prejudice of consumers;
(*c*) applying dissimilar conditions to equivalent transactions with other trading parties, thereby placing them at a competitive disadvantage;
(*d*) making the conclusion of contracts subject to acceptance by the other parties of supplementary obligations which, by their nature or according to commercial usage, have no connection with the subject of such contracts.

ARTICLE 90

1. In the case of public undertakings and undertakings to which Member States grant special or exclusive rights, Member States shall neither enact nor maintain in force any measure contrary to the rules contained in this Treaty, in particular to those rules provided for in Article 7 and Articles 85 to 94.

2. Undertakings entrusted with the operation of services of general economic interest or having the character of a revenue-producing monopoly shall be subject to the rules contained in this Treaty, in particular to the rules on competition, in so far as the application of such rules does not obstruct the performance, in law or in fact, of the particular tasks assigned to them. The development of trade must not be affected to such an extent as would be contrary to the interest of the Community.

ARTICLE 100

The Council shall, acting unanimously on a proposal from the Commission, issue directives for the approximation of such provisions laid down by law, regulation or administrative action in Member States as directly affect the establishment or functioning of the common market.

The Assembly and the Economic and Social Committee shall be consulted in the case of directives whose implementation would, in one or more Member States, involve the amendment of legislation.

ARTICLE 235

If action by the Community should prove necessary to attain, in the course of the operation of the common market, one of the objectives of the Community and this Treaty has not provided the necessary powers, the Council shall, acting unanimously on a proposal from the Commission and after consulting the Assembly, take the appropriate measures.

CHAPTER 12

Social Policy in the European Community

> Member States agree upon the need to promote improved working conditions and an improved standard of living for workers, so as to make possible their harmonisation while the improvement is being maintained. They believe that such a development will ensue not only from the functioning of the common market, which will favour the harmonisation of social systems, but also from the procedures provided for in this Treaty, and from the approximation of provisions laid down by law, regulation or administrative action.
>
> (Article 117, Treaty of Rome, p. 271)

The relative lack of progress, both in terms of thought and action, in the process of harmonizing the social security systems of the European Community is noticeable and perhaps not surprising given the complexities of the ten country systems. This chapter presents a radical view of social policy harmonization in the EEC. The first section discusses the nature of EEC social policy since 1958, and indicates its potentially significant impact on resource allocation. The finance and provision aspects of the two most expensive items of social policy budgets, health care and social security, are analysed in the second and third sections. A concluding section argues that the interpretation of the Treaty has been affected by conservative (and perhaps inevitable) political sensitivities, rather than by economic logic.

Social Policy and the Treaty of Rome: What is Social Policy?

Social policy has been defined as that work that is carried out by Directorate-General (DG) V (employment and social affairs) of the European Commission (Shanks, 1977). This directorate-general has wide terms of reference and its directorates cover general social policy guidelines, employment and vocational training, the European Social Fund, working conditions and the migrant worker, and health and safety (see Vacher (1980), p. 20).

Article 118 of the Treaty of Rome offers an alternative definition of social policy:

> Without prejudice to the other objectives of the Treaty and in conformity with its general objectives, the Commission shall have the task of promoting close cooperation between Member States in the social field, particularly in matters relating to:
>
> – employment;
> – labour law and working conditions;
> – basic and advanced vocational training;
> – social security;
> – prevention of occupational accidents and diseases;
> – occupational hygiene;
> – the right of association, and collective bargaining between employers and workers.

As in most matters (see Chapter 11 on competition policy), the interests of the directorate-generals may overlap but it seems from what the Directorate-General V does and from the Treaty of Rome, that social policy covers most aspects of the workings of the labour market, i.e. the terms and conditions of employment in its broadest aspects. However since 1958, the actions of the institutions of the EEC have been on a much narrower front. The core of social policy in this period has been concerned with work and employment, as reflected by the organization of Directorate-General V. The problems of health and social security (social protection) have been dealt with in 'a piecemeal and pragmatic' manner (Shanks, 1977), whilst the housing and education markets have been regarded as marginal and the domains of national governments.

The Interaction of Social and Economic Policy

This restricted domain of activity is perhaps surprising given the objectives of the Rome Treaty and the extent to which such social policies influence the attainment of these objectives. One interpretation of article 117 of the Treaty is that the creation of a common market will lead to the harmonization of social policies. Elsewhere the Treaty empowers the Commission to harmonize provisions laid down by the laws of member states which distort the pattern of competition within the EEC: hence the Commission can remove factors, including social policies, which prevent or distort the pattern of economic integration (article 101). It is possible that social policy harmonization is a necessary condition for the attainment of a common market in goods and services. The authors of articles 101 and 117 may be seen as arguing that the creation of a common market will lead to the harmonization of social policies, and social policies must be harmonized if a common economic market is to be created. There seems to be a hen–egg problem with this line of argument: which comes first?

The implicit thrust of article 117 and policy making in the Commission and elsewhere seems to be that the creation of a common market will lead to a harmonization of social policy. Instead the converse argument will be presented: that the process of harmonizing social policy must be much more vigorous and extensive if the goal of a common market is to be attained. Furthermore failure to formulate new initiatives in social policy harmonization may militate strongly against the creation of a common market.

The Growth of Social Policy

Since the formation of the EEC, policies concerning social security, income maintenance and the provision of health care, have grown rapidly. The coverage of state social security programmes has increased, the real value of the benefits of these programmes has risen generally, and the size of client (beneficiary) groups has grown, particularly the number of elderly and the disabled. The rapid expansion of social security expenditure has been paralleled by an escalation in social security taxation, particularly in those countries relying on this form of 'ear-marked' taxation.

Such programmes of social security redistribute income and resources from the healthy to the sick, and from tax payers in the labour force to beneficiaries outside the labour force (that is, it involves intergenerational transfers of resources). The magnitude of these transfers is not inconsiderable. Table 12.1 shows that in 1980 the projected social security expenditure level in relation to GDP over the Community as a whole was 25 per cent. The growth and national differences in these burdens can be seen from the table, with the United Kingdom and Ireland having the lowest percentages and Luxembourg and the Netherlands the highest. With static or low growing economies the burden of these expenditures can be seen to be very high.

The 'split' of social security contributions between different countries varies considerably. The contributions of employers and employees is lowest in Denmark (and hence general tax finance of social security is highest there). The UK and Ireland also use tax finance to a substantial degree. Countries such as France, Belgium

TABLE 12.1
Social Security as a Percentage of GDP

	1970	*1978*	*1980*
Belgium	18.5	26.7	25.5
Denmark	19.5	25.6	24.7
Germany	21.4	27.5	26.7
France	19.2	24.9	25.5
Ireland	13.2	–	18.1
Italy	18.8	23.6	24.5
Luxembourg	16.6	26.0	30.5
Netherlands	20.8	29.9	31.0
United Kingdom	16.3	20.1	20.6
Community as a whole	(18.2)	(25.5)	(25.0)

Source: Quoted in Euzeby (1980), p. 383.
Note: Statistics for 1970 and 1978, projections for 1980. The bracketed (Community) figures are means.

and Italy on the other hand are highly dependent on social security taxes (contributions) rather than general taxation to finance benefits.

The way in which social security finance affects total labour costs is illustrated in Table 12.2 (data for 1975). In Belgium, France and Italy they represent over 20 per cent of total labour costs. On the other hand in Denmark, Ireland and the United Kingdom such costs are relatively small.

TABLE 12.2
Social Security Costs as a Percentage of Total Labour Costs

	Manual	*White collar*	*Manual and white collar*
Belgium	23.6	19.3	22.6
Denmark	3.9	7.0	3.5
Germany	18.8	15.8	17.6
France	26.4	22.0	24.4
Ireland	10.0	11.8	10.4
Italy	29.2	25.3	28.2
Luxembourg	14.6	12.7	14.0
Netherlands	–	–	23.2
United Kingdom	11.0	14.2	11.7

Source: Euzeby (1980), p. 38; Eurostat (1977).
Note: (i) The figures in the first two columns relate to firms with 50 or more employees. The figures in the final column refer to all firms with 10 or more employees.
(ii) All industries, 1975.

The Allocative Effects of Social Security Finance

Whilst figures such as those shown in Tables 12.1 and 12.2 provide information about the macroeconomic characteristics of social security, they give little direct insight into the microeconomic effects on resource allocation. Unfortunately the state of the art is such that whilst the relevant microeconomic questions can be posed, the empirical data available to answer them are inadequate.

Social security contributions may raise the marginal cost of labour and do so differentially across the member states of the EEC. Partial equilibrium analysis would lead us to predict that a change in the price of labour would, *ceteris paribus*, induce capital migration and capital substitution. The extent of both migration and substitution would depend upon the incidence of social security contributions, and the elasticity of demand for labour.

In a competitive economy, a general tax on labour income applicable to wages in all industries, is likely to be borne by the wage earner. The worker cannot escape the tax by moving to non-taxed activities, he can only reduce his work effort but this is unlikely to be a significant factor if the aggregate labour supply is of an inelastic nature. Furthermore the split, between employers and employees, of the payroll taxes which finance social security is likely to be irrelevant in a competitive economy. If, where W = wage rate and N = man hours of employment, the demand and supply of labour are as in equations (1) and (2),

$$\text{demand for labour,}\quad W = x_1 - x_2N, \tag{1}$$

$$\text{supply of labour,}\quad W = x_3 + x_4N \tag{2}$$

The equilibrium employment level is:

$$x_1 - x_2N = x_3 + x_4N \tag{3}$$

If a tax of 50 per cent (0.5) is imposed on employers, equation (1) becomes:

$$\text{post tax demand for labour,}\quad W = 0.5\,(x_1 - x_2N, \tag{4}$$

and the new equilibrium is

$$0.5\,(x_1 - x_2N) = x_3 + x_4N. \tag{5}$$

If the tax (of 0.5) is imposed on employees, equation (2) becomes:

$$\text{post-tax supply of labour, } W = \frac{x_3 + x_4 N}{0.5}, \qquad (6)$$

and the new equilibrium is

$$x_1 - x_2 N = \frac{x_3 + x_4 N}{0.5}. \qquad (7)$$

As (5) and (7) are identical, the conclusion is that in a competitive labour market, wherever the payroll is levied (either on employers or employees), the net wage of labour declines as does employment. A graphical representation is shown in Figure 12.1.

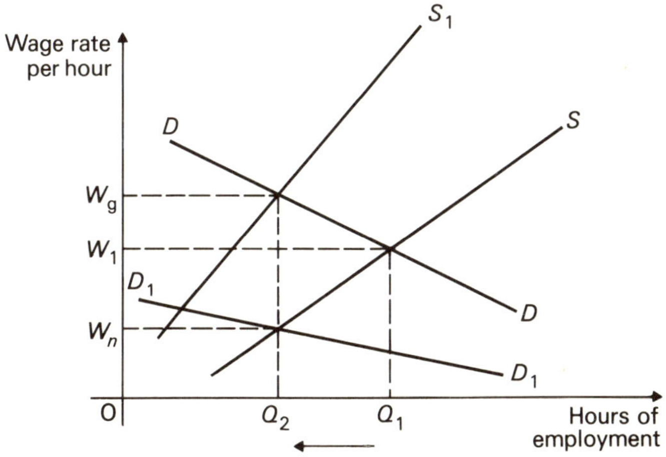

Figure 12.1 The Incidence of Payroll Taxation in a Competitive Market

After the levying of the tax, the firms pay the same gross wage rates reflected in *DD* but deduct the tax to arrive at the net wage. The net demand for labour curve is thus $D_1 D_1$ ($W_n = 0.5\,W_g$). If the tax is levied on employees, the new supply curve in $S_1 S_1$ is $1/1 - 0.5$ or twice as big as the original gross wage. Thus the level of employment falls to OQ_2 on whichever side of the market the tax is levied, the gross wage rises to W_g, and the net (of tax) wage falls to W_n.

Most labour markets are not competitive and exhibit considerable imperfections. These imperfections may permit the shifting of the incidence of the payroll tax from labour to capital. Trade-union (monopoly) power may be such that reductions in net wages may be avoided and the taxes financed by employers either out of profits (i.e. a reduced rate of return to capital or reduced returns to monopoly power) or higher prices to the consumers. The exact nature of the incidence of payroll taxes between the workers, the capitalists, or the consumers is a subject of dispute.

One study concluded that labour bears the burden of a payroll tax: it is not shifted onto capitalists (Brittain, 1971 and 1972). However there are estimation problems, and other studies, using different techniques and a US data set have concluded that labour does not bear the full burden of the employers' component of the payroll tax; the burden is only partially shifted onto labour in the short run (Leuthold, 1975).

These conflicting conclusions are not helpful in determining the allocative effects of the payroll tax. If the burden of the tax is on labour, the effects of increasing rates of taxation will be on the net wage of labour and levels of employment: reduced real wages may reduce labour supply. If the burden of the tax is on the producer, he can either finance the tax out of reduced profits, in which case the supply of investment resources is less and the demand for them is reduced as their rate of return declines, or he can shift the tax onto consumers, via price increases, in which case the burden of the tax is distributed across society in relation to the consumption of taxed goods and services.

The alternative incidence outcomes may have important consequences for relative international competitiveness and the allocation of resources within the EEC. If the incidence of all payroll taxes is on labour, then the relative international competitiveness of firms within the Community may not be affected: the taxes may not affect directly their prices or profits, they may affect labour supply only. If the incidence of the tax is on the employers, prices and profits may be affected, differentially across national boundaries in relation to the quantity of these taxes. Evidence from the reactions of capitalists in France, Netherlands and Germany to payroll taxes suggests that employers believe the latter incidence effect is the predominant one (Euzeby, 1980).

A Case Against Payroll Taxes?

If the incidence of the payroll taxes used to finance social security is on capital there will be effects on the capital–labour mix and the investment process. If the incidence of these taxes is on labour there will be effects on the supply of labour, which may differ in the short and long runs. Furthermore these labour supply effects will be supplemented by the fact that some of the welfare benefits they finance affect the relative price of leisure and may lead to further reductions in labour supply, this time amongst the welfare beneficiaries.

More information is required about the incidence of these taxes and their effects on the allocation of resources. If the incidence varies across the labour markets of the EEC there may be differential effects on the rates of return to labour and capital, and their utilization. Furthermore since the use of such taxes varies across the EEC we might again predict differential effects on resource allocation. All these allocative conclusions require more empirical investigation. However it is evident that these possible allocative effects are also associated with distributional effects of a regressive nature. Because of the characteristics of most payroll tax systems, the richer pay relatively less than the poorer sections of the labour market. The case for the abolition of the payroll tax and its replacement by income taxes, or perhaps VAT which appear to be progressive in nature, seems to be substantial (Adams, 1980).

Conclusion

It has been argued in this section that social policy has been interpreted very narrowly, and perhaps unusually, in the first few decades of the EEC. Whilst the Rome Treaty in its coverage of social policy is partial, other clauses in the Treaty (article 101) permit EEC legislative action where national policies prevent the creation of a competitive and common market. The method of financing social security may have significant effects on the allocation of resources within the EEC and it is unfortunate that the social policy activities of the institutions of the EEC have tended to pay little attention to these effects.

Harmonizing Markets in Health Care: The Treaty of Rome and Health Care

The burden of social security contributions is such that they may influence investment patterns between member countries of the EEC and one of the main services financed by such contributions in some member states is health care. The health care industry is organized in such a way that it leads to serious resource misallocation in all member countries despite the fact that the health care systems of the ten nations differ considerably. To ignore this resource misallocation, induced in part by monopoly power (created by national governments) and in part by misguided government intervention, ensures inefficient use of scarce resources. It also demonstrates illogical unwillingness to apply articles 85 to 90 of the Rome Treaty (the rules on competition) to undertakings, particularly professional associations, whose activities prevent the creation of a competitive market in health care. It is paradoxical that the Commission has initiated legislative changes creating a common market for doctors, but failed to perceive that this policy has had little effect on the inefficiency of resource allocation. The thrust of the articles in Chapters 2 and particularly 3 of the Rome Treaty and their subsequent interpretation has been misconceived at worst, and seriously incomplete at best.

The Nature of Market Failure in Health Care

The social insurance and national health service systems of health care organization have much in common. In particular membership of both schemes can lead to the removal of the price barrier to consumption. Thus, in Figure 12.2, the marginal benefit of health care curve (MB_{HC}) intersects the marginal cost curve (assumed for simplicity to be derived from an industry operating under constant returns to scale) and, without insurance or a NHS, the quantity demanded in a competitive health care market would be Q_M. The introduction of a NHS removes the price barrier to consumption, the price to the patient is zero, and Q_{NHS} would be demanded. Whether this quantity will be supplied will depend on the state which funds the services.

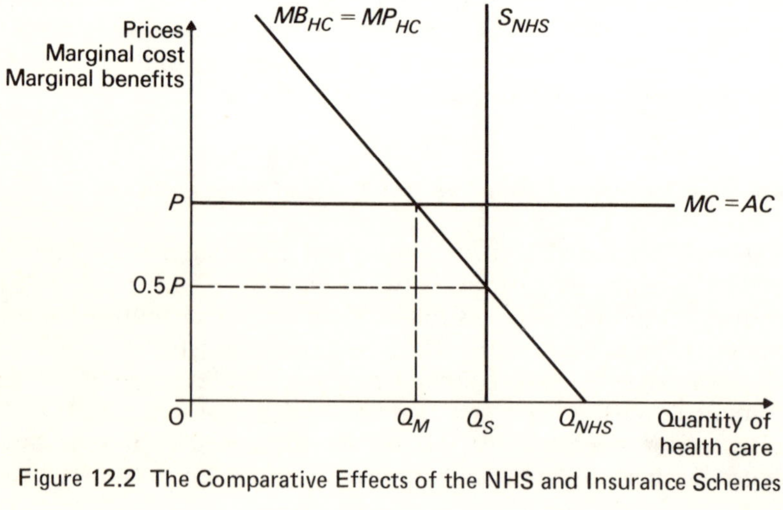

Figure 12.2 The Comparative Effects of the NHS and Insurance Schemes

All demands for health care cannot be met as they are infinite and resources are scarce. So the state may provide, as a result of political decision making, only Q_S. In which case demand (Q_{NHS}) exceeds supply and non-price rationing (according to age, health status, martial status etc.) by doctors ensures that the market is cleared so demand equals supply.

Once the individual is a member of a social insurance sickness fund, we assume for convenience that the income effects of contribution premiums is small and does not affect the shape and location of MB_{HC}, the price barrier to consumption is removed (as it is in a NHS). The individual will demand Q_{NHS} if the price is zero. However the sickness funds may be unwilling to finance the cost of supplying this quantity of care and, if so, will reduce demand by using prices. The usual price-rationing device is coinsurance, whereby the patient pays some percentage of the cost of his care. With a coinsurance term of 50 per cent, the supply-demand outcomes in Figure 12.2 are identical for a NHS and the sickness funds, although different demands will be met in each system because of the use of different rationing devices (prices and doctors' criteria) in the two systems.

This analysis assumes that the demander of health care is the patient. Whilst the initial decision to consume health care might be the patient's, once he presents himself to the system the crucial decision-making agent may be the doctor. The patient, because of uncertainty about the diagnosis and treatment of his condition, may delegate decision making to an expert agent, the doctor. The doctor may or may not use this delegated power in a way which ensures the efficient use of scarce resources. He may seek to evaluate the marginal productivity of health care (MP_{HC}), in which case, in Figure 12.2, the demand curve may now be the doctor's estimate of health care productivity at the margin. Ideally to achieve an efficient outcome, costs and benefits (productivity) at the margin should be equated and Q_M of care provided. However in NHS and insurance markets, the doctor does not bear the costs of care. He faces no cost barrier, costs are financed by the insurer or the State, and he may provide cure until its marginal product is zero (Q_{NHS}). Thus a fundamental problem in all health care markets, both private and public, is that the doctor decision taker has no incentive to evaluate and trade off the costs and benefits at the margin of his behaviour. The existing incentives of the health care market may encourage him to maximize benefits (Q_{NHS}), regardless of cost (see Chapter 11).

The power delegated to the doctor by the patient may lead to further inefficiency because it enables the doctor to generate demand for his own, and related health care, services. The doctor is the main supply side agent and the agency relationship makes him, perhaps, the main demand side agent. The hypothesis of a physician induced demand has been tested only in a limited manner but the available evidence suggests that doctors can shift demand curves for health care. For example, one study found that a 10 per cent increase in the supply of surgeons, *ceteris paribus*, leads to a 3 per cent increase in the demand for surgical activities (Fuchs, 1978). As a result increased supplies of doctors generate increased demand for care and the financial consequences of this may explain part of the rapid escalation in EEC health care budgets.

Inefficiency in Health Care Resource Allocation

These predictions of inefficient outcome can be supplemented by two other elements in the health care market matrix. Firstly a macro observation of limited association between increased inputs and increased outputs, and secondly the micro problem of evaluation.

Table 12.3 contains some macro health data showing that at this level the relationships between inputs (such as finance, doctors) and outcomes (as measured by mortality data) are unclear. For instance the data show a general trend for countries with high per capita expenditure to have a relatively low perinatal mortality rate, although Japan and the USA seem to differ. Also it seems that a high ratio of doctors to patients is associated with a relatively high perinatal mortality rate but high nurse stock figures seem to be negatively associated with mortality (see Cochrane, St. Leger and Moore (1978) for an elaboration and failure to explain these macro relationships).

Such conclusions have to be treated with caution. The output data are mortality statistics and no group of such data can summarize the health status of a country adequately. Secondly if the data are graphed, the scatter of observations is considerable and makes conclusions difficult to draw (Royal Commission on the NHS (1979), p. 22–5). It seems that the relationship between inputs and outputs is best analysed at a micro level. Unfortunately, at the micro level, the stock of knowledge about the clinical and economic aspects of medical practice is very poor. The majority of medical therapies have not been evaluated either clinically (what effect do competing therapies have on health status?) or economically (which is the least costly therapy to achieve a given health outcome?), in a scientific manner. Thus, most of the therapies in use today are employed by doctors on grounds of faith rather than scientific evidence about efficacy (Cochrane, 1972).

TABLE 12.3
Health Service 'Input' and Mortality 'Output'*

Country	*Per capita total expenditure on health US$*	*% trend GDP†*	*Doctors (per 10,000 1974)*	*Nurses (per 10,000 1974)*	*Life expectancy at age 1*		*Perinatal mortality (per 1,000 live births)*	*Maternal mortality (per 100,000 births)*
					M	*F*		
France	352	6.9	13.9	23.7	69.5	77.1	18.8	24.0
Italy	191	6.0	19.9	7.8	70.0	76.0	29.6	42.4
Netherlands	312	7.3	14.9	22.5	71.2	76.9	16.4	10.3
W. Germany	336	6.7	19.4	27.6	68.6	74.9	23.2	45.9
England and Wales			13.1	33.7	69.5	75.6	21.3	13.0
Scotland	212	5.2	16.1	45.6	67.7	74.0	22.7	21.5
N. Ireland			15.3	36.6	67.0	73.6	25.9	17.1
Finland	265	5.8	13.3	46.0	66.8	75.5	17.1	10.6
Norway	270	5.6	16.5	46.4	71.4	77.7	16.8	3.3
Sweden	416	7.3	16.2	58.6	72.0	77.4	14.1	2.7
Australia	308	6.5	13.9	54.1	68.5	75.4	22.4	11.3
Canada	408	6.8	16.6	57.8	69.7	77.0	17.7	10.8
Japan	166	4.0	11.6	16.1	70.8	76.0	18.0	38.3
USA	491	7.4	16.5	40.4	68.0	75.6	24.8	15.2

Source: Royal Commission on the NHS (1979), p. 23.
* All data refer to 1974 or nearest date.
† Trend data are used to exclude the effects of cyclical fluctuations. Full details are given in OECD (1977), p. 23.

Distributional Issues

Governments have sometimes rationalized their intervention in the health care market on grounds of 'equity'. The health care policy makers of Western Europe articulated in various ways, the objectives, usually ill defined, of greater equality in the geographical distribution of health care facilities, and more equal access to health care between the social classes. These policies have been 'explained' by economists in terms of externality models. For example, charity and the interdependence of utility functions might explain collective action to provide greater equality in health care (see Lindsay (1969), and Culyer (1971)).

The positive or scientific approach to the explanation of the government's role contrasts with the explicitly normative (Donabedian, 1971). Donabedian differentiates between the competing ideologies, liberal and socialist, and argues that the latter inevitably leads to public finance and large scale government intervention in the health care market. On this basis it would be asserted that the dominant ideology in the health policy area is socialist and thus requires government action to reduce inequality.

The implication of these arguments for EEC health care policy is that because actual markets fail due to externalities, or the frustration of ideological goals, collective action is required. However national policies and EEC policies in this area has been demonstrably inefficient: Paris has 48 per cent more doctors per head of population, and Basse-Normandie 33 per cent less doctors, than the French average; in Germany Lower Saxony is badly endowed with doctors and Hamburg well endowed (84 and 163 per cent of the national average respectively). Similar inequalities exist throughout the EEC (Abel-Smith and Maynard, 1979), and there appears to be no compensating variations in other health care inputs. If the market failures or ideology indicate that financial capacity and provision should be equalized regionally, radical new policies are required.

Similar inequalities exist within the member states of the EEC with regard to social class differences in the consumption of health care and health status. In both France and Britain the social class 'gradient' in mortality and morbidity rates has survived the 'socialization' of health care. In France, the mortality rates for working-class males aged 55 and at age 75 have been increasing relative to those of the professional and upper classes. A similar trend is evident in Britain. In both France and England the reduction in infant mortality rates over the last 30 years has been relatively greater in the lower social classes but this is due to a relative improvement in the post neonatal rates (weeks 4 to 52 of life, see Maynard and Ludbrook (1981)).

The existence of geographical and social class inequalities cannot be denied: they remain in relative terms at least as great as they were 30 years ago in many areas. However the appropriate policies to remedy these inequalities, given there are areas in which national and EEC governments are concerned, are not clear. The marginal rates of return to investment in health care may be low. The major killers in the EEC are heart disease, cancer, road traffic and drink. The mitigation of the effects of these diseases requires policies such as better exercise, more sensible diets, less smoking, road traffic legislation, and less drinking. Investments in education may give greater returns in terms of improving the length and quality of life than spending more on health care; but the effects may come only in the long run. It is unfortunate that EEC social policy action has not investigated these possibilities more thoroughly and encouraged a more efficient allocation of the Community's scarce resources.

Overview

The conclusions of this brief analysis of the health care market are important. Firstly, since 1960 the quantity of expenditure on health care has increased rapidly in all countries of the EEC and elsewhere. By 1980 countries such as Germany and the United States were spending more than 10 per cent of GNP on health services. Secondly, despite this large increase in inputs, the evidence concerning associated increases in outputs is noticeable by its absence. At the macro level the data are confusing, and at the micro level there is an absence of evaluation data, both of a clinical and economic nature. The doctor is the primary decision maker in this market, particularly because of the agency relationship, but he is not an 'expert' (he has insufficient data about therapies to claim this role) and the incentives of the health care systems offer few inducements for him to strive after this role. Thirdly, collective action has failed to remedy the significant inequalities inherited by the 'socialized' health care systems of the EEC. It is likely that these inequalities will remain substantial until more resources are put into prevention, an area of activity where there is little support from any powerful professional group.

Governments have created and sustained professional power in the health care market (illness treatment rather than prevention) and their intervention, via social insurance and National Health Services, has led to the creation of an environment which ensures that resources are used inefficiently. Resources used in health care are not available for use elsewhere in activities whose outputs may be more highly valued. The abolition of price barriers, the lack of incentives to evaluate health care outcomes and minimize costs, the failure to rectify and analyse the causes of inequality, and the uncritical support of professional power has ensured that national governments and the EEC have used resources inefficiently and prevented the creation of a harmonized and competitive health care market within the Community.

Harmonizing Income Maintenance Policies: Some Problems

Although the national social security programmes differ in scope and detail, their characteristics are similar. Most countries use payroll taxes, or contributions to sickness funds, to finance benefits, and there is extensive allusion to the principle of insurance, although most schemes are financed on a pay-as-you-go basis. In other words, 'contribution' income in a year finances the benefits for that year; so that there is redistribution from the labour force to non-workers.

The effects of a payroll tax on the allocation of resources have been discussed earlier in this chapter. Little account was taken of the precise labour supply effects of this taxation or the efficacy of expenditure on these policies in relation to national or EEC goals. Increases in Social Security taxes affect workers' labour supply decisions because the relative price of leisure is reduced. Also these taxes finance benefits which affect the relative price of work/leisure for the poor. Furthermore, in relation to externality theory these tax-transfer arrangements may be ineffective in that they do not generate efficient redistribution (Hochman and Rodgers, 1969).

These issues seem to have created surprisingly little interest within the institutions of the EEC. Perhaps, even more surprisingly there has been little analysis of the efficiency of these programmes, whether they are successful in keeping people out of poverty. The activities of Directorate-General V have been insignificant in these areas and there is little evidence of an integrated approach, in relation to the objectives set out in the Rome Treaty.

The Efficiency of Income Maintenance Policies

Most national policies aimed at maintaining income in times of unemployment, sickness, old age, disablement and related states, have objectives which are generally badly set out. The approach here is to assume that the policy objective is to bring people up to some poverty line, expressed as a percentage of national average income. If two states have similar poverty lines but the efficiency of their social programmes differ, the labour supply decisions may differ in a particular country: it may be easier to recruit labour in that country which has the infficient poverty policy. Furthermore countries may have an incentive to have inefficient poverty policies as this may induce supplies of cheap labour, lower production costs, and competitive advantages in common product markets. If poverty policies are effective, low priced labour may not be available as unemployment may be more remunerative.

Do poverty policies vary in their efficiency across the common (EEC) market? Whilst the bureaucrats in the EEC Commission have not addressed this problem, those in both the OECD and the ILO have done so. The analysis of the success of social security policies in different countries is complex because of differing definition of poverty and poor data. However the best two available sources of data indicate that the number in poverty is substantial in some countries. Table 12.4 uses OECD data and shows the extent of poverty in ten developed countries using the official or quasi-official national definitions as well as a standardized definition of poverty. The latter takes as the poverty line for a single adult, a standard equal to 66.7 per cent of average disposable income (ADI) in the

TABLE 12.4
Poverty in the Early 1970s

	Per cent of population below relative poverty line following	
	*Standardized definitions**	*National definitions*
Belgium	8	8.2
France	—	14.4
Germany	11	15.1
Ireland	16	15.0–20.0
United Kingdom	3	—
Norway	—	24.0
Sweden	5	—
Canada	3.5	—
United States	7.5	13.2
Australia	13	11.9

Source: Organisation for Economic Cooperation and Development (1976), *Public Expenditure on Income Maintenance Programmes*, p. 67.

* The derivation of these data are set out in the OECD text.

individual country and applies equivalence scales for larger families. For example, the two-persons poverty line is 100 per cent of ADI, four-persons 145 per cent of ADI, etc. (OECD (1976), p. 66). This exercise shows that in the early 1970s 13 per cent of the US population, 7.5 per cent of the UK population, and 16 per cent of France's population were living in poverty. Despite the existence of extensive welfare states, policies were deficient and large sections of the population lived in poverty.

The impact of income maintenance policies in Belgium, Great Britain, Australia and Norway can be seen in Table 12.5. Beckerman takes a poverty standard related to average disposable income but applies arbitrarily equivalence scales derived from the British Supplementary Benefits programme (see Beckerman (1979b), p. 18, footnote 7, and p. 28). Thus the poverty line for a single retired (non-retired) person is 73 per cent (62 per cent) of ADI and for two adults with two children it is 143 per cent of ADI: the OECD and Beckerman scales are thus similar but not identical. As can be seen from Table 12.5, the impact of the social security systems are not insignificant. In Belgium some 20 per cent of individuals were in poverty before benefits, and only 6.1 per cent after benefits (580,000). For

TABLE 12.5
Poverty Before and After Benefits

Item	*Belgium*	*Britain*	*Great Norway*	*Australia*
		Numbers ('000s)		
Before benefits				
Families	834	7,745	526	1,786
Individuals	1,956	12,063	985	3,185
After benefits				
Families	298	3,418	158	1,439
Individuals	580	5,374	305	2,522
		Incidence (% of total population)		
Before benefits				
Families	25.5	30.4	34.0	31.0
Individuals	20.5	22.2	24.9	24.3
After benefits				
Families	9.1	13.4	10.2	24.9
Individuals	6.1	9.9	7.7	19.2

Source: Beckerman, W. (1979a), *Poverty and the Impact of Income Maintenance Programmes*, International Labour Office, p. 25.
Note: The table gives the numbers below the poverty line and the incidence of poverty before and after Benefits in 1973 or nearest period, using a standard poverty line. All data are numbers or percentages.

Britain the equivalent figures were 22.2 per cent and 9.9 per cent (5.374 million). Thus it seems that EEC and other developed countries have a similar problem. Their welfare states remove many people from poverty but after the payment of social security benefits, a sizeable residue is left below the poverty line.

The Effects of Income Maintenance Policies on Labour Supply

The income maintenance policies whose efficiency was discussed above, give rise to two sets of labour supply effects. The taxes raised to finance benefits will affect the labour supply decisions of the tax-payer, and the benefits financed by these taxes will affect the labour supply decisions of welfare beneficiaries.

Some social security systems are financed largely out of payroll taxes and the labour supply consequences of these taxes depend on the incidence of taxation. If the burden is passed on from labour to capital or consumers, the labour supply effects may be minimal. On the other hand if labour markets are competitive, the burden of taxation will rest on labour and the taxes will reduce the opportunity cost of leisure and, *ceteris paribus*, provide an incentive for employees to work fewer hours.

If benefits are financed out of general taxation, part of that taxation, on income, may give rise to similar effects. The textbooks indicate that at the theoretical level, the labour supply effects of a progressive income tax may be more than those of an equal yield proportional payroll (income) tax: the latter creates a weaker substitution effect. Thus from the perspective of labour supply effects, policy makers seeking the creation of competitive markets, may not be indifferent to the national mixes of proportional and progressive taxation. Such a conclusion arises even without analysis of the distributional effects of such tax policies. The apparent proportional payroll tax systems are often regressive because of the use of earnings ceilings limits for contribution purposes.

The method used to finance welfare benefits has important distributional and allocative implications. Figure 12.3 shows that a social security system affects the budget constraint of the tax payer in two ways. Those to the left of the breakeven position (N), the rich, pay tax and their budget line shifts downwards: it changes from Y_1N to Y_2N. Other things being equal, a proportional payroll tax whose burden is borne by labour would lead to a shift in equilibrium points from A to B: the rich person will offer less work. The revenue raised by this taxation is used to pay welfare benefits to the poor (those to the right of N). The budget line of the poor person changes from

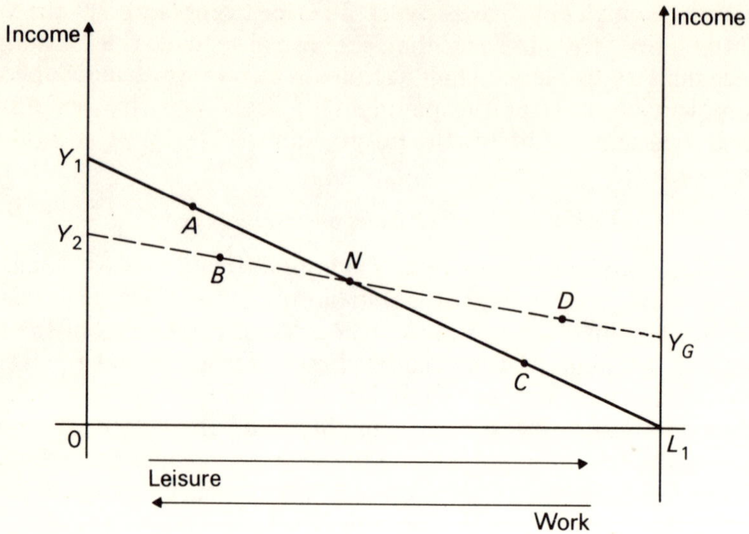

Figure 12.3 The Allocative Effects of the Finance of Social Security

Notes: To the right of *N*, benefits accrue, and to the left taxes are paid. At *N* benefits and taxes cancel out each other. Thus Y_1L_1 is the pre-tax-and-benefit budget constraint. After tax and the payment of benefits this constraint shifts to Y_2Y_G and new equilibria, *B* for the rich man who pays taxes and *D* for the poor man who gets benefits, are achieved.

NL_1 to NY_G, and, *ceteris paribus*, he will shift from equilibrium point *C* to *D*, offering less work and consuming more leisure. Thus income maintenance systems generate two labour supply effects, both in the same direction, one for taxpayers and one for beneficiaries of these tax payments. The magnitude of these changes is a matter of some empirical debate although generally this debate is about income tax *per se* and negative income tax, rather than payroll taxes and general welfare payments. The exact nature of the post-tax and post-benefit budget constraints will depend on the characteristics of the particular taxation and welfare schemes that are used. Some individuals will pay taxes and receive benefits and have their budget constraints influenced in opposite directions (such as child allowances in France).

In practice the simple adjustments depicted in Figure 12.3 may be affected by the characteristics of the labour market. Both rich and poor may be unable to adjust their work effort downwards as they might like if incentives changed: the labour contract might be fixed. This might induce changes in the quality, rather than the quantity of work: more on-the-job leisure might be consumed (long tea breaks, bad time keeping etc.). Neoclassical analysis and the associated empirical work has taken little notice of such possibilities.

The exact extent of labour supply disincentive effects is a matter of dispute (Godfrey (1975), Pechman and Timpane (1975)). The conclusion seems to be that such effects do exist, both for taxpayers and beneficiaries, but their magnitude is quite small. However the data base from which these conclusions have been drawn is limited and more research work is required.

Conclusion: An Evaluation of Social Policy in the EEC

The social policy activities of the European Commission have been limited and are incomplete in conception and execution. Until recently little attention has been paid to the form of financing social security even though payroll taxes are in widespread use, raise significant amounts of revenue, and may have significant, and differential across the Community, effects on the allocation of resources and employment.

Despite the potential broad interpretation which could be given to articles 117–18, and 100–1, social policy action has tended to avoid the major resource user areas of health, income maintenance, housing and education. The first two of these markets have been discussed in relation to the achievement of a common market. The Community has tended to extend (such as by the 1976 directive affecting the recognition of medical training) professional power in medicine and has done little to remedy its defects. These defects have led to a rapid expansion of resource usage and a paucity of data about the efficiency of these allocations.

Income maintenance policies have effects on the labour supply of tax financers and welfare beneficiaries. Countries such as Britain and Denmark which have pursued more egalitarian policies may have affected work incentives more than those countries with less concern for redistribution (such as France and Italy). Furthermore these latter countries have tended to finance social security by payroll taxes and VAT rather than progressive income taxation; the latter is likely to affect the relative price of leisure more than the former and to have greater redistributive effects.

These policies require careful analysis. What are their objectives? Why is government, nationally and internationally, concerned with the finance and provision of such goods and services? Are such policies provided efficiently, or cost-effectively in the case of policies whose outputs are unclear? Policy makers always and everywhere must ask why? what? how much? how? to whom? and ensure that their resultant policies minimize the use of scarce resources.

Social policy initiatives from the European Commission could cover a wide range of issues related to the general labour market and manpower policy but not discussed in this chapter. For example, policies concerning employment and unemployment both nationally and regionally, labour market information, mobility, and industrial training and retraining. The scope for market supplementing policies in these areas is large and any improvements in efficiency which result may also be substantial. Unfortunately the analysis of social policy and labour policies has been very limited and will remain so until economic analysis is used more comprehensively and political responses to such analysis are forthcoming. The objective of a competitive common market in goods and services within the EEC is unlikely to be achieved until more care is taken to analyse and ameliorate the obstacles to trade which are created by the social and labour policies of member countries. One challenge of the 1980s is to determine whether the problems created by such policies can be mitigated effectively and rapidly.

References

Abel-Smith, B. and Grandjeat, P. (1978) *Pharmaceutical Consumption*, Social Policy Series No. 35, Brussels and Luxembourg, Commission of the European Communities.

Abel-Smith, B. and Maynard, A. (1979) *The Organisation, Financing and Cost of Health Care in the European Community*, Social Policy Series No. 36, Brussels and Luxembourg, Commission of the European Communities.

Adams, D. W. (1980) 'The distributive effects of VAT in the United Kingdom, Ireland, Belgium, and Germany', *Three Banks Review*, No. 128, December, pp. 21-37.

Anderberg, M. R. (1973) *Cluster Analysis for Applications*, London, Academic Press.

Angus, R. (1979) *Collaborative Weapons Acquisition: The MRCA (Tornado)–Panavia Project*, Aberdeen Studies in Defence Economics 12, Centre for Defence Studies, University of Aberdeen, October.

Argy, V. and Hodjera, Z. (1973) 'Financial integration and interest rate linkages in the industrial countries', *IMF Staff Papers*, Vol. 20, pp. 1-77.

Arrow, K. J. (1962) 'Economic welfare and the allocation of resources for invention', in *The Rate and Direction of Inventive Activity*, National Bureau of Economic Research, Princeton University Press.

Bacon, R., Godley, W. and McFarquhar, A. (1978) 'The direct costs to Britain of belonging to the EEC', *Cambridge Economic Policy Review*, No. 4, pp. 44-9.

Baker, S. A. (1980) 'European Monetary Union and the demand for international reserves', *Bulletin of Economic Research*, Vol. 32, pp. 97–101.

Balassa, B. (1962) *The Theory of Economic Integration*, London, Allen and Unwin.

Balassa, B. (1975) 'Monetary integration in the European Common Market', in B. Balassa (ed.), *European Economic Integration*, Amsterdam, North-Holland.

Balassa, B. (1977) '"Revealed" comparative advantage revisited: an analysis of the export shares of the industrial countries 1953–71', *The Manchester School,* Vol. 45, No. 4, December, pp. 327–43.

Balassa, B. (1979) 'The changing international division of labour in manufactured goods', *Banca Nazionale Del Lavoro Quarterly Review*, No. 130, pp. 243–85.

Bank of England (1980) *Monetary Control*, Cmnd. 7858, London, HMSO.

Basevi, G. (1975) 'The All Saints' Day Manifesto for European Monetary Union: a currency for Europe', *The Economist*, Vol. 257, 1 November 1975, pp. 33–8, London. (Reproduced in M. Fratianni and T. Peeters (1978) (eds), *One Money for Europe*, London, Macmillan.)

Becker, G. S. (1975) *Human Capital*, 2nd edn, New York, Columbia University Press for the National Bureau of Economic Research.

Beckerman, W. (1979a) *Poverty and the Impact of Income Maintenance Programmes*, Geneva, International Labour Office.

Beckerman, W. (1979b) 'The impact of income maintenance payments on poverty in Britain', *Economic Journal*, Vol. 89, No. 354, pp. 261–79.

Berglas, E. (1976) 'On the theory of clubs', *American Economic Review*, Vol. 68, May, pp. 116–21.

Bhagwati, J. N. (1971) 'The generalized theory of distortions and welfare', in J. N. Bhagwati (ed.), *Trade, Balance of Payments and Growth*, Amsterdam, North-Holland, pp. 69–90.

Biehl, D. (1978) 'The role of public finance in European integration', *Integration*, No. 3.

Blinder, A. S. and Solow, R. M. (1973) 'Does fiscal policy matter?', *Journal of Public Economics*, Vol. 2, pp. 319–37.

Brams, S. J. (1975) *Game Theory and Politics*, New York, The Free Press (Collier-Macmillan).

Brams, S. J. (1976) *Paradoxes of Politics*, New York, The Free Press (Collier-Macmillan).

Brennan, G. B. and Flowers, M. (1980) 'All Ng up on clubs?', *Public Finance Quarterly*, Vol. 8, No. 2, April, pp. 153–69.

Brittain, J. A. (1971) 'The incidence of social security payroll taxes', *American Economic Review*, Vol. 61, March, pp. 110–25.

Brittain, J. A. (1972) *The Payroll Tax for Social Security*, Washington, Brookings.

Brunner, K. (1976) 'Inflation, money and the role of fiscal arrangements: an analytical framework for the inflation problem', in M. Monti (ed.), *The New Inflation and Monetary Policy*, London, Macmillan.

Buchanan, J. M. (1965) 'An economic theory of clubs', *Economica*, Vol. 32, February, pp. 1–14.

Cairncross, A. (1974) *Economic Policy for the European Community*, London, Macmillan.

Callaghan, T. A. Jr. (1975) *US–European Economic Co-operation in Military and Civil Technology*, Center for Strategic and International Studies, Georgetown University, Washington DC.

Cherif, M. and Ginsburgh, V. (1976) 'Economic interdependence among the EEC countries: an unconventional view', *European Economic Review*, Vol. 8, pp. 71–86.

Cochrane, A. L. (1972) *Effectiveness and Efficiency: Random Reflections on Health Services*, London, Nuffield Provincial Hospitals Trust.

Cochrane, A. L., St. Leger, A. S. and Moore, F. (1979) 'Health service "input" and mortality "output" in developed countries', *Journal of Epidemiology and Community Health*, No. 32, pp. 200–5.

Collins, D. (1975) *The European Communities: The Social Policy of the First*

Phase, London, Martin Robertson.

Colman, D. (1978) 'Some aspects of the economics of stabilisation', *Journal of Agricultural Economics*, Vol. 29, pp. 243-56.

Cooper, M. H. (1975) *European Pharmaceutical Prices 1964-1974*, London, Croom Helm.

Cooper, M. H. and Maynard, A. (1971) *The Price of Air Travel*, London, Institute of Economic Affairs.

Cooper, M. H. and Maynard, A. (1972) 'The effect of regulated competition on scheduled air fares', *Journal of Transport Economics and Policy*, Vol. 6, No. 2, pp. 167-75.

Cooper, R. N. (1969) 'Macroeconomic policy adjustment in interdependent economies', *Quarterly Journal of Economics*, Vol. 82, pp. 1-24.

Corden, W. M. (1972) *Monetary Integration*, Princeton Essays in International Finance No. 93, Princeton Uniersity Press.

Corden, W. M. (1974) *Trade Policy and Economic Welfare*, Oxford, Clarendon Press.

Crockett, A. D. (1977 and 1979) *International Money*, London, Nelson.

Culyer, A. J. (1971) 'Medical care and the economics of giving', *Economica*, Vol. 38, No. 151, pp. 295-303.

Currie, D. (1976) 'Some criticisms of the monetary analysis of balance of payments correction', *Economic Journal*, Vol. 86, pp. 508-22.

Davies, D. L. (1971), 'The efficiency of public and private firms', *Journal of Law and Economics*, Vol. 14, pp. 149-61.

Davies, D. L. (1977) 'The efficiency of public and private firms', *Journal of Law and Economics*, Vol. 20, 223-6.

De Grauwe, P. and Peeters, T. (1978) *The E.M.S. after Bremen: Technical and Conceptual Problems*, Leuven International Economic Research Paper No. 17, Leuven.

Demsetz, H. (1969) 'Information and efficiency: another viewpoint', *Journal of Law and Economics*, Vol. 14, No. 1, pp. 1-22.

Denton, G. (1978) 'Reflections on fiscal federalism in the EEC', *Journal of Common Market Studies*, 1978.

Denton, G. (1981) *The European Community Budget*, Oxford, Philip Allan.

Department of Health, Education and Welfare (1979) *New Drug Evaluation Project: Briefing Book*, Food and Drug Administration, Bureau of Drugs, Maryland.

Dernburg, T. F. (1970) 'Exchange rates and co-ordinated stabilization policy', *Canadian Journal of Economics*, Vol. 3, pp. 1-13.

Dernburg, T. F. (1974) 'The macroeconomic implications of wages retaliation against higher taxation', *IMF Staff Papers*, November.

Donabedian, A. (1971) 'Social responsibility for personal health services: an examination of basic values', *Inquiry*, Vol. 7, No. 2, pp. 3-19.

Donges, J. B. (1981) *What is Wrong with the European Communities?*, Occasional Paper 59, London, Institute of Economic Affairs.

Dosser, D. (1973) 'Notes on some public finance issues as they relate to economic union', in EEC *European Economic Integration and Monetary Unification*, Brussels, EEC.

Dosser, D. (1974) 'Development of a European Community budget', in G. Denton (ed.), *Economic and Monetary Union in Europe*, London, Croom Helm.

Dosser, D. (1981) 'The Value-Added Tax in the UK and the Community', in F. Forte and A. Peacock (eds), *Issues in Tax Policy*, Oxford, Basil Blackwell.

Dosser, D. and Pinder, J. (1974) *Economic Union in the EEC*, London, Croom Helm in association with the Federal Trust.

Downs, A. (1957) *An Economic Theory of Democracy*, New York, Harper and Row.

EEC (1970a) 'A plan for the phased establishment of an economic and monetary union', *Bulletin of the European Communities*, Supplement No. 7, Brussels.

EEC (1970b) 'Report to the Council and the Commission on the realisation by stages of economic and monetary union', *Bulletin of The European Communities*, Supplement No. 11, Brussels (Werner Report).

EEC (1975a) 'Action programme for the European aeronautical sector', *Bulletin of the European Communities*, Supplement No. 11, Luxembourg.

EEC (1975b) *Report of the Study Group 'Economic and Monetary Union 1980'*, Brussels (Margolin Report).

EEC (1975c) 'Stocktaking of the Common Agricultural Policy', *Bulletin of the European Communities*, Supplement No. 2, Brussels.

EEC (1976) *Ninth General Report on the Activities of the European Communities 1975*, Brussels and Luxembourg.

EEC (1977a) *Report of the Study Group on the Role of Public Finance in European Integration*, Brussels (MacDougall Report).

EEC (1977b) *The Common Agricultural Policy*, Brussels, Directorate General for Press and Information.

EEC (1978a) *Financing the Community Budget - The Way Ahead*, Brussels.

EEC (1978b) *Report on Some Structural Aspects of Growth*, COM (78) 255 final, 22 June, Brussels.

EEC (1978c) *The Rules Governing Medicaments in the European Community*, Brussels and Luxembourg.

EEC (1978d) 'Where the fish are', *European Community*, No. 5, pp. 8-12.

EEC (1979a) 'Air transport: a community approach', *Bulletin of the European Communities*, Supplement No. 5, Brussels.

EEC (1979b) *First Report of the Committee on Proprietary Medicines*, Brussels and Luxembourg.

EEC (1979c) *The Agricultural Policy of the European Community*, 2nd edn, Luxembourg, Office for Official Publications of the European Communities.

EEC (1980a) *Ninth Report on Competition Policy*, Brussels and Luxembourg.

EEC (1980b) *Report from the Commission to the Council on the Scope for Convergence of Tax Systems in the Community*, Brussels.

El-Agraa, A. M. (1980a) 'The Common Agricultural Policy', in A. M. El-Agraa (ed.), *The Economics of the European Community*, Deddington, Oxford, Philip Allan.

El-Agraa, A. M. (1980b) *The Economics of the European Community*, Deddington, Oxford, Philip Allan.

Eurostat (1980) 'Note on social protection aspects of the Second European Social Budget', *Eurostat*, 5 March.

Euzeby, A. (1980) *Social Security Financing Methods and the Effect on Employment*, V/519/1/79, Brussels, Commission of the European Communities.

Foch, R. (1970) *Europe and Technology*, Atlantic Papers 2, Paris, Atlantic Institute.

Foot, M. D. K. W. (1981) 'Monetary targets: their nature and record in the major economies', in B. Griffiths and G. E. Wood (eds), *Monetary Targets*, London, Macmillan.

Forte, F. (1979) *Report on the Economic Effects of Budget and Financial Transfers in the Community*, Brussels, EEC.

Fuchs, V. (1978) 'The supply of surgeons and the demand for operations', *Journal of Human Resources*, Vol. 13, Supplement, pp. 35-56.

Gaitskell, H. T. N. (1933) 'Four monetary heretics', in G. D. H. Cole (ed.), *What Everyone Wants to Know About Money*, London, Gollancz.

Godfrey, L. G. (1975) *Theoretical and Empirical Aspects of the Effects of Taxation on the Supply of Labour*, Paris, OECD.

Godley, W. (1980) 'The United Kingdom and the Community Budget', in W. Wallace (ed.), *Britain in Europe*, London, Heinemann, pp. 72-86.

Goodhart, C. A. E. (1976) *Money, Information and Uncertainty* (2nd edn), London, Macmillan.

Gowland, D. H. (1978) *Monetary Policy and Credit Control*, London, Croom Helm.

Gowland, D. H. (1979) (ed.) *Modern Economic Analysis*, London, Butterworths.

Gowland, D. H. (1981) *Controlling the Money Supply*, London, Croom Helm.

Greenwood, A. (1975) 'Response to research policy article on MRCA', *Research Policy*, No. 4, pp. 207-10.

Hamada, K. (1974) 'Alternative exchange rate systems and the interdependence of monetary policies', in R. Z. Aliber (ed.), *National Monetary Policies and the International Financial System*, Chicago and London, University of Chicago Press.

Hamburger, M. J. (1978) *The Demand-for-Money in the UK and Germany*, FRBNY, mimeo.

Hartley, K. (1969) 'Estimating military aircraft production outlays: the British experience', *Economic Journal*, December, Vol. 74, pp. 861-81.

Hartley, K. (1974) *A Market for Aircraft*, Hobart Paper 57, London, Institute of Economic Affairs.

Hartley, K. (1977a) 'Training and retraining for industry', in *Fiscal Policy and Labour Supply*, Conference Series 4, London, Institute for Fiscal Studies.

Hartley, K. (1977b) *Problems of Economic Policy*, London, Allen and Unwin.

Hartley, K. (1980) 'The economics of bureacracy and local government', in *Town Hall Power or Whitehall Pawn?*, Readings 25, London, Institute of Economic Affairs.

Hartley, K. (1981a) 'The aerospace industry: problems and policies', in H. W. de Jong (ed.), *The Structure of European Industry*, The Hague, Martinus Nijhoff.

Hartley, K. (1981b) 'The political economy of NATO standardization and industrial policy', *NATO Review*, June, Brussels, NATO.

Hartley, K. (1981c) 'The political economy of NATO weapons procurement policies', in M. Edmonds (ed.), *International Arms Procurement*, Oxford, Pergamon.

Hartley, K. and Corcoran, W. (1975) 'Short-run employment functions in the UK aircraft industry', *Applied Economics*, Vol. 7, December, pp. 223-33.

Hartley, K. and Cubitt, J. (1977) 'Cost escalation in the UK', in *The Civil Service*, Expenditure Committee, HC 535-III, Appendix 44, July, London, HMSO.

Hartley, K. and McLean, P. (1981) 'UK defence expenditure', *Public Finance* (forthcoming).

Hartley, K. and Tisdell, C. A. (1981) *Micro-economic Policy*, London, Wiley.

Hayek, F. A. (1978) *Denationalisation of Money - The Argument Refined*, Hobart Paper 70, London, Institute of Economic Affairs.

Hazlewood, A. (1979) 'The end of the East African Community: what are the lessons for regional integration schemes?', *Journal of Common Market Studies*, Vol. 18, pp. 40-58.

HC 254 (1977) *Cumulative Effect of Cuts in Defence Expenditure*, Defence and External Affairs Sub-Committee, London, HMSO.

Heath, B. O. (1979) 'MRCA Tornado: achievement by international collaboration', *Aeronautical Journal*, September, Royal Aeronautical Society, pp. 329-43.

Helpman, E. and Hillman, A. L. (1977) 'Two remarks on optimal club size', *Economica*, August 1977, pp. 293-5.

Hill, B. E. and Ingersent, K. A. (1977) *An Economic Analysis of Agriculture*, London, Heinemann.

Hinckley, B. (1976) (ed.) *Coalitions and Time*, Sage Contemporary Social Issues, No. 27.

Hochman, H. H. and Rodgers, J. D. (1969) 'Pareto-optimal redistribution', *American Economic Review*, Vol. 59, No. 3, pp. 542-57.

Hodge, M. and Wallace, W. (1981) (eds) *Economic Divergence and the European Community*, London, Allen and Unwin for Royal Institute of International Affairs.

Holmes, J. M. (1972) 'Monetary and fiscal policies in a general equilibrium model under fixed exchange rates', *International Economic Review*, Vol. 13, pp. 386-98.

Hood, C. and Wright, M. (1981) (eds) *Big Government in Hard Times*, London, Martin Robertson.

Houthakker, H. S. and Magee, S. P. (1969) 'Income and price elasticities in world trade', *Review of Economics and Statistics*, May, p. 73.

Irving, R. W. and Fearn, H. A. (1978) *Green Money and the CAP*, Wye College (University of London), Ashford, Kent.

Johnson, H. G. (1968) 'The implications of free or freer trade, for the harmonization of other policies', in H. E. English (ed.), *World Trade and Trade Policies*, Toronto, University of Toronto Press.

Johnson, H. G. (1971) 'Problems of European Monetary Union', *Journal of World Trade Law*, Vol. 5, pp. 377-87.

Johnson, H. G. (1972) 'The monetary approach to balance of payments theory',

Journal of Financial and Quantitative Analysis, Vol. 7, pp. 1555-71.

Johnson, H. G. (1975) *Technology and Economic Interdependence*, London, Macmillan, Chap. 3.

Josling, T. (1973) 'The Common Agricultural Policy of the European Economic Community', in M. B. Krauss (ed.), *The Economics of Integration*, London, Allen and Unwin, pp. 267-96. (Adapted from *Journal of Agricultural Economics*, Vol. 20, 1969, pp. 175-91.)

Josling, T. (1974) 'Agricultural policies in developed countries: a review', *Journal of Agricultural Economics*, Vol. 25, pp. 229-64.

Josling, T. (1979) 'Agricultural protection and stabilization policies: analysis of current neomercantile practices', in J. S. Hillman and A. Schmitz (eds), *International Trade and Agriculture: Theory and Policy*, Boulder, Colorado, Westview Press, pp. 149-62.

Kemp, M. C. (1977) 'Monetary and fiscal policy under alternative assumptions about international capital mobility', *Economic Record*, Vol. 53, pp. 589-605.

Kennedy, G. (1979) *Burden Sharing in NATO*, London, Duckworth.

Klepsch, E. and Normanton, T. (1978) *Report on European Armaments Procurement Cooperation*, Working Documents 83/78, Luxembourg, European Parliament.

Koester, U. and Tangermann, S. (1977) 'Supplementing farm price policy by direct income payments: cost-benefit-analysis of alternative farm policies with special application to German agriculture', *European Review of Agricultural Economics*, Vol. 4, pp. 7-31.

Laidler, D. (1978) 'Difficulties with European Monetary Union', in M. Fratianni and T. Peeters (eds), *One Money for Europe*, London, Macmillan.

Laidler, D. (1980) 'The case for flexible exchange rates in 1980', paper presented at the Salford Conference on European Monetary Union.

Layton, C. (1969) *European Advanced Technology*, PEP, London, Allen and Unwin.

Leuthold, J. (1975) 'The incidence of the payroll tax in the United States', *Public Finance Quarterly*, Vol. 3, January, pp. 3-13.

Levacic, R. (1976) *Macroeconomics*, London, Macmillan.

Lindsay, C. H. (1969) 'Medical care and the economics of sharing', *Economica*, Vol. 36, No. 144, pp. 351-62.

Machlup, F. (1977) *A History of Thought on Economic Integration*, London, Macmillan.

Machlup, F. (1980) 'My early work on international monetary problems', *Banca Nazionale Del Lavoro, Quarterly Review*, Vol. 133, pp. 113-46.

Maynard, A. and Ludbrook, A. (1981) 'Thirty years of fruitless endeavour?', in J. van der Gaag and M. Perlman (eds), *Proceedings of the 1980 World Congress in Health Economics*, Amsterdam, North-Holland.

McKinnon, R. I. (1974) 'Sterilisation policies in three dimensions ...', in R. Z. Aliber (ed.), *National Monetary Policies and the International Financial System*, Chiacgo and London, University of Chicago Press.

McKinnon, R. I. (1979) *Money in International Exchange*, Oxford, Oxford University Press.

Meeks, G. (1977) *Disappointing Marriage: A Study of the Gains from Merger*, Occasional Paper 51, Department of Applied Economics, University of Cambridge.

Metcalf, D. (1969) *The Economics of Agriculture*, Harmondsworth, Penguin.

Ministry of Technology (1969) *Productivity of the National Aircraft Effort*, Elstub, London, HMSO.

Morris, C. N. (1980) 'The Common Agricultural Policy', *Fiscal Studies*, Vol. 1, pp. 17-35.

Mueller, D. C. (1979) *Public Choice*, Cambridge Surveys of Economic Literature, Cambridge, Cambridge University Press.

Mundell, R. A. (1964) 'Capital mobility and size: reply', *Canadian Journal of Economics and Political Science*, Vol. 30, pp. 421-31.

Musgrave, R. and Musgrave, P. (1980) *Public Finance in Theory and Practice* (3rd edn), New York, McGraw-Hill.

Nelson, J. R., Konoske-Dey, P., Fiorello, M. R., Gebman, J. R., Smith, G. K. and Sweetland, A. (1974) *A Weapon System Life Cycle Overview: The A7D Experience*, Rand R-1452, Santa Monica.

Neubauer, W. (1973) 'European integration policy today: alternatives to the Werner plan', in EEC 'European Economic Integration and Monetary Unification', *Report of the Study Group on Economic and Monetary Union*, DG II, Brussels.

Ng, K. Y. (1973) 'The economic theory of clubs: Pareto optimality conditions', *Economica*, Vol. 40, August, pp. 291-8.

Niehans, J. (1968) 'Monetary and fiscal policies in open economies under fixed exchange rates: an optimising approach', *Journal of Political Economy*, Vol. 76, pp. 893-943.

Niskanen, W. A. Jr. (1971) *Bureaucracy and Representative Government*, Chicago, Aldine-Atherton.

Nobbs, R. (1979) 'Air industry policy report: political choice in the aerospace sector', in G. Ionescu (ed.), *The European Alternatives*, Leiden, Netherlands, Sijthoff and Noordhoff.

Oates, W. (1972) *Fiscal Federalism*, New York, Harcourt Brace.

Oates, W. (1977) 'Fiscal federalism in theory and practice: applications to the European Community', in EEC *Report of the Study Group on the Role of Public Finance in European Integration*, Brussels, EEC.

OECD (1970) *Gaps in Technology: Analytical Report*, Paris.

OECD (1976) *Public Expenditure on Income Maintenance Programmes*, Studies in Resource Allocation, Paris.

OECD (1977) *Public Expenditure on Health*, Studies in Resource Allocation, Paris.

Olson, M. Jr. (1965) *The Logic of Collective Action*, Cambridge, Mass., Harvard University Press.

Olson, M. Jr. and Zeckhauser, R. (1968) 'An economic theory of alliances', *Review of Economics and Statistics*, Vol. 48, August, pp. 266-74.

Parkin, M. (1976) 'Monetary union and stabilisation policy in the European Community', *Banca Nazionale Del Lavoro, Quarterly Review*, No. 29, pp. 222-40.

Pavitt, K. (1976) 'The choice of targets and instruments for government support of scientific research', in A. Whiting (ed.), *The Economics of Industrial Subsidies*, London, HMSO.

Peacock, A. T. (1979) 'Stabilisation and distribution policy', in A. T. Peacock, *The Economic Analysis of Government and Related Themes*, Oxford, Martin Robertson, Chap. 11.

Pechman, J. A. and Timpane, P. M. (1975) (eds) *Work Incentives and Income Guarantees*, Washington, Brookings.

Peltzman, S. (1976) 'Towards a more general theory of regulation', *Journal of Law and Economics*, Vol. 19, No. 2, pp. 211-40.

Pinder, J. (1981) 'Integrating divergent economies: the extranational method', in M. Hodges and W. Wallace (eds), *Economic Divergence in the European Community*, London, Allen and Unwin.

Readman, P. (1974) *The European Monetary Puzzle*, London, Michael Joseph.

Richardson, Sir G. (1978) 'An account of monetary policy: the Governor's Mais Lecture', *Bank of England Quarterly Bulletin*, Vol. 18, No. 1.

Riemsdijk, J. F. van (1973) 'A system of direct compensation payments to farmers as a means of reconciling short-run to long-run interests', *European Review of Agricultural Economics*, Vol. 1, pp. 161-89.

Riezman, R. (1979) 'A 3 x 3 model of customs unions', *Journal of International Economics*, Vol. 9, pp. 341-54.

Ritson, C. (1973) 'The Common Agricultural Policy', in *The European Economic Community: Economics and Agriculture*, Open University.

Ritson, C. (1980) 'Self-sufficiency and food security', Centre for Agricultural Strategy, Paper 8, University of Reading.

Rolls Royce (1978) *Report on Visit to the USA*, August, private data, Specifications and Brochures Dept., Aero Division, Derby.

Roper, D. E. (1971) 'Macroeconomic policies and the distribution of the world money supply', *Quarterly Journal of Economics*, Vol. 85, pp. 119-46.

Royal Commission on the National Health Service (1979) *Report*, Cmnd. 7615, London, HMSO (Chairman, Sir Alec Merrison).

Salant, W. S. (1977) 'International transmission of inflation', in L. B. Krause and W. S. Salant (eds), *Worldwide Inflation: Theory and Recent Experience*, Washington DC, Brookings.

Saptsford, D. (1981) *Labour Market Economics*, London, Allen and Unwin, Chap. 6.

Saul, S. B. (1975) 'MRCA: comment on the article by W. B. Walker', *Research Policy*, No. 3, pp. 373-4.

Shanks, M. (1977) *European Companion*, Vol. 33, August, London.

Shoard, M. (1980) *The Theft of the Countryside*, London, Temple Smith.

Shone, R. (1978) 'The monetary approach to the balance of payments: stock-flow equilibria', *Department of Economics Discussion Paper No. 60*, University of Stirling.

Smith, A. (1776) *An Inquiry into the Nature and Causes of the Wealth of Nations* (Everyman edn 1910), London, Dent.

Stigler, G. (1971) 'The theory of economic regulation', *Bell Journal of Economics and Management Science*, Spring.

Swan, D. (1973) *The Economics of the Common Market* (3rd edn), Harmondsworth, Penguin.

Swan, D. (1978) *The Economics of the Common Market* (4th edn), Harmondsworth, Penguin.

Tiebout, C. (1956) 'A pure theory of local expenditures', *Journal of Political Economy*, Vol. 64, No. 5.

Tinbergen, J. (1952) *On the Theory of Economic Policy*, Amsterdam, North-Holland.

Treaty of Rome (1973) *Treaties Establishing the European Communities* (English version), Brussels and Luxembourg, European Communities.

Tsiang, S. G. (1975) 'The dynamics of international capital flows and internal and external balance', *Quarterly Journal of Economics*, pp. 195-214.

Tucker, G. (1976) *Towards Rationalising Allied Weapons Production*, Atlantic Papers 1, Paris, Atlantic Institute.

Turnovsky, S. J. (1979) 'Optimal monetary and fiscal policies in an open dynamic economy', *Scandinavian Journal of Economics*, Vol. 27, pp. 400-14.

Turnovsky, S. J. and Kaspura, A. (1974) 'An analysis of imported inflation in a short-run macroeconomic model', *Canadian Journal of Economics*, Vol. 3, pp. 355-80.

Vacher (1980) *European Companion*, London, Kerswell Ltd.

Vaubel, R. (1978) 'Strategies for currency unification: the economics of currency competition and the case for a European parallel currency', *Kieler Studien No. 156*, Tubingen, Germany, J. C. B. Mohr.

Volcker, P. A. (1977) 'A broader role for monetary targets', *FRBNY Quarterly Review*, 1977, pp. 23-8.

Walker, W. B. (1974) 'MRCA: a case study in European collaboration', *Research Policy*, No. 2, pp. 280-305.

Wishart, D. (1978) *Clustan: User Manual*, Edinburgh, Program Library Unit, Edinburgh University.

Wood, G. E. (1974) *European Monetary Union*, Surrey Economic Paper 6, Guildford, University of Surrey.

Woolley, P. (1974) 'Integration of capital markets', in G. Denton (ed.), *Economic and Monetary Union in Europe*, London, Croom Helm.

Index